CELEBRATING
50 YEARS
Texas A&M University Press
publishing since 1974

Run for Your Lives!

RUN FOR YOUR LIVES!

Gender and the Runaway Scrape

LINDA ENGLISH

TEXAS A&M UNIVERSITY PRESS
College Station

Copyright © 2024 by Linda English
All rights reserved

First edition

♾ This paper meets the requirements of ANSI/NISO Z39.48-1992 (Permanence of Paper). Binding materials have been chosen for durability.

Library of Congress Cataloging-in-Publication Data

Names: English, Linda, 1969– author.
Title: Run for your lives! : gender and the Runaway Scrape / Linda English.
Other titles: Elma Dill Russell Spencer series in the West and Southwest.
Description: First edition. | College Station : Texas A&M University Press, [2024] | Series: Elma Dill Russell Spencer series in the West and Southwest | Includes bibliographical references and index.
Identifiers: LCCN 2023057970 | ISBN 9781648432194 (hardcover) | ISBN 9781648432200 (ebook)
Subjects: LCSH: Women pioneers—Texas, South. | Frontier and pioneer life—Texas, South. | Texas—History—Revolution, 1835–1836—Women. | Texas—History—Revolution, 1835–1836—Refugees. | Alamo (San Antonio, Tex.)—Siege, 1836—Evacuation of civilians. | BISAC: HISTORY / Women | HISTORY / Military / United States
Classification: LCC F390 .E53 2024 | DDC 976.4/03—dc23/eng/20231220
LC record available at https://lccn.loc.gov/2023057970

For my father, Joe

Contents

Acknowledgments ix

Introduction
  The Runaway Scrape 1

1 A Sanctity No More
   The Building and Burning of Homes 20

2 Gendered Confrontations on the Road to Safety 44

3 Deserters, Noncombatants, and Criminals
   The Fulfillment and Failures of Manly Obligations 63

4 Manliness and the Texas Enemy
   The Dishonorable and the Depredators 84

5 Gendered Heroism
   Pamelia Mann and Sam Houston 104

   Conclusion
   Remembering the Last Months of the Texas Revolution 127

Notes 137
Bibliography 165
Index 177

Acknowledgments

Like most projects, the idea for this book began as a curiosity. When a friend mentioned it in passing, I knew very little about the Runaway Scrape, but I was intrigued. I remembered the scene of public chaos in the 2004 movie version of *The Alamo* with Billie Bob Thornton and Dennis Quaid, parts of which I have shown in class to my Texas history students. Quite a while back, I remember reading a well-written article on the Runaway Scrape by Fane Downs that stuck with me over the years; however, mentions of the event in subsequent readings tended to be scant or elusive (for me, up until Light Cummins's more recent contribution to *Women and the Texas Revolution* in 2012). And so, the digging into the Runaway Scrape began. As I pored through relevant documents, the story that emerged in my head centered on women and men desperately trying to meet the expectations of the moment—expectations that were often steeped in the gendered norms of the period. I had no idea whether a book-length account was possible, but here we are. A portion of Chapter 2, "Gendered Confrontations on the Road to Safety," appeared in article form in *American Nineteenth Century History*.

    I presented early versions of my research at academic conferences, specifically the Annual Conference for the Western History Association; the Texas State Historical Association Annual Meeting; the Berkshire Conference on the History of Women, Genders, and Sexualities; the Rural Women's Studies Association Conference; the Central Texas Historical Association Annual Conference; and the South Texas Historical Fall Conference. In each instance, I received valuable feedback from audience members and panel commentators, including from my good friend and fellow panelist Sarah Eppler Janda. I also gave public talks on the topic to the Texas General Land Office, the Friends of the San Felipe de Austin State Historical Site, and the Dustin Michael Sekula Memorial Library in Edinburg, Texas. My project also benefited from in-house feedback from the University of Texas

Rio Grande Valley (UTRGV)'s History Department Colloquium series; I appreciate all who attended and provided collegial responses and support. Some of my colleagues went above and beyond in their willingness to read drafts and offer critical feedback. A special thanks to four of my department colleagues who provided comprehensive chapter critiques: Drs. Jamie Starling, George Diaz, Friederike Bruehoefener, and Megan Birk. I also want to thank Dr. Kristin Shamas, who read the full draft and provided insightful comments and encouragement. Finally, I want to thank the anonymous readers assembled by the Texas A&M University Press for their constructive suggestions on how to improve the work.

No field depends on and benefits more from the work of archivists than does history. I visited numerous archives researching materials for this project and want to thank the staff at the Dolph Briscoe Center for American History at the University of Texas at Austin, the Austin History Center, the Alamo Research Center (formerly the Daughters of the Republic of Texas Library), the Woodson Research Center, Fondren Library at Rice University, the Albert and Ethel Herzstein Library at the San Jacinto Museum of History, and the Archives and Information Services Division, Texas State Library and Archives Commission. I received research travel monies from the UTRGV's Faculty Research Council and monetary support from the Department of History for travel and book expenditures.

I said it before, and I'll say it again. Where would we be without our friends? For me, my circle of friends are a constant source of support and joy (a special thanks to my book/movie club for the delightful distraction). The same goes for my family, especially my son, Alexander, who makes me immensely proud every day. No person has been of more assistance to me on the completion of this book than my husband, Christopher Davis. Chris read multiple drafts of my monograph and was my sounding board throughout, but more important, he provided me with encouragement, assurance, and love.

Finally, this book is dedicated to my father, Joe English, who died in the final stages of its completion. My dad was proudly supportive of his family. My brother, Jeff, and I mourn his loss and profound presence in our lives. While he loved all history, Joe was especially partial to Texas history. Along with thousands of enthusiastic visitors who make their way to San Antonio each year to visit the centerpiece of Texas history, my father loved his trip to the Alamo in 2010, talking about the site and its history to all who would listen in the years that followed.

RUN FOR YOUR LIVES!

INTRODUCTION

The Runaway Scrape

> *To provide for and protect our wives and children is a sacred duty, prompted by nature and sanctioned by every manly feeling.*[1]
>
> **—David G. Burnet,**
> *Interim President of the Republic of Texas*

At the age of 85, Rosa [von Roeder] Kleberg relayed in German the story of her first experiences in Texas to her grandson, Rudolph Kleberg Jr., who in 1898 published the account in *The Quarterly of the Texas State Historical Association* in two volumes. Titled "Some of My Early Experiences in Texas," Kleberg's reminiscences described the dramatic events surrounding her family's plight during the harried last months of the Texas Revolution. She recalled that, initially, "things were now quiet," suggesting a kind of calm-before-the-storm atmosphere: "But when the news of the fall of the Alamo came, there was great excitement."[2] Some families opted to abandon Texas altogether, but for Rosa's family, who held "no property elsewhere," leaving the state was simply not an option; instead, it was decided that the young, hardy men in the family (who included Rosa's husband and brothers) would enlist in the army, while her father, Ludwig von Roeder, would stay with the rest of the family. The remaining von Roeders joined the throngs of Texas families who sought the safety of the Louisiana border, hundreds of miles out of the reach of the advancing Mexican army. With a large traveling party and only one big ox-wagon, the family was compelled to travel light and leave much of their valued possessions behind. Before leaving their home, the von Roeders buried their fine linens, jewelry, and other valuables under a large copper kettle and covered it with soil and ashes. Fortunately, the items survived the family's retreat and eventual return.[3]

It was a harrowing journey for the family. Rosa remembered, "My father and I drove our cattle and packed horses; and I carried my daughter Clara, who was then a child of a few months, upon the saddle in front of me."[4] Incessant rain, swollen rivers, and hordes of families—forty to fifty deep—all attempted to cross waterways at the same time with cattle, tousled belongings, and rickety wagons, creating logjams at river crossings, "and the noise and confusion was terrible," Rosa recalled. Further exasperating the situation, Rosa's pregnant sister-in-law, Pauline von Roeder, gave birth to a son, Louis von Roeder, while the family was holed up at a camp near Clear Creek in southern Harris County.[5] The von Roeders intended to remain at the camp to allow Pauline time to recuperate, but the threat of an approaching army forced them to press onward. Along the road, the refugees met not only scores of other families heading to safety but also able-bodied men shirking their martial responsibilities by fleeing the battlefield. With her own husband and brothers fighting for the Texas cause on the frontlines, a resentful Rosa noted, "Deserters were constantly passing us on foot and on horseback. The old men with the families laughed at them and called to them, 'Run! Run! Santa Anna is behind you!'"[6] Decades after the fact, Rosa Kleberg's story featured all the relevant players in the "great excitement" that characterized the last months of the rebellion: soldiers on the front, deserters, an invading army, and a frightened civilian population—all facing intense pressure and scrutiny during these tumultuous few weeks, each jockeying to overcome formidable odds as Texas devolved into chaos.

Before it became the Republic of Texas in 1836, the state of Coahuila y Tejas underwent a bloody revolution that commenced in the fall of 1835 with canon fire at Gonzales, Texas, and ended with a decisive victory for Texas forces at the Battle of San Jacinto in April 1836. The Runaway Scrape, as it was called, denotes a particularly dire period for the Texas revolutionaries and their families.[7] During this turbulent episode, Santa Anna's forces were on the march, General Sam Houston and the Texas army fell back toward Louisiana and the United States to avoid the assault, and much of Texas thought the cause was lost. Elderly men, women, children, and enslaved persons left behind on plantations and small farms responded to this crisis by joining the retreat, essentially running for their lives. Most were new arrivals to the state who had just begun establishing their homesteads before deserting them in terrified haste. It was under these circumstances that the von Roeder traveling party, led by its patriarch, Ludwig von Roeder, decided to join the panicked exodus to the Sabine River and the safety of the American border.

A multitude of grievances drove the Texians (as they called themselves) to engage in armed insurrection against their government, including cultural differences, permissive Mexican colonization laws and oversight, concerns over taxes and slavery, and a consolidation of power by centralist forces within Mexico under the direction of General Antonio López de Santa Anna.[8] In an abrupt shift in policy, the Law of April 6, 1830, countered the permissive colonization laws of the 1820s by restricting future immigration from the United States. The Siete Leyes (or Seven Laws) served as the final straw for both Anglos and Tejanos, pushing even reluctant Peace Party adherents into more militant stances. Implemented by Santa Anna in 1835, the Siete Leyes included provisions that dissolved the federal Constitution of 1824 and abolished state legislatures (including Coahuila y Tejas). Initially elected as a federalist, Santa Anna's calculated shift to conservative centralism drew support from the church and the military, allowing him to consolidate his power with potent institutional allies. By October 1835, Santa Anna had abolished all state legislatures and transitioned them to departments run by governors who answered to him. The spirit of the Constitution of 1824 and aspirations of a constitutionally based republic that divided federal power with states dissipated with the rise of an autocratic regime under the command of the formidable general.

Once word of Santa Anna's power grab reached Texas settlements, rebellion ensued. Texians kicked off their revolt against the centralist government with the battle of Gonzales in October 1835. Located on the Guadalupe River, the small settlement of Gonzales possessed a much-desired cannon, loaned to them by the Mexican army for defense against Indian attack. As tensions escalated, the demand for its return from the Mexican military prompted the small group of Texians stationed at Gonzales to respond: "Come and Take It." The Texas unit, roughly 150 volunteers, used the cannon to lob the first shots of the Texas Revolution on October 2, 1835. After a slew of victories for the Texas forces in the fall of 1835, the tables turned with the arrival of Santa Anna's large army into Texas in early 1836. Defeats at the Alamo and Goliad in March 1836 impelled General Houston and what was left of the Texas army to retreat toward the Louisiana border. Some feared the army would keep going. A soldier under Houston's command recalled, "Many of the boys believed that Houston would never halt as long as the road was open to the Sabine."[9] At the Colorado River, Houston made the controversial decision to fall back and not engage the advancing Mexican threat. It was initially thought that Houston's forces would stand their ground and thwart the Mexican army from crossing the river; however, the general, upon hearing news of the Goliad massacre and reports that their combatants—stationed across the river—had received reinforcements, decided to retreat from the Colorado and fight another day, allowing more time to better equip and train his recruits.

The fall of the Alamo and the Goliad massacre were seminal events that directly precipitated what Rosa Kleberg described as the "great excitement" among the civilian population as it fled in terror from the anticipated arrival of Santa Anna's troops. As evidenced by the thousands of tourists who visit the mission fortress each year, the thirteen-day Alamo standoff that took place in late February and early March is by far the most well-known battle of the 1836 campaign. Despite their steadfast determination, the defenders of the Alamo were simply outnumbered. Estimates of Mexican troop levels are murky, but Santa Anna crossed the Rio Grande in mid-February with at least two thousand men headed to San Antonio on a collision course with the Alamo defenders, who numbered less than two hundred at their apex (after scant reinforcements from Gonzales).[10] The first Mexican soldiers arrived at the Alamo site on February 23, and troop levels steadily increased thereafter. On the second day of the siege, Lt. Col. William Barret Travis sent a letter addressed to "The people of Texas & all Americans in the world" requesting aid "with all dispatch" and declaring his resolve to never surrender, ending his letter with the commitment "victory or death."[11] The large force of troops, numbering roughly four hundred, stationed at Goliad under Col. James W. Fannin's command would not be coming to the assistance of those at the Alamo. With less than two hundred available men, the defenders of the mission were on their own. General Santa Anna ordered the attack before dawn on the morning of March 6, 1836, and the victory for the Mexican army soon followed. Few survived the carnage.[12]

Two weeks later, the Texas forces endured another stunning loss. Houston instructed Colonel Fannin to fall back from Goliad to a more defensive location at Victoria in mid-March. However, Fannin delayed the retreat until the morning of March 19; unfortunately, the decision proved costly for the Texas forces. Near Coleto Creek in Goliad County, Fannin's garrison found themselves surrounded and outnumbered by Mexican General José Urrea's troops—their position was vulnerable and their provisions (including water and ammunition) were running out. After a day and evening of exchanging volleys, Fannin, realizing his vulnerabilities, surrendered to Urrea, and his men were marched, as prisoners of war, back to Goliad. Despite Urrea's plea for clemency and adherence to customary rules-of-war for soldiers who surrendered on the field, Santa Anna ordered the immediate execution of the Goliad prisoners, whom he labeled as pirates unworthy of conventional war protections. The execution of the men under Fannin's command took place on March 27, 1836. Thus, two decisive victories for the Mexican army occurred within weeks of each other. With Santa Anna's forces unleashed in the state, marching toward civilian settlements, the home front proved to be a largely unstable, insecure, and transitory space rather than a safe place of refuge.

Families in South Texas communities, including San Antonio, began leaving their homes as early as January 1836 when the first rumors spread that the Mexican forces were marching north. Tensions mounted from there. Word of the distressing March defeats for the Texas army caused Texians to hurriedly throw what belongings they could onto any means of transport possible and head east. Consequently, March and April of 1836 marked the peak period of the Runaway Scrape. While the Texas forces under Houston represented a large contingent of those on the retreat, the majority of people falling back were not soldiers, but civilians. They were the men (often elderly or maimed, but not exclusively so), women, children, and enslaved persons who resided in the vulnerable territory that spanned from south central Texas to points farther east. In addition to the terror generated by the advancing Mexican army, the chaos created by war also provided the opportunity for increased Native American raids, particularly by Kiowa and Comanche warriors. How frightening was the atmosphere? According to her later account, Anne Fagan Teal recalled a man on horseback riding through the country shouting, "Run, run for your lives; Mexicans and Indians are coming, burning and killing as they come."[13] Indeed, there were threats from all sides.

During the frenetic last months of the Texas Revolution, when the situation seemed most perilous, anxieties among Anglo Texians reached a fever pitch, and heated rhetoric proliferated. Fear and suspicions amplified questions of loyalty to the Texas cause: Were you doing enough to support the rebellion? For anxious Texas revolutionaries, the stakes could not be higher. There was no room for half-hearted commitments and zero tolerance for cowardice. Amid this environment, a decidedly gendered component seeped through impassioned, sometimes malicious, pleas for support. Gender serves as a critical analytical tool for understanding the social dynamics of the last months of the Texas Revolution. This is not a history of men's experiences during the 1836 military campaign or women's tribulations during the flight to Louisiana; it is a history of both. It examines women *and* men as gendered subjects. This study explores dominant perceptions of nineteenth-century gender norms and expectations that permeated historical accounts of this turbulent period. As Joan Wallach Scott argues in her influential article "Gender: A Useful Category of Historical Analysis," gender is not a reference nor reduction to biological sex, but rather, "gender becomes a way of denoting 'cultural constructions'—the entirely social creation of ideas about appropriate roles for women and men."[14]

Scott's definition of gender is rooted in two propositions: "Gender is a constitutive element of social relationships based on perceived differences between the sexes, and gender is a primary way of signifying relationships of power."[15] She counsels historians "to examine the ways in which gendered identities are substantively constructed and relate their findings to a range of activities, social organizations, and historically specific cultural representations."[16] Examining gender entails both exploring the process of *becoming gendered*—learning of culturally and historically specific social roles associated with women and men and used to describe someone as masculine or feminine—and understanding gender difference in relation to power (i.e., analyzing gender difference in relation to social division).[17] Gender cannot be studied without exploring relationships to other aspects of status and identity.[18] Nor can gender be examined in isolation from competing notions of masculinity and femininity; indeed, gender historians analyze "the changing meaning and value attached to maleness and femaleness and the relationship between the two."[19] Both power dispensations and social constructions of what it meant to be a man or a woman and, importantly, who fell short of this mark provide the basic analytical frameworks for this analysis of 1830s Texas.

In March and April of 1836, when the outcome of the Texas Revolution stood on a precipice, the pressure mounted for Texas men to act "manly," which necessitated they meet their enemy on the battlefield, not desert nor retreat from the fight. Arguments for enlistment often relied on gendered tropes—accusations of unmanliness, loutishness, and wanton failure to protect women and children—to make their case, escalating in frequency and intensity when the rebellion's outcome seemed most bleak. Their enemy was cast as weak, uncommitted, dishonorable, and savage—their leader, craven and uncivilized. The secretary of war, Thomas J. Rusk, implored Texas men to think about the consequences of desertion: "Will you continue to do so—will you permit the deaths of your murdered countrymen to go unavenged—will you abandon helpless women and children to their fate?"[20] Similarly, in his bid to attract recruits for the rebellion, interim president of Texas, David G. Burnet, proposed an essentialized definition of manly obligations, particularly in relation to their female counterparts: "To provide for and protect our wives and children is a sacred duty, prompted by nature and sanctioned by every manly feeling."[21] Texas men who refused their call to duty provided grounds for administrators, soldiers, and civilians to question their manliness—masculine presumptions they embedded in both the sacred and natural world. This analysis builds on existing scholarship on prevailing hegemonic notions of masculinity in the early nineteenth century, examining Texas men in the context of increasingly complex, often competing, expressions of manliness that proliferated in antebellum America.

The chaos of war and turmoil of the Runaway Scrape affected gender expectations for women as well. Before, during, and after the nineteenth century, women's gender identity was inextricably tied to their roles as mothers, wives, and daughters. Foundational to nineteenth-century notions of womanhood was the centrality of the family and home. In their capacities as mothers and wives, women assumed the responsibility of fostering and enriching the domestic space; further, their obligations included developing and molding the character and behaviors of those within the household. Reflecting on the role of women in the family, one Texas woman wrote: "Here the devoted wife and affectionate mother, the gentle sister and obedient, confiding daughter, exerts a conservative influence on all within the sacred precincts."[22] According to this view, women elicited order and restraint within the household. The displacement of war meant the sacrifice of homes that served as familial sanctuaries—a consequential application bestowed upon even the crudest of structures carved out of the Texas prairie. Many Anglo families were just getting started on the processes of breaking ground and building livable dwellings in the late 1820s and early 1830s. Once the revolution and retreat began, family homes could no longer be deemed places of comfort and sanctuary. This new reality was particularly traumatic for women.

While a rather short campaign from a military perspective, the Texas Revolution and the flight to the safety of the Louisiana border created a liminal space that afforded some women leadership and decision-making roles. As one historian notes, "The Runaway Scrape thus represented a rare moment in early nineteenth-century Texas when by chance many women found themselves independently empowered to provide for the safety and security of their families."[23] Especially for women in Texas, the threat of an invading army cast them out of their protected private sphere and into a dangerous, often brutal, environment.[24] This was not the case for all women, however. Rosa Kleberg's narrative indicates that not all traveling parties headed to the Sabine were either led by women or devoid of men. In some instances, women grappled for power and decision-making roles with men in their refugee groups; in other cases, women ceded leadership decisions to their male counterparts. Moreover, there are examples of women who confronted men along the way who often sought to assume authority over the situation; these men included enlisted spouses (and sometimes teenaged sons) who left the fighting to see to the well-being of their wives, mothers, and children.

The exigencies of war created new spaces for women to exert discernable levels of agency and brashness when it came to their male counterparts; indeed, there are examples of men who admired demonstrations of female pluck during the unrest, recording anecdotes of women's heroism in their personal accounts. And yet, there were temporal limitations to such attitudes. Toward the end of the Revolution, accusations abounded of men acting like women (i.e., weak and unmanly) and women acting like men (i.e., brazen and authoritative); on the surface, gendered expectations appeared scrambled and strained. However, a closer examination of such animated language exchanged during this period indicates more bombast than actual social tension. Criticisms lobbed at men who chose not to fight, for example, were intended to provoke shame and invoke action, specifically enlistment to the army. References to manly obligations and the threat to women and children were useful talking points. As related to gender, any shifting of attitudes and expectations proved short lived. Commenting on the aftermath of wartime conditions, a preeminent historian of the Texas Revolution noted, "While the processes that gripped Texas during the previous year clearly reflected revolutionary dynamics, the brevity of the experience limited the degree to which revolution had wrenched apart the political order and social fabric."[25] The fate of one storied Texas woman, Pamelia Mann, who was known for her impudent encounter with the commander of the Texas army during the Runaway Scrape, suggests that women who threatened gender expectations (i.e., by acting too much like men) in the post-Revolution period faced consequences, sometimes severe.

Research for this book draws from extant memoirs of witnesses of the Runaway Scrape, women's and men's diaries and reminiscences—often written decades after the war. In the case of women's memoirs, these accounts serve not only to memorialize the trials and triumphs of 1836 but also to insert women into the story of events. To date, there is wide scholarship on the Texas Revolution, concentrated especially on storied battles, heroes, and military strategies. The countless biographies of the military heroes of the Revolution reflect the heavily masculine bias in the historiography, focusing on figures such as Davy Crockett, William B. Travis,

James Bowie, Juan Seguin, and Sam Houston.²⁶ In the past and present, the Texas Revolution is perceived as predominantly a male episode, consistent with much of Texas history. In focusing almost exclusively on the exploits of mythic male adventures in shaping the history of the state, historian Angela Boswell points out that "such myth not only omits the women from these activities, it conceals the reality of women's lived experiences—their history."²⁷ Positioning women into this iconic event, especially for Texas history aficionados, does not come without challenges. Undeniably, the Texas Revolution occupies a hyper-elevated role in Texas cultural memory and identity. In *Texas Identities: Moving Beyond Myth, Memory, and Fallacy in Texas History,* Light Townsend Cummins and Mary Scheer emphasize the contribution of myth and memory to Texas identity, noting that "one's place in the political, economic, and social order also determined identity, such as that of women who were outside the male sphere of power and politics that defined Texas identity as masculine."²⁸ While Texas is particularly notorious for its male centricity, it continues to be a problem for the broader study of the American West as well. In an analysis of books recognized as the best in the field of the American West (published between 2000 and 2010), Margaret Jacob's notes that "none of the books *completely* ignores women, yet in most cases, their inclusion is minimal (often just a few sentences), tokenistic, or uninformed by the most recent scholarship."²⁹ Despite decades of publications by gender historians of the American West, she concludes that western women's and gender history have made little impact on the larger field of western history.

As was the case for Rosa Kleberg, some women told their Revolution stories to family members who assembled and edited the information into narrative form and submitted them for publication in journals such as *The Quarterly of the Texas State Historical Association*. Rosa's grandson, Rudolph Kleberg Jr., also compiled the narrative of his great aunt, Caroline Ernst von Hinueber, publishing her account, "Life of German Pioneers in Early Texas," in the journal in 1899.³⁰ One of the most well-known, detailed accounts of the Runaway Scrape is Dilue Rose Harris's reminiscences, which were published in a three-part series in *The Quarterly* in 1900, 1901, and 1904 when Harris was in her mid-seventies.³¹ A young girl at the time of the Texas Revolution, not quite eleven years old, Harris augmented her account by incorporating material from her father's, Dr. Pleasant W. Rose, journal. In the 1890s, she worked in consultation with two Texas historians, George P. Garrison and Adele Looscan, to bring her story to life. In another account, Clarinda Pevehouse Kegans, who was also a young girl at the time of the Runaway Scrape, wrote down her experiences of early life in Texas and left them to the care of her family. Her great-great granddaughter published a fictional account of the Runaway Scrape based on excerpts from Clarinda's unpublished and unbound memoirs.[32] Despite the flaws of reminiscences and memoirs, which sometimes include self-aggrandizement and whitewashing, they provide an important window into personal perceptions of the past, reflecting established and provisional social dynamics.

Other women's memoirs recounting their experiences in early Texas were published as full-length books, such as those by Ann Raney Coleman, Mary Sherwood Wightman Helm, and Mary Crownover Rabb.[33] Coleman began writing her memoir in 1875 but did not complete the project until 1889. She sent her manuscript to her niece, Alice Smith, who laboriously copied it into final form; however, it did not see publication until the 1940s when it fell into the "lap from a blue sky" of Dr. Samuel E. Asbury, a faculty member at Texas A&M College, after being sold to a manuscript repository several years after her niece's death. On the historical significance of Coleman's journal, Asbury wrote to a Texas state archivist: "You fear that the Ann Raney documents are not important, but they are very important. The dates are important and the addresses of Ann are particularly important."[34] While not a famous figure in Texas history, Coleman had a valuable story that relayed the less-chronicled female experience before, during, and after the Texas Revolution. Not all manuscripts were published, however. The narratives of Harriet A. Ames, Mary A. Baylor, and Rosalie B. Hart Priour all found their way into the archival collections at the Dolph Briscoe Center for American History at the University of Texas.[35] Other women's stories surfaced in local newspaper articles, magazines, oral interviews, and personal correspondence.

This study also relied heavily on the reminiscences of men who published partial and full accounts of their experiences during the Texas Revolution, once again, often many decades after the fact. Two personal histories proved especially valuable: Creed Taylor's *Tall Men with Long Rifles: The Glamorous Story of the Texas Revolution, As Told by Captain Creed Taylor, Who Fought in That Heroic Struggle from Gonzales to San Jacinto* and Noah Smithwick's *The Evolution of a State or Recollections of Old Texas Days*.[36] Creed Taylor

Figure 1. Providing one of the most well-known and detailed accounts of the Runaway Scrape, Dilue Rose Harris published her story in a three-part series in *The Quarterly of the Texas State Historical Association* in 1900, 1901, and 1904. *Courtesy of the Nesbitt Memorial Library Archives*

told his story to historian James T. DeShields, who subsequently arranged and edited the material. In prefacing his narrative, Taylor stated: "I may not be capable of posing as a historian; but having personal knowledge of most of the stirring episodes transpiring in the course of our fight for liberty, I shall attempt to tell the story of my part of that glorious struggle."[37]

Smithwick initially recounted his version of the 1836 campaign to the *Galveston-Dallas News* but was later encouraged to publish his memoirs in book form. In response to the request, his daughter compiled the material into a full-length manuscript, a project completed when Smithwick was eighty-nine years of age. Another fruitful source was *The Diary of William Fairfax Gray: From Virginia to Texas, 1835–1837*. Historian Paul Lack published the diary, which chronicled Gray's travels through Texas in the spring months of 1836, including a valuable record of the proceedings of the Convention of 1836 as well as his participation in the Runaway Scrape.[38]

Other enlisted men's stories found their way into both published and unpublished venues. S. F. Sparks relayed his experiences of the Texas Revolution in an article that appeared in *The Quarterly* in 1908; Beulah Gayle Green edited and published Robert Hancock Hunter's diary as a book in 1936.[39] Located at the Austin History Center, the unpublished transcript of John Milton Swisher's *Early Days in Texas: Reminiscences of Colonel Swisher* describes his military experiences during the Revolution.[40] George P. Garrison published Col. Guy Morrison Bryan's account of the rebellion in *The Quarterly* in 1901 (which was initially relayed to his daughter and compiled by Garrison). However, Bryan provided Kate Scurry Terrell with a more detailed account of the Runaway Scrape in correspondence exchanged with Terrell in 1895. Written in his mid-seventies, the letter recounts his experience as a seventeen-year-old teenager traveling with his mother to the safety of the Louisiana border during the Runaway Scrape.[41]

Like many of my predecessors, the research for this book drew heavily on several volumes of John Jenkins's *Papers of the Texas Revolution* for pertinent letters, ordinances, army orders, and proclamations issued by political and military operatives in 1835 and 1836, including letters from regular soldiers and civilians reaching out to authorities on matters germane to the rebellion. It is hard to overstate the comprehensiveness of this collection. Published in 1973 by Presidial Press, Jenkins's ten-volume collection is a massive compilation of primary documents, arranged by date and easily accessible for scholars of the revolutionary period. Thorough in scope, the volumes include not only documents from the Texas side but also correspondence from Mexican officials. John Holmes Jenkins III, was a historian, publisher, and bookseller who was honored with a lifetime fellowship to the Texas State Historical Association in 1967 in recognition of his scholarly contributions to Texas history.[42]

Prior to this book, there was no full-length monograph focused exclusively on the Runaway Scrape; however, select narratives of women's experiences during the last months of the Texas Revolution appear in articles by historians such as Stephen Hardin, Fane Downs, and Light Townsend Cummins. The latter appears in an award-winning collection, edited by Mary Scheer, that examines the full scope of women's experiences during the Texas Revolution, including Tejana, Black, and Native American women's experiences.[43] Before these publications, historical examinations of the Runaway Scrape are sparse. Carolyn Callaway wrote a master's thesis on the Runaway Scrape for the University of Texas in 1942, providing an insightful scholarly examination of what she termed "An Episode of the Texas Revolution."[44] Earlier still, it is also worth mentioning the preliminary work on the subject by Kate Scurry Terrell, who published a short chapter on the Runaway Scrape in *The Comprehensive History of Texas, 1685-1897* (published in 1898), which drew upon a handful of indispensable firsthand accounts, including her exchange with Guy Bryan.[45]

This book builds on previous scholarship of the Runaway Scrape by expanding the scope and placing gender at the center of analysis. In chapters focused on male power dynamics, examining questions of patriarchy, chivalry, honor, and manly obligations, there are several references to southern notions of nineteenth-century masculinity. Why the emphasis on the South as a regional influence and on southern culture more specifically? By the early 1830s, most of the new arrivals who settled in Texas came from the American South. Initial migrants came from neighboring states, such as Louisiana, Arkansas, and Mississippi; however, over the course of the 1820s and early 1830s, Anglo colonists migrated from all regions of the South.[46] With ample land and an agreeable climate, Texas proved ripe for an expansion of the South's "peculiar institution." Permissive colonization laws in the mid-1820s encouraged Anglo immigration from the United States, typically through empresario contracts. The prospect of cheap land and exemptions from customs duties spurred population growth. New arrivals to Texas established homesteads as subsistence farmers in often remote frontier settings (planting gardens and raising a limited number of domestic animals); colonists broke ground for their crops while often residing in little more than tent structures or one- or two-room cabins. Earlier arrivals, especially those engaged in cotton production, who were able to rely on an abundant supply of enslaved labor, established more sophisticated plantation homes. At whatever stage of settlement—either just starting out or more established—production of a cash-crop, typically cotton, was a top priority. At the time of the Revolution, a population of enslaved people, numbering around five thousand, lived in Anglo households located on the fertile lands in south central and southeastern Texas, drawing from the Brazos, Colorado, and Trinity rivers. Settlements on the lower Brazos and Colorado were especially vulnerable to the Mexican advance. With cotton and slavery firmly entrenched, most Anglo Texas households by the 1830s were southern in nature, relying on racial and gender distinctions shared by their American brethren in states located south of the Mason-Dixon line.

There was an obvious class aspect to slave ownership. Stephen F. Austin, the state's most famous and successful empresario who later became known as the father of Texas, not only was a slaveholder himself but worked to solidify the institution under the complexities of Mexican law. For example, to work around the constitutional restrictions on slavery, in the early months of 1828, Texas introduced a system wherein enslaved persons were "freed" before entering Mexican Texas and then brought into the state as permanently indentured servants working to pay their former masters for manumission. This newly imagined contract system between master and "servant" may have renamed chattel slavery, but the mechanics of the American system of slavery remained in place.[47] Through his role as an empresario, Austin received generous land grants from the Mexican government and became one of the wealthiest and most influential figures in the state. Under Austin's guidance, slavery proliferated in the state. Probably the most famous enslaved person of the Texas revolutionary era is "Joe," held in bondage by slaveholder William Barret Travis, who was one of the few survivors of the battle of the Alamo. Reminiscences of the Runaway Scrape by Dilue Rose Harris, Ann Raney Coleman, and Mary Sherwood Wightman Helm include references to enslaved people in their traveling parties who ended up doing much of the heavy lifting during the trek. While the stressful panic of the Runaway Scrape affected all, bondwomen and men alleviated some of the blistering physical demands of the journey for those wealthy enough to exploit their labor.

As Santa Anna's forces bore down on the farms and plantations in south central Texas in March and April of 1836, the civilian reaction was swift and frenetic. One firsthand account reports seeing a fully set dinner table in their travels, complete with biscuits, potatoes, and fried chicken, left unconsumed by a family who fled their home in haste—the sanctity of the family table summarily interrupted by the immediate threat of a nearby invading army. Chapter 1 traces how the Runaway Scrape upended any sense of domestic security for Texas families, generating a sense of trauma and loss for Texas women. Because women's identities were interwoven with their roles as mothers and wives and they were charged with the responsibility of maintaining the integrity of their homes, the panicked events of the spring of 1836 loomed large. In their hurried exodus, Texas women sacrificed prized possessions, large and small, even burning their homes and crops ahead of the Mexican army's advance. Many Anglo newcomers had just laid down roots in Texas, so the loss of their new homes was especially difficult. Some turned to their faith for strength. For women living through these tumultuous last weeks of the Texas Revolution, it was not only structures and material goods that were at risk but also the very notion of the family home as a space for safety and domestic tranquility.

Chapter 2 continues to focus on women's experiences during the Runaway Scrape, but not exclusively. This chapter examines the gendered contestations between predominantly Anglo women and the men who joined the retreat to the Louisiana border. In many instances, women negotiated power and decision making with men deemed frail, elderly, or generally unfit to fight. Female-led groups encountered men along the way who often sought to assume authority over the situation; these men included spouses and sons who left the fighting to see to the well-being of their wives, mothers, and children. If men supposed that women would wither in the face of danger or meekly acquiesce to their demands, they were often proven wrong. The road to safety proved fertile ground for testing the limits of assumed power. In the mayhem of the race to the Sabine, extant records reveal numerous accounts of women who challenged the authority, decision making, character, and even manliness of their male counterparts during the early months of 1836. To protect their families or properties, some women issued these challenges to men with pistols in their hands, ready to fire if necessary.

Chapter 3 shifts gears by primarily concentrating on the experiences of Anglo Texas men in the late stages of the Revolution and the engagement of gendered language by those both on and off the battlefield. In particular, this chapter focuses on deserters as well as men who chose not to fight in the first place. After the fall of the Alamo and the Goliad massacre, amid a growing sense of despair, the leaders of the Texas Revolution deployed an all-encompassing strategy to compel men to join the Texas cause. Hoping to exploit their martial tendencies, military and government officials exerted virtually every tactic at their disposal to rally Texas men to the front, including shame, alarm, and a multitude of threats. Authorities employed gendered rhetoric intended to humiliate Texas men for failing to come to the aid of Texas women and children. Beginning at the Colorado river, Houston's decisions to retreat and postpone the fighting to another day left the women and children on Texas farms and plantations at risk to an invading army. The Texas commander's military strategy created the predicament that compelled men to choose between two manly obligations: to protect their families or stay in the fight. Texas men grappled with appropriate expressions of their manliness—a microcosm of larger competing notions of nineteenth-century manhood. The chapter also addresses noncombatants (men who chose not to enlist) as well as the criminal element (men who exploited a frightened populace fleeing the rapidly approaching threat).

Chapter 4 continues to examine the use of gendered language in the last difficult months of the 1836 campaign. In this instance, the chapter examines how Texas rebels cloaked their cause in the language of liberty—a fight against the tyrannical aims of a "cruel despot." Further, they aligned their objectives with the Spirit of '76 and the revolutionaries who fought a similar campaign against the British a half century earlier. During the Runaway Scrape, there were *two* perceived enemies that posed a looming threat to the civilian population of the state: the invading Mexican army and Indigenous tribes who launched raids on frontier settlements, which escalated in frequency during the 1836 rebellion, especially in East Texas. From the perspective of Texas government and military officials, both Santa Anna's army and Native Americans waged a dishonorable war against the women and children of the state. Texians did not shroud their fight against Native Americans in the language of liberty; rather, this fight was against a supposed enemy who threatened depredations on Texas households—perceived sites of domestic tranquility—that southern patriarchs were obligated to protect. In their desperate appeal for troops, including military reinforcements from the United States, residents of East Texas resorted to the threat of Native Americans ravaging the region's women and children as their pivotal argument for intervention. The looming threat compelled supporters of the insurgency to rely on gendered language, often alarmist in tone, to draw attention to the danger posed to Texas women and children, both real and imagined.

Chapter 5 compares the experiences of two heroes of the Texas Revolution: Pamelia Mann and Sam Houston. During and immediately after the 1836 military campaign, Houston faced questions regarding his courage and character. At the peak of hostilities, his critics claimed that he failed to display a sufficient level of martial acumen, shirking from his enemy in retreat. As the rebellion teetered on a precipice, there was simply no room for cowardice; gendered expectations held by the populace insisted that men needed to act like men—demanding that they neither retreat nor desert. Ultimately, things worked out fine for the future president of the Republic of Texas. In contrast, the plucky antics and spirited demeanor of Pamelia Mann, a woman who challenged Houston and his men when they tried to impress her oxen during the Runaway Scrape, fared less well in the post-Revolution period. While her contemporaries found it amusing for Mann to act like a man in the chaos of war and the ensuing Runaway Scrape, as Texas settled into a peacetime Republic, the supposition that followed was that men and women should also settle into their expected roles. Mann struggled in this new environment, underscoring a larger question about just how revolutionary the Texas Revolution was when it came to issues of gender.

The book is focused on a brief period of time—less than two months—and yet, from a gender perspective, this is an especially revealing historical moment. The tensions that arose during the Runaway Scrape provide an important window into both shifting and stable gender dynamics in 1830s Texas. The threat of an invading army jangled the nerves of not only the heavily outnumbered Texas army but also the vulnerable civilian population. For the men, women, and children who took to the road hoping to survive the Mexican advance, the ensuing escape to the Louisiana border created trauma and, at times, tensions between participants. During the last months of the Revolution, fear of defeat prompted larger questions of what it meant to be a man or to be woman in a period of war and retreat. Everyone needed to do their part toward the success of the rebellion. Men could rise to the challenge and fulfill their manly obligations on the battlefield or fail to do so. For women, the Runaway Scrape sometimes opened new opportunities for leadership and decision making, although that was not always the case. How stable were new configurations of gender roles and expectations? As it turns out, they were as fleeting as the rebellion itself.

1
A SANCTITY NO MORE

The Building and Burning of Homes

It was about three o'clock in the afternoon when we bid goodbye to the old home, never expecting to see the dear spot again. It was not a palatial house, the furniture was scant and rude; there was no organ or piano, but few pictures and books, no carpets, but it was home *in every sense to us.*[1]

—Creed Taylor

In her reminiscences of her early years in Texas, Ann Raney Coleman relayed a touching story about the fate of a prized china set she stashed among her possessions prior to embarking on the journey to Louisiana. With the Mexican army fast approaching, only seven miles away from their home, Ann's family needed to both move quickly and pack light. She admitted that it would not do to take anything that would retard their progress. Still, the decision on what to leave behind was not an easy one for Ann. In the years preceding, she strove to create a comfortable, though modest, home for her small family, which she now had to leave behind. She wrote: "I packed up our china set and put them in the wagon, and thought my husband would think that they were my little boy's clothes and mine, a foolish thought."[2] Having lost both her parents only a few years earlier (shortly after their arrival to Texas), Ann also packed letters and papers that belonged to her parents, "all the remembrance I had of them," along with a few other small mementos. Ann's scant keepsakes took up little space in the wagon; thus, she had largely kept to the plan to pack sparingly.

Unfortunately for Ann, her husband, John Thomas, was adamant about keeping their load light, monitoring not only his wife's provisions but also those of the enslaved laborers who accompanied the family on their trek. There was little room for missteps. Despite the runaways' quick getaway from the Mexican advance, the army continued its pursuit and were gaining on them. Further, the family was hobbled by oxen moving too slowly to keep up with the rest of their traveling party; consequently, Ann's husband overhauled the wagon to lighten the cargo. In doing so, he threw "something belonging to the Negroes which he had told them not to take." During the reshuffle, Ann's husband discovered her china set and proceeded to remove it from the wagon and set it on the roadside, affirming his role as the family patriarch and primary decision maker. She entreated her husband to take it along, but he rebuffed her request, arguing that if they did not travel faster, they would be taken prisoner by their enemy. Stressing the financial loss of their much more expensive homestead, Thomas stated: "You have thousands of dollars behind, independent of that little trunk of china." Ann admitted that what he said rang true, but she "kept a sullen silence for several hours."[3]

Ann's failed attempt to keep some remnant of her home in the face of the total loss of her household possessions provides a window into the many privations of the Runaway Scrape: the sacrifice of homes that served as familial sanctuaries occurring alongside the trauma of an invading

Figure 2. Mrs. Ann Raney Coleman. While not published during her lifetime, Ann Raney Coleman's reminiscences were assembled into a monograph titled *Victorian Lady on the Texas Frontier: The Journal of Ann Raney Coleman of Whitehaven*. The collection was edited by C. Richard King and published posthumously by the University of Oklahoma Press in 1971. *Courtesy of the University of Oklahoma Press*

army threatening Texas men, women, and children. An essential tenet of nineteenth-century notions of womanhood was the centrality of the family and home as foundational institutions of society.[4] The home was perceived as a bulwark against outside threats. Women's identity was tied to their roles as mothers, wives, and daughters; in these roles, they assumed the responsibility of fostering and enriching the domestic space. Men assumed the role of head of the household, although such roles became more tenuous in times of war and tumult. Whether they did so enthusiastically or reluctantly, women followed their husbands and fathers in the 1820s and 1830s to the Texas frontier, establishing homes on often contested terrain.

While dwellings in frontier Texas were often rudimentary compared to their eastern and southern counterparts, they were still homes—a place of shelter and safety for early migrants to the state.

Prescriptive literature produced during this period focused on women's responsibilities in the domestic sphere. For example, Lydia Howard Sigourney counseled young ladies on the importance of establishing a comfortable home and its distinct importance in women's lives. In *Letters to Young Ladies,* first published in 1834, she wrote: "Since the domestic sphere is entrusted to our sex, and the proper arrangement and government of a household are so closely connected with our enjoyments and virtues, nothing that involves the rational comfort of home is unworthy of attention."[5] Writing on her experiences in early Texas, Mary Sherwood Wightman Helm reiterated that the family and, by extension, the home remained in the purview of women as "sacred precincts." She wrote: "Here woman, by her unostentatious and hallowed influence, reigns preeminently. She may not preside in Church or State, but she trains the hand that ministers in the one and guides in the other."[6] Busy with the labor demands of the frontier, women in isolated cabins and on modest farms in rural Texas likely had little room—literally and figuratively—to stock up on advice books from writers like Sigourney; still, there is little doubt that they took pride in their homes and saw its governance as part of their prime responsibilities.

In her examination of women's lives in early nineteenth-century Texas, Adrienne Caughfield argues that "the colonists needed everything possible to make themselves more comfortable and give the land the feeling of home. It is at this point that women's roles—whether as bastions of virtue at home or an influential force elsewhere—became crucial and where the call to bring civilization to the wilderness grew louder."[7] Within this framing, women were tasked with the responsibility of creating a sense of home on the Texas frontier. Indeed, Ann Raney Coleman was engaged in such a project. However, just as many women were making headway on this front, the exigencies of war and invasion forced them to leave their home improvement efforts behind. The Runaway Scrape upended any sense of domestic security, generating a sense of trauma for Texas women. Because women's identities were interwoven with their roles as mothers and wives, and they were charged with the responsibility of maintaining the integrity of their homes, the panicked events of the spring of 1836 must have been perceived as an existential threat. For women living through these turbulent last weeks of the Texas Revolution, it was not only structures and material goods that were at risk but also the very notion of the family home as a space for safety and tranquility.

Laura Clark Shire's work on the central role of white women and expansionist domesticity in the US colonization of Florida, *The Threshold of Manifest Destiny*, offers a useful comparative model to the experiences of white women who moved to Texas in the late 1820 and early 1830s. Shire's book examines a similar time period (1830–1840), and most of the subjects of her study were recent migrants to the former Spanish territory. She also situates women and their newly established households at the forefront of her analysis. Shire explores the sensationalist press accounts of the Seminoles Wars in Florida that concocted and promoted Indian depredations narratives in which white women and their children suffered injury or death or lost property when attacked by Seminoles. Relying on gory, bloodcurdling stories, Shire notes that "these tales glossed over Indian removal and the expansion of slavery and framed the conflict in Florida as a noble war being waged for the protection of white women and children."[8] Depredation narratives paid special attention to the destruction of families and the domestic spaces that white women created in Florida: "Along with the material consequences, depredations were also attacks on white women and children, the families who transformed property into a 'true home.'"[9] Shire's analysis never loses sight of women's roles as settler colonizers, complicit in the violence and volatility that accompanied their migration into Seminole territory. Throughout the period, women in Texas faced the threat of Indian attack; however, in the early months of 1836, their biggest concern was an advancing Mexican army and the devastations they assumed would follow.

In describing his own family's flight from the Mexican forces, Creed Taylor expressed a sense of loss similar to that of Ann Raney Coleman when it came time to leave the family home. From their location on the Guadalupe River, the Taylor family watched squads of men make their way to the battlefront, sometimes stopping in for food and water before pushing on to Gonzales. However, Taylor explained, the tide turned and the men returned from the front "great excited, halting only long enough to shout, 'The Mexicans are coming, Houston is making for the Trinity, the Sabine! Flee for your lives.'"[10] The panicked reports prompted the Taylor family to hurriedly ready for their departure. Taylor's mother prepared their packs for the "sad" trip. Taylor noted, "It was about three o'clock in the afternoon when we bid goodbye to the old home, never expecting to see the dear spot again. It was not a palatial house, the furniture was scant and rude; there was no organ or piano, but few pictures and books, no carpets, but it was *home* in every sense to us." He continued, "It was humble but very dear, and the children cried all evening and that night till sleep finally came to their tired bodies. If mother shed a tear I never knew it though there was an unusual huskiness in her voice that day."[11] Like Coleman, Taylor's mother created a home for her family and grieved for its loss, vowing that her boys would seek revenge for the upheaval.

The Taylor family's humble home was not unlike many frontier Texas homes, scant in furniture and primitive in condition. It is important to note that most Anglo Texans were new arrivals in the late 1820s and early 1830s; accordingly, many were in the early stages of establishing their farms and plantations. Cultivating a productive farm entailed clearing land and planting crops, grueling work that was often the critical first step for a newly arrived family.[12] Although nineteenth-century prescriptive literature propagated domesticity as a woman's true calling, almost all women (except a precious few elite women) labored both inside and outside of their homes, especially in new frontier settlements.[13] In his examination of two counties in the Florida Panhandle during the same period, historian Edward Baptist argues that on the plantation frontier, "women's labor was as essential as that of adult men. Consigned by custom and law to the direction of the male head of household, women performed almost every kind of task on small farms."[14] Erecting a permanent shelter in a new environment took time and resources. Mary Sherwood Wightman Helm described the interior of her new home on Matagorda Bay when she and her husband first landed in January 1829: "A large fire in the centre, a mosquito-net covering a rude bed at each corner of the room, the whole building being without joists or tennents [sic], but simply forked sticks drove into the ground to support poles on which cross-poles were laid to sustain the mattress, while perpendicular poles the mosquito net—a thing quite indispensable."[15] Vulnerability to the elements prompted the couple to erect a tent inside their fifty-square-foot home to shut out the weather and rain.

Despite their modest beginnings, the couple would climb, socially, into Texas's most elite circles—Mary's husband, Elias Wightman, founded the town of Matagorda and was employed by Stephen F. Austin as a surveyor for his colony. As a reward for his service, Elias Wightman was given a land grant on Caney Creek, near the present-day town of Sargent.[16] In 1837,

Figure 3. Map of Texas settlements. *Courtesy of Erin Greb Cartography*

Wightman was elected as one of the first justices of the peace for the newly established Matagorda County. Perhaps it was her family's elevated status that prompted Mary Sherwood Wightman Helm, in her description of the Runaway Scrape, to write: "The sick and the young and the helpless found graves all along the way; they had left comfortable homes surrounded by luxury and abundance."[17] Her observation that most people who joined the march to safety left "luxury and abundance" underscores rather stark differences in class in early Texas, particularly as reflected through property ownership (including enslaved persons). Not all Texians were leaving "luxury and abundance" behind. The sacrifice of those leaving property that represented the entirety of their wealth was especially acute. Of course, *any* home—rudimentary or otherwise—would be more comfortable than the outdoor conditions and extreme weather Texians faced along the road to the Louisiana border.

Ann Raney Coleman admitted that when she first arrived in Texas in 1832 with her mother and sister (her father came earlier), what constituted a home was often little more than a two-room log cabin with an entry running through the middle of the structure. She recalled the lack of privacy of such dwellings and the forced intimacy they entailed, at times tight proximity with virtual strangers. Witnessing her discomfort with sharing a bedroom with "gentlemen," the "ladies," also present in the cabin, counseled Ann that "'by the time you have been in Texas a few months, if you travel the country, you will have to sleep with the man and his wife at the house you visit,' as houses were only log cabins with two rooms, one for the house servants, the other for the family."[18] The advice proved prescient as, two weeks later, Ann found herself sleeping in a married couple's bed as she visited friends in the country: "I had to sleep with the man and his wife. I slept at the back of the bed, the wife in the middle and the man in the front." Such rudimentary living was meant to be temporary as the newly arrived focused on establishing their farms. She noted that making money was the primary concern for Anglo newcomers, "all things else were subsidiary to it." When it came to class dynamics, log cabin living cut across socioeconomic lines; Ann observed that "this was the way most of the wealthy planters lived when we first arrived in Texas."[19]

In a letter dated May 31, 1836, to her sister's in-laws in Kentucky, Colgate D'Eve Donaldson provides constructive insights into both the Runaway Scrape and the rustic living conditions in which she found herself during the spring/summer of 1836. At the time of the letter, the widowed Colgate resided with her sister, Charcila ("Chess"), and her sister's husband, William Moore, in a cabin located above the mouth of the west side of Neches River in East Texas "where William has concluded to remain for some years."[20] Like the Sabine River, the Neches River drains into Sabine Lake on the Texas-Louisiana border, which became the desired destination of many fleeing the invading Mexican army for safety. Part of the impetus behind Colgate's letter was to provide her initial impressions of Texas to the Kentucky kin and advise them on whether they should similarly migrate to the state. Further, Colgate sought to counter her brother-in-law's extraordinarily positive assessments of Texas. And while she had many qualms about the state, she shared her brother-in-law's optimism regarding the fertility of the land. She wrote that she had not seen the interior of the state, "but what I can judge from the time I have been here every account of William was correct, all the grains, fruits, vegetables, game and fish of the temperate zone as well as the tropics can be and is cultivated and grown here with the greatest success." She continued, "Emigrants by providing themselves with bread and salt the first year, can with the least industry live like Nabobs."[21]

However, despite the favorable climate and land, Colgate D'Eve Donaldson did not find Texas to be a suitable match for her in-laws and friends in Kentucky—at least not in the early months of 1836 when the state was consumed by war. Texas was too raw, too crude in condition. She explained: "Notwithstanding all that I have stated of Texas, and 'tis all true, I say *do* not come neither you nor Mr. Harlan; the country is too new and unsettled; the houses few and uncomfortable, workmen, & material rare and not good, commerce too uncertain, and of course groceries not easily procured, these are all mountainous objections when brought home to our own selves as I can tell from experience."[22] Creating a comfortable life amidst such scarcity and uncertainty proved to be a daunting, perhaps unattainable, pursuit in a state too early in its evolution. For Colgate, the negatives clearly outweighed the positives when it came to Texas.

One can imagine that the context of war and people fleeing for their lives also marred the letter writer's opinion of the state. Given their location near the Louisiana border, Colgate and her sister's family were well placed to witness the arrival of scores of Anglo Texans as they raced to the safety of the border, and she was deeply disturbed by what she saw:

"Of all the distresses I ever saw or read, of the miserable flight of those poor flying wretches exceeded, they came in miserable carts and wagons tyed together with raw hide, covered with blankets, sheets or quilts as they had them, with ragged bits of harness holding to those apologies of vehicles the largest and finest oxen you can possibly imagine—(where there was a horse, he looked like dog meat)—filled with a portion of their plunder, (for in their terror they left nearly all behind) and women and children."[23]

She continued, "Numbers came on horseback two or three thick without hat or shoes many of them, hundreds of a day came in tired and worn down themselves and their cattle, begging for something to eat." She noted that since their group arrived with provisions before the throngs of civilians from the interior, William, who was a merchant by trade, sold his goods "at a fair price" and "did not take advantage of the times."[24]

There was a decidedly class aspect to Colgate's perception of the primitive conditions of the state. Colgate's deceased husband, William Donaldson, was a diplomat, and the couple lived in France for several years before returning to the United States—a setting quite at odds with frontier Texas.[25] In describing the family's cabin, Colgate wrote: "We have a small shantee [sic] built in appearance and comfort a counterpart of those little huts of the workmen, on the turnpike road between Maysville and Lexington, about 10 feet square for our beds and furniture which consists of three tables, five chairs (borrowed) a looking glass which William place [sic] *slanting* in the old fashioned way, for his special benefit, I presume, since no one else consults it." On the kitchen, she sardonically wrote: "Our kitchen is wide commodious and airy, as it is out of doors, and when it rains we cook in the house." Despite her cynicism, Colgate admitted, "We are more elegantly accommodated than anyone here, all being in miserable tents, which neither excludes sun or rain." An interesting footnote to Colgate D'Eve Donaldson's story is that when her sister tragically died of complications during childbirth in 1838, she married her sister's husband, William Moore, and helped raise his two daughters.[26]

The adjustment to country life and rudimentary living was not an easy transition for many Anglo Texas women. Rustic cabin life was quite standard, especially for the new arrivals. As historian Mark Carroll notes, "Texas remained a primitive farming society to the end of the antebellum period. As late as 1850, 96 percent of Texans lived in remote rural areas."[27] Even the farmhouses of established settlers who were able to upgrade from cabin living to more spacious dwellings offered few amenities: "Hand-hewn and mud-chunked, with a gabled clapboard roof and dirt floor, they proved oppressively hot in the summer, drafty and cold in the winter."[28] In *Texas Roots: Agriculture and Rural Life Before the Civil War,* Allan C. Jones details the building process and layout of the typical one-room log house erected by Texas colonists. Upon arrival to their plots of land, settlers' initial priorities were planting a corn crop and creating makeshift shelters, such as crude lean-to structures. After breaking the land and cultivating their first crops, they could focus on a more permanent structure. Colonists felled logs fourteen to eighteen feet long and rolled or dragged them by oxen to the cabin site. Those with enslaved people avoided much of the truly arduous, backbreaking work. Most houses had puncheon floors made of split logs or thick slabs smoothed by an adze. Doors were made with similar materials. One-room cabins typically featured a single small hide- or wood-covered window located high on the wall near the fireplace, which provided light for cooking and other domestic chores. Furniture, such as chairs, benches, and stools, were made from rough lumber and rawhide.[29]

Such cabins, while austere in condition, provided much-needed protection for new arrivals to the state from an array of potential hazards. Rural Texans grappled with isolation, threat of Indian attack, and extreme weather. Caroline Ernst von Roeder von Hinueber, who migrated to Texas when she was eleven years old, provided the following description of her first house: "This was a miserable little hut, covered with straw and having six sides, which were made out of moss. The roof was by no means waterproof, and we often held an umbrella over our bed when it rained at night, while the cows came and ate the moss." When she landed in Texas, Caroline was among the earliest German children to settle in the Mexican state of Coahuila y Tejas, her family being the first German family to arrive in the state in 1831. Caroline's father, Friedrich Ernst, was later regarded as the father of the immigrants for his role in spurring German migration during the period of the Texas Republic. She noted that conditions were a great deal worse in the winter: "My father had tried to build a chimney and a fireplace out of logs and clay, but we were afraid to light a fire because of the extreme combustibility of our dwelling. So we had to shiver."[30]

Harriet A. Ames wrote about her difficult adjustment to rural living: "When I went to Texas, country life was a sealed book to me. I knew how to make a stylish dress; all about the fashions; and how to dress my hair in the latest mode of coiffure, and how to make a living in New Orleans."[31] Harriet's sister-in-law taught her how to raise chickens, set a hen, milk cows, and make butter—common female responsibilities on a farm. She noted that she was just beginning to enjoy country life when the Runaway Scrape intervened. What initially prompted Harriet and others in her community to "flee for their lives" was a misunderstanding—someone had set a fire in the canebrakes, which apparently popped like "volleys of gunfire." A man named Norton, whom Harriet described as a "very hard drinker," mistook the cane fire as a Mexican attack, shouting that the Mexicans were "burning and murdering as they came."[32] Consequently, she and her neighbors immediately fled in a panic. Before the group became aware of the mistake and returned to their homes, they were met by Col. Robert Potter, secretary of the Texas Navy, and two or three others who informed them that he had orders to remove all the people from the area to Galveston for safety, at which point they could board ships to points east.

Written at the age of eighty-three, Harriet's reminiscences detail her experiences before and after the Runaway Scrape. She arrived in Texas from New Orleans in 1836 with her husband, Solomon Page. Rather than seeing his enlistment as a sign of bravery, Harriet believed her husband abandoned her and their children when he chose to join the Texas army. For Harriet, her husband's first and foremost responsibility was to protect his family. Destitute and isolated, she could not believe that her husband would leave her and the two children with no provisions while he went to war. When she asked him what she and the children were going to do survive, he replied, "You will have to do the best you can." To which she responded, "'If you go off and leave us to starve, … I hope that the first bullet that is fired will pierce your heart, and just leave you time enough to think of the wife and children that you left to die of starvation in this wilderness."[33] After the war, given her clear sense of betrayal, she brazenly refused her husband's attempts at reconciliation when he sought to reunite with his family.

Decades after the Revolution, Harriet remembered with vivid detail the trauma of the escape. On the night of the Norton panic, she had planned to visit a neighbor and was dressed for such a social occasion. After the pronouncements that the Mexicans were "murdering and burning" nearby, the scramble to get out of the area was immediate—with no time for Harriet to change clothes. Reflecting on these events, she remembered feeling distressed and embarrassed by her appearance. She wrote, "One would have imagined that I was some very strange animal, indeed, to see the amount of open-eyed and openmouthed attention that I received. I should never forget the dress that caused me such uncomfortable regard. It was black silk, somewhat the worse for wear after my forced march over Texas prairies."[34] She added, "With it I wore a white crape shawl and a black velvet hat with trimmings of white satin ribbons and feathers." Rather extravagant attire for travel in the rain and mud. Harriet recalled the difficult trek across the prairie carrying her youngest baby, "who seemed to grow very heavy as the way grew longer."[35] She eventually made it safely to Galveston under the protection of Colonel Potter, who gave the family refuge on a naval ship.[36]

In Harriet Ames's case, the group's decision to leave in haste was based on a false rumor; however, for many Texas families, reports (both real and imagined) that the Mexicans were fast approaching compelled them to hurriedly escape their homes with little time to plan for travel or fortify their belongings. Upon hearing the disturbing news of the defeat of the Texas forces at the Alamo, Jane Hallowell Hill recalled: "Mother was so distressed when she heard of the fall of the Alamo that she only took one trunk, some bedding and provisions, leaving a good supply of everything at home. On our return we only found most of the books. The Mexican army had camped within five miles of our house and burned the fence rails to make their fires."[37] During her escape to the Louisiana border with her parents, Mary A. Baylor remembered a detailed scene of one family's abrupt departure: "One day we passed a house with all of the doors open, the table had been set, all of the victuals on the table and even the chairs set up in their places, on the table was a plate of buiscuit [sic], a plate of potatoes, fried chicken (a real nice dinner had been prepared), coffee pot on the table, pitcher of milk." She continued, "It was supposed the owner had left in a hurry."[38] So, in this instance, Baylor witnessed a fully set dinner table—a rather nice dinner—that was ultimately left unconsumed by the family who occupied the house. The immediate threat of a nearby opposing army summarily interrupted the sanctity of the family table. Baylor's description provides an indispensable glimpse into both the comforts of family life and the disruptive nature of the onset of war to domestic security.

Guy Morrison Bryan recalled similar scenes of hurried departures to what Baylor witnessed during her family's escape. At the time of the Runaway Scrape, in the spring of 1836, Bryan was a teenager traveling with his mother to safety toward the Louisiana border and away from Gen. Antonio López de Santa Anna's invading army. Decades later, in his mid-70s, Bryan was asked by a historian in 1895 to provide a detailed account of his experiences during these turbulent months; he gave a lengthy response.[39] After hearing of Gen. Sam Houston's retreat at the Colorado, Bryan described the intense panic that spread among the civilian population: "Some families left their homes with tables spread for the daily meal, all hastily prepared for flight, as if the enemy were at their doors and that flight was the only means to avoid capture and death." He wrote, "As I learned afterwards, some secreted themselves in cainbreaks [sic] on the Brazos bottoms and the late Gov. Smith with his family sought protection in the thickets of Clear Creek. Such was the confusion, dismay and distress that many forgot to take with them provisions for their support."[40] On farms and plantations across the state, Texas families no longer felt safe in their homes.

Bryan's letter also sheds light on the conditions of the Runaway Scrape itself—both the physical and mental stresses endured by fleeing families in the early months of 1836. He described the excessive rains, overflowing rivers, conditions of the roads, and the bottlenecks of frightened and desperate people at ferry crossings. He also addressed the fear of an advancing army so prevalent among the line of runaways: "Sometimes from false reports coming from behind that the enemy were rapidly approaching, would produce a panic, then you would see some throwing out of their wagons, bed clothes, provisions, and what little they had, whipping up their horses & fleeing as fast as they could, spreading dismay among those ahead."[41] Fear of the approaching Mexican army or Indian attack, led some traveling families to dump their limited material goods over the Texas prairie. These were not simply luxury items but staples necessary for subsistence. Such actions prompted Bryan's mother to comment: "What good can they expect to come to them from throwing away their provisions and clothes, if the enemy are coming, they can't get away by throwing away the articles they will so much need. But these people were panic-stricken and not responsible for what they did. O! the cruel runaway scrape—how much of distress, suffering and loss it caused!!"[42]

Before frightened Texans took to the road, they needed to decide what to do with their belongings—what to leave and what to take—and, further still, what to do to with their immovable possessions, specifically their crops and homes. As Guy Bryan observed, many families chose to hide most their belongings and travel light. According to Rosalie Bridget Hart Priour, whose reminiscences were composed in 1860, the residents of the town of Labardee were told that attack from five hundred Mexicans and Indians was imminent and they needed to leave the area immediately. Town residents, comprised mostly of women and children, were told to take "nothing but provisions for two days and one frying pan, one coffee pot and skillet." They were also allowed to take one change of clothes. Priour recalled that "everybody buried their valuables before leaving." In one instance, she noted that a "Mrs. Synot tied some money in a handkerchief and putting the rest in a chest, together with her jewelry and other valuables, moved her bed, dug a hole and buried them under the bed, then removing as far as possible all traces of the ground having been disturbed, replaced the bed where it normally stood."[43] Having some money on hand would obviously be beneficial for the journey ahead; however, there was clearly a desire on Mrs. Synot's part to squirrel away some of the family's fortune for their return, operating under the assumption that she would eventually return.

Below the heading "While Houston Battled at San Jacinto: Pioneer Women Left Record of Panic That Spread Over Texas When Mexican Invasion Was On," the *Dallas Morning News*, on April 24, 1927, published in its news feature section the experiences of one pioneer woman's plight during the Runaway Scrape, including her community's efforts to hide the family property from the advancing Mexican army. The feature writer noted, "One pioneer Texas woman has left us a record of her experiences at that time, which shows the less spectacular, but no less heroic side of the Texas war for independence." In the article, the woman recalled that "all went to work to hide our goods. Our crockery was sunk in the margin of Cany Creek, our beds were carried to a thicket and a rude shelter put over them; and our bushels of potatoes were piled in one large heap covered with straw and earth." She continued, "One cart carried only such things to support life. We left luxuries and groceries for only a limited amount could be carried."[44] There was plainly some hope on the part of this pioneer woman that the items that constituted her home—her crockery, beds, food items, and luxuries—might survive the onslaught of an invading army and be retrievable upon her homecoming.

Caroline Ernst von Roeder von Hinueber's father not only constructed the rudimentary shelter discussed earlier but also oversaw the family's escape during the Runaway Scrape. In April 1831, Caroline's father, Friedrich Ernst, received a land grant from the Mexican government that enabled him to establish a farm where he grew fruit trees and tobacco. Because of a letter conveying his enthusiasm on the positive attributes of his new land, which was subsequently published in a German newspaper, Ernst started the first steady stream of German migration to Texas; inspired by Ernst's messaging, thousands under direction of the Adelsverein moved to Texas in the mid-1840s.[45] When the Revolution broke out, Ernst initially planned to shelter his family in place until he got word that, amidst the chaos of war, the Kickapoo Indians were launching raids on Texas settlements. Such news prompted Ernst to prepare his family to join the massive exodus of civilians fleeing to the Louisiana border. The German traveling party included the Ernst family as well as thirteen other men and their families.[46]

In her memoirs, Caroline explained that her father stashed many of their belongings before their flight, alleviating some of the challenges they would face when they returned to the farm. She stated, "After the war, times were hard. However, my father had buried a good many things and thus succeeded in keeping them from the Mexicans." She recalled her father's strategy for protecting the family's valuables: "He had placed two posts a considerable distance apart and had buried his treasures just midway between them. The posts had both been pulled out and holes dug near them, but our things had not been found. Our house and garden had been left unharmed, though those of our neighbors had been destroyed." She rationalized the discrepancy in property damage between her family and her neighbors was because one of the German families was Catholic and had brought "all of their holy relics to our place and set up several crosses in our garden."[47] The theory was that, because most soldiers in the Mexican army were Catholic, they would respect the property of fellow Catholics.

As was the case with Ann Raney Coleman and her cherished china set, Texas women made gut-wrenching decisions about whether they should bring items of sentimental value on the journey or leave them behind and risk losing them forever. Recording the experiences of her great aunt, Maria Bachman Atkinson, during the Runaway Scrape, M. Jourdan Atkinson relayed the family's efforts at protecting a prized family heirloom—a Seth Thomas mantel clock. Maria and her husband, John Atkinson, settled in Austin's Colony between the Brazos and Colorado rivers with their eight children. The children ranged in ages: Sarah (age sixteen), Elizabeth (age fourteen), John (age twelve), Catherine (age ten), Alexander (age seven), Nancy (age five), Mary Ann (age three), and Henry (one year, nine months). Like many Texas families, Maria's was left to navigate the troublesome escape without the assistance of her husband, who was "somewhere with Houston's army" at the time of the Runaway Scrape; instead, she had to rely on her children to assist with the travel preparation. Unlike families with more abundant means, the Atkinson family did not have enslaved laborers to depend on. Hampering their travel further was that the family had no access to a wheeled vehicle. Maria and the children emptied the cabin, "buried all nonperishables except their most precious possession, the thigh-high Seth Thomas mantel clock, and planted the earth to mustard."[48]

According to Jourdan Atkinson's account, the only option to transport their minimal belongings was a makeshift sled: "They took the barrel from the waterslide (a heavy, clumsily built sled), loaded on to it a box in which they put provisions, the clock, and some balls of spun cotton, and yoked the slide to their pair of oxen. They left with the baby boy and the smaller girls riding on the sled with the box as they lumbered down to Groce's Crossing on the Brazos."[49] At Groce's Crossing (also known as Groce's Landing), the proprietor, plantation owner Jared Groce, intervened in the family's plight, providing the travelers with a high-wheeled Mexican cart and a promise to take care of their prized belongings—the clock and the balls of cotton. Realizing the challenge ahead, Maria agreed to leave the items with Groce.

Unfortunately, her cherished possessions did not fare well in the wartime turmoil. When she returned to Groce's Crossing, she found her box broken open and the clock's lead weights missing. Apparently, Houston's army impressed her items for the war effort: "the lead to mold into bullets and the cotton to braid into bridles for the horses."[50] Maria took the clock home, minus the lead weights, with the hope that it could be repaired in the future.

Understandably, a thigh-high mantel clock would be an odious burden for families seeking to move swiftly out of harm's way; however, even small, prized possessions needed to be sacrificed. Clarinda Pevehouse Kegans was just shy of twelve years old when hostilities broke out in Texas. She described the ordeal of preparing for the journey to the Sabine as well as the fate of her most precious possessions: "Papa had made a little box for me the year I was ten. It had a butterfly on the lid and he said it was to keep my treasures. My treasures were the two glass buttons keepsakes from Grandma's dress and a scrap of blue ribbon and a pressed flower."[51] When Clarinda's family started packing for their journey, her mother told her she couldn't take the little box, scolding her that it wasn't necessary. This assertion did not sit well with little Clarinda, who noted that her mother "had made room for the family violin and our study books. I didn't think they were necessary." She was also troubled that her mother rebuked her in front of her grandfather. Ultimately, the episode prompted her to go off to cry. An individual of elevated status in Texas, Clarinda's grandfather, Alexander Hodge, owned Hodge's Plantation and served as the local magistrate. He was a serious man who "didn't take time for us children."[52]

The concern over protecting the family holdings prompted Hodge to order his bondsmen to drive their cattle to the bottoms in the hope that the Mexican army would not find them. As the family embarked on their journey eastward, Clarinda observed smoke rising above the trees across the country. She stated, "I knew the settlers were burning their homes and things before they left. Mama had refused to set fire to ours, said we would be back home soon."[53] Unlike Maria's family, the Hodge-Pevehouse traveling party benefitted from their enslaved laborers, although Clarinda still found the flight too terrible to describe. On the second day of the trek, the group stopped to set up camp and, to Clarinda's surprise, her grandpa pulled the little butterfly box out of his pocket. Despite feeling tired and scared, Clarinda revealed that "when I saw Papa's little box, then I knew that he and Grandpa, who had never said half a dozen words to me, loved me after all. I threw my arms around his neck and cried." The "serious man" clearly had a soft spot for his granddaughter, perhaps recognizing the benefit of small comforts during a frightening ordeal. She concluded her story be saying, "The box and Grandma's buttons were precious then as they are to this day."[54] While Clarinda's grandfather ultimately spared her the sorrow of giving up her precious mementos, other Texas women were not so fortunate.

The burning of homes across the countryside that Clarinda witnessed underscores the challenging dilemma Anglos in Texas faced before they joined the panicked exodus to the Louisiana border. Should they burn their homes and crops to thwart their enemy's seizure of the fruits of their hard-earned labor or leave them intact, hoping they would withstand the Mexican advance? Creating homes and productive farms out of the Texas wilderness was a daunting, laborious task for settlers. It must have been an unbearable sight for the Texas families who chose this option, watching their hard work and sacrifice go up in flames as they fled to safety. Their homes were their sanctuaries. Just as Guy Bryan's mother questioned the efficacy of throwing away provisions and clothes in the escape, which "they will so much need," Clarinda's mother expressed similar doubt on the practicality of burning one's home to frustrate the Mexican army.

Despite such reservations, contemporaneous accounts suggest that many Texas civilians decided to burn their homes before the Mexican advance, and further evidence shows that the Texas army also engaged in the torching of towns. In a letter to the *Columbus Herald,* later published in the *Baltimore Gazette and Daily Advertiser,* one eyewitness account described the "terrors of the war," particularly the massacre of Fanin's forces at Goliad. Included in the account was a report on the status of several Texas towns: "San Phillippe is burnt (by the citizens) and there is probability that Brazoria and Washington have shared the same fate."[55] It was not the citizens, but the captain of the San Felipe militia, Mosely Baker, who was ordered to burn down the town to prevent the Mexican army from using logs from structures to build rafts to cross the Brazos. Operating on a false report that the Mexican army was within a few miles of the town, Baker's company torched the town of San Felipe on March 29, 1836. While Sam Houston disclaimed giving the order to burn San Felipe, after the war, the Board of Examination, responsible for reimbursing damaged or impressed property claims to citizens in the post-Revolution era, paid most claims for the destruction of San Felipe property as an official act of the army.[56]

In a similar instance involving the Texas army, after the fall of the Alamo when panic gripped the civilian population, a soldier named Quintus Allen wrote to a friend in Mississippi advising against a proposed move to Texas: "You ask whether I would advise you to come to Texas now. No; I wouldn't just now, if ever." Allen was reacting to the regression of the state as it spiraled into war and devastation. The letter dated March 15, 1836, from a Texian Army Camp on the Navidad River relayed the following eyewitness account of the burning of the town of Gonzales: "Soldier John Sharp said: 'Captain Karnes told us orders were to burn the town. We made quick work of it.' Tall spires of flame from the blazing houses lit up the countryside."[57] He noted that the fleeing townspeople were frightened by explosions, which they thought were from cannon fire by their enemy; however, the explosions were due to the blowing up of barrels of gin and wine.

The impetus behind Texians' decision to burn their plantations, farms, and towns to the ground was to prevent the Mexican forces from exploiting valuable Texas resources, specifically wood for fires and much-desired food, which was in short supply. Enemy or ally, armies on the march regularly appropriated what they needed from civilian caches. It is not evident that the Mexican army was any more ruthless in their treatment of Texas property than any advancing army—they took what they needed and continued their pursuit of Houston's forces. Sometimes their needs were vast. Samuel Rogers described his family's return from the Runaway Scrape: "We returned home at last but found nothing as the Mexicans had carried off everything. Of about a hundred head of cattle they had taken all but one."[58] In fact, the preemptive destruction of property by Anglo Texans irked the invading army. In a letter to his superior, Gen. Joaquim Ramirez y Sesma reported to General Santa Anna on the Texians' propensity for burning property:

> I immediately sent to the inhabitants one of the proclamations in English, which your Excellency addressed to the People of Texas; notwithstanding which, they have so consummated their barbarous conduct, by burning down entirely three houses which stood on the road to the river, and the whole town, with the grain, furniture, and all that it contained; after they set fire to everything, without exception, they fled. The craft and boats on the river are all burnt, and although I have found a ford for the infantry, a day's work is necessary to enable me to transport the artillery, baggage, and horses, across, as impediments have been placed on each side.[59]

If the Texians sought to frustrate the Mexican army with their tactics, their plan worked. The burning of homes and crops was a tactical decision made in the throes of retreat, but it yielded long term consequences for families who returned home to charred landscapes, forced to start anew the arduous process of settlement. There is a certain hypocrisy to the who-burned-the-town debate—the army or civilians. During the same period in Florida, Laura Clark Shire notes that fire and the destruction of property figured prominently in Indian depredation narratives, as American narrators attributed the use of fire as a practice of "Barbaric" Seminoles, ignoring that American troops plundered and burned any Seminole villages they encountered during the First, Second, and Third Seminole Wars.[60] In these narrated accounts, authors "offered readers scenes of devasted domestic tranquility as sensational proof that the Seminoles had violated all of the family and domestic relationships that Americans held to be sacred and natural."[61] Publishers expected American audiences to feel heightened sympathy for white women who watched their sacred spaces burning to the ground.

Disposing of their cherished possessions, large or small, created a significant sense of loss for frightened Texas families, but it was just one of many difficulties. Their fears were myriad—the rapidly advancing Mexican army, the threat of Indian raids, deep concern for their loved ones on the battlefront, and, finally, the task at hand—their desperate need to navigate extreme circumstances to safety, often with children in tow. The conditions were treacherous; it rained continuously during the spring of 1836, resulting in swollen rivers and streams that proved difficult to cross. In addition to rising waters, diseases (such as measles, sore eyes, whooping cough, and cholera) spread throughout the makeshift camps.[62] In such time of crisis, it is no surprise that fleeing colonists during the Runaway Scrape turned to religion for solace. Bereft with grief after hearing about the loss of her son at the Alamo and distraught with fear about her husband's condition as well as her youngest son, Thomas, Mrs. Frances Sutherland wrote to her sister conveying her sorrow: "My poor William gone, Sutherland in the army, me with my three little daughters and my poor Thomas wandering about, not knowing what to do or where to go. You will guess my feelings were dreadful, but ever the Lord supported me, and was on our side for I think I may boldly say the Lord fought our battles." Mrs. Sutherland attributed the Texas army's defeat of Santa Anna's forces at San Jacinto to divine intervention: "Some say our army fought double their number and who dares say that the Lord was not on our side. Mr. Sutherland's horse was killed under him, but the Lord preserved his life and brought him back to his family."[63]

In her reminiscences, Rosalie Bridget Hart Priour recounted the many misfortunes her family endured upon their arrival to the state; in such difficult times, Rosalie's parents found comfort in their belief in God. The first struggle the family contended with was the death of her father, who had fallen sick on the voyage to Texas and passed away shortly after docking. She wrote: "Soon after landing Father asked Mother to take him out walking and let him see what kind of country he was in. He had not gone far when he begged to return as he felt too weak to go any further." Later that night, he succumbed to his illness, but not before imparting his last wishes for his daughters to his bereaved wife: "Above all things teach them to love God and keep good company."[64] Six weeks later, the now-fatherless family met another challenge that pressed them to the brink. An outbreak of flux spread throughout their new community. Rosalie's mother and another woman were the only persons available to take care of the sick. The other lady would "go from house to house doing what she could to relieve the suffering." Rosalie's mother was charged with the strenuous task of washing for the entire community, washing twelve dozen pieces of clothing a day. When it was too late for her to wash, she would go among the sick and help make them comfortable for the night. Even eight-year-old Rosalie was called upon to cook, clean, and take care of her little sister, while her mother labored to keep up with the community's needs. However, with all their exertions, "they could not save all, a great many died." On the tragedy, Rosalie wrote: "As my mother always said 'God always fits the back for the burden.' If he had not given her superhuman strength she must have succumbed under the troubles of that year."[65] Shortly thereafter, the family would be thrust into the chaos of fleeing the Mexican forces; no doubt, once again relying on their faith to see them through the trauma.

In a separate account of the Runaway Scrape, Mary Crownover Rabb described the dangers all around, including sickness and the death of her child: "I was vary sick while we was campt thare but however we got to come home in the fall and stay untell the first of Febewary 36 then we was all drove out of ouer houses with ouer little ones to suffer with cold and hungry and little Lorenzy not three months old when we started died on the road [sic]."[66] The loss of homes and valued possessions paled in comparison to the loss of a family member along the road. A woman of the Methodist faith, Mary turned to her religion to help cope with her loss during the Runaway Scrape: "How many tryels and trubbles have we past threw to gether here in texas and no opportunity of going to church yet god was mindfull of us and blesst us and gave us his sparit and made us feel that we was his [sic]." Musing on her experiences during the Texas Revolution years later, she wrote "runing from Maxicans and Indians who would have thought we would have lived to be as old as we are yet god is with us and that to Bless [sic]."[67]

Piety was not solely under the preserve of women. In her memoir, Clarinda Pevehouse Kegans wrote about her grandfather's faith and its role in getting them through their panicked escape to the Louisiana border: "Grandpa was a religious man and every day he read us a chapter from his Bible and said a prayer for our men. I prayed every day for Papa and I know everybody else was also praying. That was all we could do for them." Clarinda expressed some doubt as to the efficacy of her prayers: "I had my doubts that it would be much help because I had said prayers for the men at the Alamo and Goliad and they had not been answered, but I was afraid not to. I have learned since those years to have greater faith. He does answer our prayers." The conclusion of the war saw the return of the men in Clarinda's family, including her father. Indeed, her prayers were answered. Sadly, her beloved grandfather, the man who shepherded the women and children of the Hodge/Pevehouse family to safety during the Runaway Scrape, died from illness and exhaustion shortly after their return to Oyster Creek in August 1836.[68]

Despite these expressions of faith, the observation of religion in Texas proved to be both varied and inconsistent, in part because, outside of the places of worship for the state-sanctioned Roman Catholic religion, Texas did not have institutionalized Protestant churches (the religious preference for most Anglo Texans). Even Catholic churches were in decline in the 1830s. Centers with concentrations of Anglo settlement in Texas, such as Nacogdoches, remained without religious services for much of the period. On the paucity of Protestant churches, Mary Sherwood Wightman Helm wrote: "In this experience she [Helm] lived some fourteen years of frontier life, on the extreme border of Southwestern Texas. Seven years of that time not the remotest sect dare preach Protestantism, on account of the laws of Mexico."[69] As historian Paul Lack noted, "Texas had the practice if not an official theory of toleration. This situation emboldened Protestant activity in the early 1830s, despite Austin's continued concern that 'fanatical' preachers might provoke the attention of Mexican authorities."[70] There were clearly believers among those who migrated to Texas in the late 1820s and early 1830s, particularly Methodists and Presbyterians,[71] but they practiced their faith without authorized churches, sometimes in informal settings like Sunday schools and camp meetings.[72] Lydia Ann McHenry, who arrived in Texas in 1833 and settled in Austin's Colony, participated in the first Methodist camp meeting in Texas, which took place at Caney Creek in 1834. McHenry stayed active in the Methodist church and is credited with nurturing the spread of the faith in the state both before and after the revolutionary period.[73]

The weakness of formal institutions of religion in the state garnered discomfort on the part of some Anglo Texans who worried about the moral health of residents. In her letter to relatives in Kentucky, where she advised them to refrain from moving to the state, Colgate D'Eve Donaldson wrote: "The morals of the people here I believe are better than one has a right to expect from the lawless state of the country, but sorry as I am to say that religion is more ridiculed than tolerated, no place to worship nor not the remotest disposition to erect any—not seeing the use of such a place." On religion, she continued, "I have heard people laugh and say those who came here have soon lost it all, and come to their senses—which proves to them 'tis all false. I have endeavored to convince them that Christians are still human nature [emphasis in original] and liable to err, but all in vain they find it more convenient to continue in their own selfish opinions."[74] Notwithstanding Colgate's harsh evaluation of the state of religion in Texas, during the Runaway Scrape (and beyond), many terrified Texians turned to their faith for reassurance.

Returning to their homes after the trauma of the Runaway Scrape, Texians faced the daunting challenge of starting over. In her letter to her sister, Mrs. Sutherland wrote: "When I received your letter I had been away from home with a distracted mind and had been wandering about ever since till three weeks ago this day we got back to our house where we found nothing in the world worth speaking of not one mouthful of anything to eat, but a little we brought home with us. God only knows how we will make out."[75] The family was devastated by what they saw upon their return. Rosa Kleberg noted that "times were very hard" when they returned to their farm: "Our house had been partly consumed by fire, and our crop of corn and cotton was, of course, totally destroyed." There was no money and a shortage of provisions in the newly independent Republic. To address such shortages, Rosa wrote: "I sold some fine linen table cloth which I had brought from Germany for rice and flour."[76] As in the Runaway Scrape itself, in the aftermath of war, women continued to make sacrifices when it came to their treasured possessions. Just as they created homes out of the Texas wilderness, after the conclusion of the Texas Revolution, women were tasked with the challenge of starting over, creating, once again, a domestic space that rendered comfort and safety for their families. After a turbulent few months, the hope was that stability would follow Texas independence.

2
GENDERED CONFRONTATIONS ON THE ROAD TO SAFETY

Madam, you ought to be the man such times as these. You could defend yourself and property well if you had no husband. I should not have taken the girl from you, for I believe you would stay in the country and defend yourself and your property.[1]

—**Comments to Ann Raney Coleman**

Creed Taylor, a fifteen-year-old soldier and scout in the Texas army, witnessed the tribulations of the Texas Revolution firsthand. After the fall of the Alamo in early March, Creed and his brother left the ranks briefly to accompany "his mother and the children to a place of safety" during the Runaway Scrape before returning to fight in the battle of San Jacinto, which took place the day before he turned sixteen. His reminiscences, dictated and published by James T. DeShields as *Tall Men with Long Rifles: The Glamorous Story of the Texas Revolution, As told by Captain Creed Taylor, Who Fought in That Heroic Struggle from Gonzales to San Jacinto*, narrates the peaks and valleys of the rebellion of 1835–1836—described by the editor as the staggering defeats, glorious victories, and countless depredations in between. Indicative of DeShields's intense veneration of the "glamorous" Texas Revolution, his foreword to Taylor's memoirs proclaimed, "Ours was certainly the most heroic struggle for liberty in all American history."[2] Creed Taylor was a little more circumspect. In his own words, Taylor offered "A true account of this colorful episode, including all of its pathetic incidents."[3] There was nothing glamorous about Taylor's description of the Runaway Scrape. On the frightened refugees, he recalled: "Old men, frail women, and little children, all trudging along. And though I have passed through the fields of carnage from Palo Alto to Buena Vista, I never witnessed such scenes of distress and human suffering."[4] The Taylor family, led by the two enlisted brothers, felt a modicum of safety when they reached a secluded section of what is now Grimes County, well ahead of the Mexican forces. Several other families also halted their escape in this vicinity. Feeling that their mother and younger siblings were finally out of the reach of the approaching Mexican forces, the brothers returned to the field.[5]

Although it is commonly held that most participants of the Runaway Scrape comprised "thousands of refugees, largely women, children, and slaves," not all traveling parties were devoid of men.[6] In many instances, women negotiated power and decision making with men deemed feeble, elderly, and generally unfit to fight. It should also be noted that many of the men who avoided war were in perfectly good health. Female-led groups encountered men along the way who often sought to assume authority over the situation; these men included spouses and sons who left the fighting to see to the well-being of their wives, mothers, and children. Gendered contestations arose between those who took to the roads, particularly between Anglo women and the men who joined the retreat to the Louisiana border. By positioning and problematizing the role of men in their interactions with women during the Runaway Scrape, this chapter enriches previous scholarship that depicted the civilian exodus as a largely female event. Amid the chaos (and likely because of it), there are numerous examples of women who challenged the authority, decision making, character, and even manliness of their male counterparts during the early months of 1836; in fact, some of these criticisms were directed at those occupying the highest positions of authority in the war-torn state.

When referenced, traditional accounts of the Runaway Scrape—both scholarly and popular—tend to emphasize the noble and daring efforts of the women leading their families from Santa Anna's forces, with little in the way of subtlety or critical analysis. Describing the stoic feats of women during the Scrape, one newspaper article waxed poetically: "This was harrowing and weakening to these brave women, but hope never failed them. Glorious women! Their husbands achieved glory and gave a new nation to the world at San Jacinto. But these women on that marvelous retreat gave as bright a luster to the annals of Texas as the men did."[7] To be sure, the situation was dire, requiring heroics from participants on multiple fronts, but such a cloying, one-dimensional rendering of women's actions during the escape does little to advance historical inquiry. Even less attention has been paid to the gender and race dynamics between women, enslaved persons, and the men not engaged in the fighting during the panicked exodus. Given the participation of thousands of Texans and the surprisingly numerous records of the event from both male and female diarists, there is certainly room for more nuanced scholarship that delves further into the Runaway Scrape, exploring aspects of gender beyond female heroism and sacrifice. During the early months of 1836, women exhibited not only courage, but a willingness to assert themselves, take up arms (in some instances), and challenge the authority of Anglo Texan patriarchs (when necessary). While traditional historic rendering of the Runaway Scrape acknowledges the gritty courage of Texas frontier women, it limits the scope of women's experiences as supplemental, transitory, and peripheral to the masculine heroics of revolutionary warfare.

If the vast majority of Texas men left their homes to join the fight, who were those considered unsuitable for war? According to Kate Scurry Terrell, a nineteenth-century chronicler who created a record of the Runaway Scrape based on firsthand accounts: "All the able-bodied men of the settlements were with the army, only a few men and boys being left to guard the homes. On the women—brave wives and mothers of brave men—fell the responsibility of protecting the families."⁸ It is worth noting that Terrell's description left out the role of bondsmen in providing protection to women and children. Dilue Rose Harris, whose reminiscences provide some of the most comprehensive details of this episode, described the pivotal role that one enslaved man, bonded to the family, played in events: "The old negro man, Uncle Ned, was left in charge. He put the white women and children in his wagon. It was large and had a canvas cover. The negro women and children he put in the carts. Then he guarded the whole party until morning."⁹ For one little white boy in the Dilue's traveling party, Uncle Ned provided extra support. Little Eli Dyer kicked and cried for Uncle Ned until he came and got him, after which, "He slept that night in Uncle Ned's arms."¹⁰ Dilue was barely eleven years old at the time of the Runaway Scrape but recollected the event vividly in her later memoirs, which were written in the late 1890s.

Traveling with her sister, an orphan girl, the family's enslaved persons, and several neighbors (including men), Mary Sherwood Wightman Helm remembered not only the contributions of their family's bondspeople on their successful journey to safety but also the preeminent roles they played in other families' plights. When her traveling party arrived on the bank of the Bernard River, Mary registered surprise that her neighbors refused to help the women scale down their supplies and cross the river on a makeshift raft. Consequently, the women and their enslaved laborers went to work: "So all the women and the few colored ones of my family, especially our man of color, who was as much at home in the water as out of it, or we might not have succeeded."¹¹ Taking a schooner to Beaumont, Mary observed the throngs of families, with "despair on their faces," looking to escape the danger by ship. She noted, "There were very few white men; negroes seemed to be protectors of most of the families."¹² "Uncle" Jeff Parsons, a man bonded to the Sutherland family, accompanied his mistress on her quest to the safety of the Sabine and provided a similar account of the despair among the populace to the *Galveston News;* years after the fact, he recalled: "I can't begin to describe the scene on the Sabine. People and things were all mixed up, and in confusion. The children were crying, the women praying and the men cursing."¹³

In explaining why her father did not join the fighting, Dilue Rose Harris stated that while most neighboring men with families joined Houston's army, "Father and Mr. Shipman were old, Adam Stafford a cripple, and they stayed at home."¹⁴ Dilue's father, Dr. Pleasant Rose, served as a physician in the War of 1812 and was approximately fifty-six years old at the time of the Runaway Scrape, placing him at or very near the uppermost age boundary for military service.[15] In March 1836, newly appointed President David Burnet ordered that "All persons citizens [sic] of Texas over the age of 18 years and under the age of 56 years are subject to military duty."[16] Thus, Dilue's father just barely escaped conscription. The Harris family migrated to Texas on April 28, 1833, the date of Dilue's eighth birthday. Her record of the events of 1836 is based not only on her own reminiscences but also on her father's journal; regrettably, for future researchers and other interested parties, the latter source was "unfortunately destroyed."[17] After the Revolution, Dilue settled in the Houston area and later married Ira Harris, a former Texas Ranger; the couple would have nine children.

Clarinda Pevehouse Kegans was similar in age to Dilue Rose Harris at the time of the Runaway Scrape—she was just shy of twelve years old. In Kegans' case, her grandfather, Alexander Hodge, led their family's traveling party away from the Mexican advance. At seventy-six years old, Hodge was long past the age for military service. In her memoirs, Clarinda dedicated ample time to praising the efforts of her grandfather in keeping their family safe, but she also acknowledged the role of the family's enslaved laborers in their escape: "too terrible to describe but we made it only with the help of our slaves and Grandpa. The slaves were so strong, good and kind. Joshua was a slave boy about eighteen and he made a harness to wear so Mary Jane Dunlavy could ride in it. She was only four and could not walk for long."[18] On moving their belongings, Clarinda wrote: "The slaves had a hard time keeping the carts from turning over and keep them moving but they did. They were experts at that I think."[19] So in addition to dealing with the stress of fleeing an advancing army and negotiating the elements, family bondspeople, particularly the men, absorbed the physical burden of hauling goods (and apparently children, in this instance). However, outside of brief mentions by Harris, Helm, and Kegans, the effort to laud enslaved persons—either male or female—for their contributions to the Runaway Scrape is exceptionally rare in the records.[20] Given that this was Texas in the nineteenth century, it is hardly surprising that African Americans were largely left out of heroic stories of the Revolutionary experience of 1836.

It was not age but health that kept Ann Raney Coleman's husband from serving in the Texas forces. In her detailed account of the Runaway Scrape, she explained that after the call to arms to join Col. James W. Fannin's army stationed at Goliad reached their plantation on the Brazos River in

1836, her husband declined: "My husband had one of his arms broken in two places by the fall of a tree, which disabled him so much he could not do good and efficient service, but sent his overseer, Mr. George Paine, as his substitute."[21] When she married John Thomas on February 14, 1833, at the age of twenty-two, Ann was not an especially young bride, at least according to the practices of the day.[22] Her "advanced" age, however, did not prevent her husband from referring to her as "my child" and casting himself in a dual role: "My child, I will be a father as well as a husband."[23] Having lost both of her parents only months beforehand, Ann felt especially vulnerable, calling herself an "orphan" and stating that she "had need of a father's and a husband's care."[24] At fifteen years her senior, her husband was in his late thirties when hostilities broke out. There was certainly an age discrepancy between the couple, but not a significant one, at least from a generational perspective. So, in some of the most richly detailed accounts of the Runaway Scrape—the recollections of Dilue Rose Harris, Clarinda Pevehouse Kegans, and Ann Raney Coleman—it was men, not women, who made the decisions for their respective traveling parties.

Besides age and physical disability, small numbers of men were allocated to protect women and children in specific communities. Nacogdoches, for example, was granted thirty men to protect the town and surrounding farms. Even though the community was hundreds of miles from Santa Anna's advancing army, anxious townspeople worried about the acute and imminent attack of hostile indigenous tribes. There was some concern on the part of army officials that persons in East Texas used the threat of Indian attack as an excuse to avoid providing the Texas forces with much-needed horses, wagons, and foodstuffs and, worse still, a justification for dodging military service.[25] Many women shared their concerns. Recounting his and his mother's experiences during the early part of 1836 in East Texas, John G. Rusk Jr. stated that "we were in the greatest danger in Nacogdoches. Only thirty men were detailed to guard the town which contained, beside them, only women and children."[26] Significantly, Mary Rusk's husband, Thomas J. Rusk, served as Secretary of War for the recently declared independent Republic of Texas. According to her son, his mother had little patience for the fragile dispositions of the men left to protect herself and her female companions: "One thing was noticeable, what few there were who had refused to join the army (on the plea of having to protect the women and children) were panic stricken and wild with excitement." The women busily occupied themselves with placing their little ones in the wagons.

Rusk continued, "I noticed the quiet self-control of the women contrasted with the wild terror of the men who did not go with the army."[27] Written decades after the fact, Rusk's testimony accomplished two feats: it extolled the stoic fortitude of his mother and her companions and tacitly jabbed at the men not engaged in combat.

In their panic-stricken state, the men would "ride at full speed along the line of wagons loaded with women and children, shouting 'the Indians are coming,'" according to Rusk. Concerned that such shouting would further alarm her children—beyond the circumstances of the escape itself—Mrs. Rusk would say as "each of these men rushed by with his evil tidings, 'don't be alarmed, our army is between us and the Mexicans and the thirty men at Nacogdoches will fill as many bloody graves before the Indians can reach us.'"[28] While such words offered immediate calm and comfort to her frightened children, Mrs. Rusk plainly harbored suspicion regarding the bravery of men not serving on the battlefield. More ire still was leveled at men who chose to neither protect the home front nor join the frontlines—noncombatants and deserters. Outside of the critique of distressed men brimming in wild terror from the Mexican threat, the Rusk story underscores the fact that most women during the flight to Louisiana were busy taking care and providing for their families and had little time to focus on unnecessary provocations.

In *The Texas Revolutionary Experience*, a seminal work on the political and social aspects of the Texas Revolution, Paul Lack argues that there was a class component to the men who chose not to fight and that "those who shirked military participation often had the most to protect in a material sense."[29] In a number of cases, Lack demonstrates that a large number of wealthy Anglo Texans failed to take up arms against Santa Anna's forces, ultimately joining the exodus east. One group overrepresented in the ranks of war evaders was elected public officials—many of whom promoted the initial call for independence, preceding and contributing to the outbreak of hostilities. Some of the elected officials could be excused from service because of advanced age, but that was not true for all. In one local political body—the Department of the Brazos—a considerable portion of its top political leaders avoided military service, including many who were of age for conscription (the average among this group being forty). Many among this faction of wealthy nonmilitants owned land and bondspeople. With that said, Lack contends that a more significant economic fact was that "a sizable number derived their income from nonagricultural pursuits; that is, they were lawyers, physicians, surveyors, or merchants."[30] An important factor in whether they chose to fight or flee was whether they were married with children. According to Lack, men of means who stayed home "more often than not had wives and children."[31]

Lack develops his assumptions regarding the men who did not fight, not simply by looking at individual cases of wealthy males avoiding service, but also by looking at broader patterns that emerge from draft records and conscription reports. A lone conscription record from the Austin district, listing fifty draft evaders from the area, highlighted that the majority of men recorded in the report possessed several characteristics of affluence, including owning considerable land and enslaved persons. In the end, Lack concludes that this data reinforced "the conclusion of widespread avoidance of military service by local leaders."[32] To offset their lack of participation, some men of wealth and status demonstrated their commitment to the Texas cause by sending substitutes to serve on their behalf (to be sure, a less personally hazardous show of support for the war effort).[33] In a cart-before-the horse move, the constitutional outlines for an independent republic were of central concern to those engaged in the rebellion; consequently, interim government officials and representatives from each of the settlements of Texas focused their efforts in early March on establishing the foundations for a new nation, debating their ideas at the General Convention held in the town of Washington. Men of wealth and influence swelled the ranks of executive officers as well as the fifty-nine delegates from Texas localities who drafted and approved the Texas Declaration of Independence on March 2, 1836. Of course, their efforts would be moot if they didn't first *win* their independence from Mexico.

As they focused on administrative matters, government representatives located in Washington-on-the-Brazos were also vulnerable to Santa Anna's invading forces; indeed, fear of attack prompted the hasty decision to move the seat of government to Harrisburg in mid-March to avoid any chance of a Mexican onslaught. This decision exacerbated public anxiety and further propelled the panicked exodus of civilians to the Louisiana border. A sharp rebuke from General Houston followed, wherein the commander of the Texas forces blamed the seemingly rattled decision to move government operations as a contributing factor to the Runaway Scrape. Indicative of his disdain, Houston wrote in late March: "For Heaven's sake, do not drop back again with the seat of government! Your removal to Harrisburg has done more to increase the panic in the country than anything else that has occurred in Texas, except the fall of the Alamo."[34] For their part, administrative officials, including interim President David Burnet, countered that it was Houston's decision to retreat at the Colorado that accounted for the desperate rush of Anglo Texans to the American border. Each sought to scapegoat the other for the panicked state of the Texas populace.

Houston was not alone in his criticism. Grumblings about the cowardice of government leaders, particularly those involved in the Convention, permeated among the civilian population as well. William Fairfax Gray attended the Convention until its adjournment in mid-March and joined the government in its retreat in the weeks that followed. In a diary entry from mid-April, Gray described the derisive comments of a woman he encountered in his travels across Texas. Mrs. Jackson was a "fine looking woman," who was "in great wrath against the Texeans [sic] for bringing on the war and its consequences." She was apparently eloquent in her vituperation against members of the late Convention, "particularly her neighbor Judge West, whom she called *Lawyer* West, in allusion to his early vocation, and said he ran off to Washington after signing the Declaration of Independence, before the ink was dry, and in his panic forgot his hat and coat, and came home bareheaded."[35] The following day, Gray noted the scores of Texas families waiting to be ferried across swollen rivers: "There are at least 1,000 fugitives here, among them Menefee, A. B. Hardin, Smith, Jno. Fisher, all members of the Convention."[36]

Further criticisms of Convention participants stemmed from the hypocrisy exhibited by some of its most vocal members who demanded that Texas men support the rebellion by joining their countrymen on the battlefield—at times, shaming them into service—when they themselves refused to serve in the army and fled with their families to safety. Lack points out that it is unfair to cast this aspersion on all Convention members and that enlisted men exaggerated the lack of martial display by political leaders. He noted that twelve delegates besides those who had already been in the army served in the six months after March 17, bringing to thirty-six (or 61 percent) the number who volunteered over the course of the war.[37] Recruitment efforts by government and military officials directed at men who failed to respond to the call to arms continued well into the spring crisis; indeed, the advancing Mexican army and its subsequent victories at the Alamo and Goliad only served to amplify the need for new enlistments. Of course, such developments also had the reverse effect of elevating fear and heightening the desire for many men to protect themselves and their families from the approaching onslaught by fleeing from the danger.

In his memoirs of the Texas Revolution, S. F. Sparks, who as a teenager served in the Texas army, recalled his encounter with a family being led by its male head-of-household as they fled the Mexican forces during the Runaway Scrape—or so it seemed. Sparks described the atmosphere of the period as "a complete panic." In this instance, a man, his wife, and three to four children joined the retreat, driving ten or twelve head of cattle east. His wife and youngest child rode a pony alongside. A group of people passed them and urged them to go as fast as they could because the Mexicans were close behind. Apparently, the news was more than "the heroic man" could stand and "he told his wife that it would be better for one of them to escape, than for all to be killed; then he took her and the child off the horse, left them in the road and came on and crossed the river."[38] Unruffled, the wife and her children continued to drive the cattle along the route, crossing the river, and coming across the husband an hour later as he sat under a tree. She told him, "Now you get behind this breastwork of cotton bales and fight." Despondent, he replied that it wasn't worth fighting and they would all be killed. She replied, "Well, I will. If I can get a gun, I'll be durned [sic] if I don't go behind that breastwork and fight with those men."[39] Sparks's messmate gave the woman an old musket and she remained half the night behind the makeshift fortifications, presumably fighting alongside the men. One can guess that Sparks's description of the husband as a "heroic man" was meant as sarcasm. The episode clearly highlights the husband's failure to step up and fulfill his manly responsibilities—a failure observed not only by his wife but also by passing soldiers (including Sparks). In Sparks's account, it appears that the wife expected her husband to get more in touch with his bellicose side and emerge the hero. At the very least, he needed to stay and protect his family. In this anecdote, the husband failed on all counts.

The desperate circumstances of the Runaway Scrape also forced women to take action to protect their families, even if that meant standing up to their husbands. Rosalie Hart Priour's mother, Elizabeth Hart, found it necessary to challenge her new husband's authority in—what turned out to be—a life-and-death decision during the exodus from Santa Anna's forces. According to her autobiography, Priour's father, Tom Hart, died shortly after the family landed in Texas in 1834. On his deathbed, he secured a promise from his wife to treat his children kindly, educate them, and "keep my children from bad company."[40] Soon after, Priour's mother remarried Mr. John James, a widower with two young sons (ages five and three) and one illegitimate son (age fifteen). Six weeks after their nuptials, hostilities broke out in Texas, and James joined a company of soldiers at Laberdee (better known as La Bahia, the mission near Goliad) under Philip Dimmit's command until the unit disbanded in January 1836, after which he joined Ira Westover's company. Ordered to move to safer territory, Elizabeth and children left their homestead, temporarily stationing themselves at Victoria, Texas.[41]

After his youngest son became dangerously sick, James was given permission to take a leave of absence from his civil and military responsibilities (he had served as *síndico procurador,* or city attorney, for Refugio).[42] His civil duties in the ayuntamiento caused him to be furloughed at Refugio, where he also served in Hugh McDonald Frazier's militia. Once reunited with his family, James ordered them to move to the fort at Laberdee where he could better watch over them. Unfortunately, the fort was in the line of fire for an attack by "ten-thousand Mexicans and Indians." Given her promise to her first husband, Elizabeth refused to put her children in harm's way by taking her children into "bad company." The couple was at a stalemate. Despite Elizabeth's pleas, Priour's stepfather chose to separate his new family, taking his sons with him and then placing them at Nicholas Fagan's home on the San Antonio River for safekeeping.[43] For her part, Elizabeth and her two daughters made their way to the coast to board a steamship to New Orleans (calamities ensued, and the passengers ended up landing in Mobile, Alabama). James tried to save the ayuntamiento archives from the Mexicans but was captured and imprisoned (placed in confinement with Colonel Fannin's men after their surrender at Goliad). With Fannin, John James was killed during the Goliad massacre on March 27, 1836—with the fate of his two boys uncertain. On this, Rosalie wrote, "When we were informed of Fannin's massacre, Mother wanted to go back to the San Antonio River to get my two stepbrothers, but the officers would not listen to her entreaties."[44] Elizabeth Hart returned to Texas in 1839 to search for the boys but was unsuccessful in her quest.[45] Had the boys stayed with their stepmother, they would have, in all likelihood, safely docked in Mobile, Alabama, with their stepsisters—hundreds of miles from the death and mayhem in Texas.

As noted, it was a previous injury that prevented Ann Raney Coleman's husband, John Thomas, from joining his fellow Texans on the frontlines; instead, the family traveled together toward the safety of the US border. In addition to referring to his twenty-two-year-old wife as "my child" and appointing himself husband and father to her, Thomas used the harried circumstances of the Runaway Scrape to teach his wife a valuable life lesson. Dreadfully tired from the march, Ann recalled that she never slept at night for fear of attack by either Indians or Mexicans. Rather, both she and her husband slept at noon, "when the Negroes got dinner and the horses were turned out to graze, and then only slept for a short time." On one occasion during their trek, Ann slept through the loud commotion of her group breaking camp and taking back to the road, despite being called "a great many times and paying no attention to their call." Ann awoke to a deserted camp—her husband, child, and traveling companions left her behind. She wondered, "Had he [her husband] done this to punish me not to play the same thing over again?" Quickly, she mounted her horse and raced after the group. After speeding over the prairie, she caught up with the caravan's wagons an hour later. She was so "put out" with her husband's treatment toward her that she kept in the rear of the wagons until they stopped for the night, writing, "I looked what I felt, hurt to the core."[46]

Later that evening, Thomas came to help her off her horse, but she refused his assistance. He was displeased with her response, explaining to his wife, "My child, I know you are angry with me, but I had to do something to alarm you or you would have given me a great deal of trouble in the future." Not content with this rationale, Ann countered, "I had been woman enough to pass through trials that a man strong in physical strength alone could pass through and that he need not doubt my mental faculties any more than my physical ones." Further, she continued, "I myself was the last consideration in danger, that I thought only of him and my child, but that now I began to think him lacking in his affection for me." Ultimately, Ann forgave her husband, but she noted that "I did not forget this adventure, always telling my husband he was a different man, that the war had changed his nature."[47] In a later episode during the journey, the couple came across a "bad creek or river." Ann's husband and horse passed the creek without her, leaving her to find her own way across. One of the gentlemen in their traveling party asked Ann, "Where is your husband? Passed over and left you behind?" To which she replied, "Yes, sir." He called to another gentleman to help Ann across the creek, commenting, "It is a lady who has got no husband."[48] Ann blushed at the remark.

These incidents were neither the first nor the last time Ann Raney Coleman would find cause to question her husband's decision making during the spring months of 1836. As the traveling party drew closer to the Louisiana border, an altercation developed between her husband and two men regarding compensation for an enslaved girl "about ten years of age," who was in the couple's possession and served as their young son's nurse. The men claimed that John Thomas still owed them fifty dollars for the girl and, if he didn't pay, they would take her as security. When she saw that her husband was going to let them take the girl, Ann apparently threatened the men with a pistol, declaring, "If my husband chooses to let you have that girl that is paid for up to fifty, I will not. You must kill me first." Her husband took the pistol from her hand and said that he could tend to his own business. Before they left with the enslaved girl, one of the men said to Ann, who was visibly upset, "Madam, you ought to be the man such times as these. You could defend yourself and property well if you had no husband. I should not have taken the girl from you, for I believe you would stay in the country and defend yourself and your property."[49]

Ann's decision to include this story and, in particular, this obvious slight against her husband's manhood in her memoir is telling on multiple counts. In the eyes of this male contemporary, it was Ann who "ought to be the man," for she would have better defended their property. She exhibited martial traits, while her husband exercised restraint; indeed, she did so with a pistol in hand. If it were up to Ann, she not only would have fought for the young girl but (by extension) also would have stayed and fought for their property against the invading forces. In essence, she would have fought for Texas. Her husband failed not only to fight harder for their property—an enslaved girl—but also to fight for their property in a larger sense. Upon learning that John Thomas negotiated and settled their estate before crossing the Texas border, "without my knowledge or signature," Ann was extremely dismayed. Her husband sold their property for a little over two thousand dollars, though it initially cost him eleven thousand, which, according to Ann, "was defrauding his wife and child out of their rights." He did so because "he thought that the Mexicans would run the country. It was better to take this two thousand dollars for it than to get nothing." It does not appear that Ann agreed. After Texas independence, Ann begged her husband to go back to their plantation, but "I could not prevail with him to return." Apparently, the toll of the traumatic escape as well as "many circumstances which happened on our travel made him disgusted with the country"; in the end, the couple incurred a significant financial loss.[50] It is significant that decades after these events took place, Ann deemed these areas of disagreement with her husband important enough to include in her memoirs chronicling the Runaway Scrape.

As part of the landed slaveholding elite, John Thomas conformed most closely to southern notions of masculinity—rooted in celebrations of honor, land independence, and patriarchal control of women, children, and enslaved laborers.[51] When it came to property, Thomas was the principal decision maker for the family. In casting himself as father and husband, he ostensibly conflated some of these patriarchal responsibilities. Southerners left an indelible print on social and cultural development of early Texas. Patriarchal masculinity provided every southern man with the right to exert authority over his own household and property that lay within its boundaries.[52] As an expression of such privilege, Ann's husband claimed the right to teach his wife life lessons, even those that placed her safety in peril while they escaped to the safety of the American border—a somewhat suspect application of familial protection.

The examples of women challenging their husband's authority during the Runaway Scrape point to a larger question of whether the exigencies of war provided a forum for women to confront the broader patriarchic dynamics so prevalent in nineteenth-century America. An ongoing debate among gender historians of the Civil War centers on whether wartime circumstances created new opportunities for women in the postwar environment, especially in the wider social and political world. In her early and influential *The Southern Lady: From Pedestal to Politics, 1830–1930*, Anne Firor Scott argues for the liberating influence of the Civil War and the subsequent postwar transformation that afforded southern women new opportunities to work outside the home, attend college, and engage in reform and suffrage activities.

Other gender historians caution against reading too much, in terms of liberation and change for women, into the postwar environment.[53] Southerners were hopelessly conservative on matters of gender, and most expected ascribed gender roles to return to normal after the war. As George Rable notes, "Men and women alike seem to have assumed that wartime arrangements would be temporary, that women still performed largely *auxiliary* tasks in the economy, and that peace would return women to the domestic circle."[54] If post–Civil War southern society provided little opportunity for women to challenge gender expectations, it is unlikely the Texas Revolution went any further in mounting a serious challenge to the power dynamics between men and women after the war. After all, the Texas Revolution was twenty-five years earlier and a much shorter military campaign than the American Civil War. Further still, given that many Anglo migrants arrived in Texas only a few years before the outbreak of hostilities, Texas farms and plantations were unsettled, frontier outposts compared to their mature southern counterparts.

Gender confrontations during the war were another matter, however. In *Occupied Women: Gender, Military Occupation, and the American Civil War,* editors LeeAnn Whites and Alecia P. Long collected numerous accounts during the Civil War wherein women challenged the authority of occupying men and mounted resistance in both obvious and subtle modes. These historians argue against the perception of women as hapless victims or collateral damage of military occupation and that "women in occupied areas during the Civil War were not simply preoccupied, that is, basically rendered either inert or of little structural consequence by their domestic status in the face of military force. Rather, they were occupied, as in busy and responsive, in the face of an occupying military presence."[55] These examples of women who exhibited spirited resistance to occupation during the Civil War (in the 1860s) are, perhaps, a more apt framework for comparison with the women who challenged men during the Runaway Scrape (in the 1830s). In both cases, the anxious circumstances of war provided the opportunity for women to challenge men, at least in the short term.

Outside of gendered contestations between men and women along the road, and the perils therein, the tangible dangers of the Runaway Scrape were ever-present: fear, discomfort, and death followed the trail of refugees east in their effort to escape the advancing Mexican forces. Worse still, the elements worked against them—it rained continuously during the spring of 1836, resulting in swollen rivers and streams that proved difficult to cross. Travelers bogged down at riverbanks, waiting for days for an opportunity to ferry across flooded waterways. In her reminiscences, Dilue Rose Harris described a backlog of "fully five thousand people at the ferry" trying to cross the San Jacinto River, and her traveling party waited for three days before they could cross: "Every one [sic] was trying to cross first, and it was almost a riot."[56] Traveling with her father and a large group of German immigrants, Caroline Ernst von Roeder von Hinueber witnessed a similar scene at the Brazos River, where there were so many people assembled at the ferry that it would have taken several days for them all to cross; as a result, her family pitched camp in the middle of the Brazos river bottom.[57]

Besides rising waters, disease—measles, sore eyes, whooping cough, and cholera—spread throughout the temporary camps set up by travelers.[58] The trip was especially arduous on young travelers. At one site, roughly three

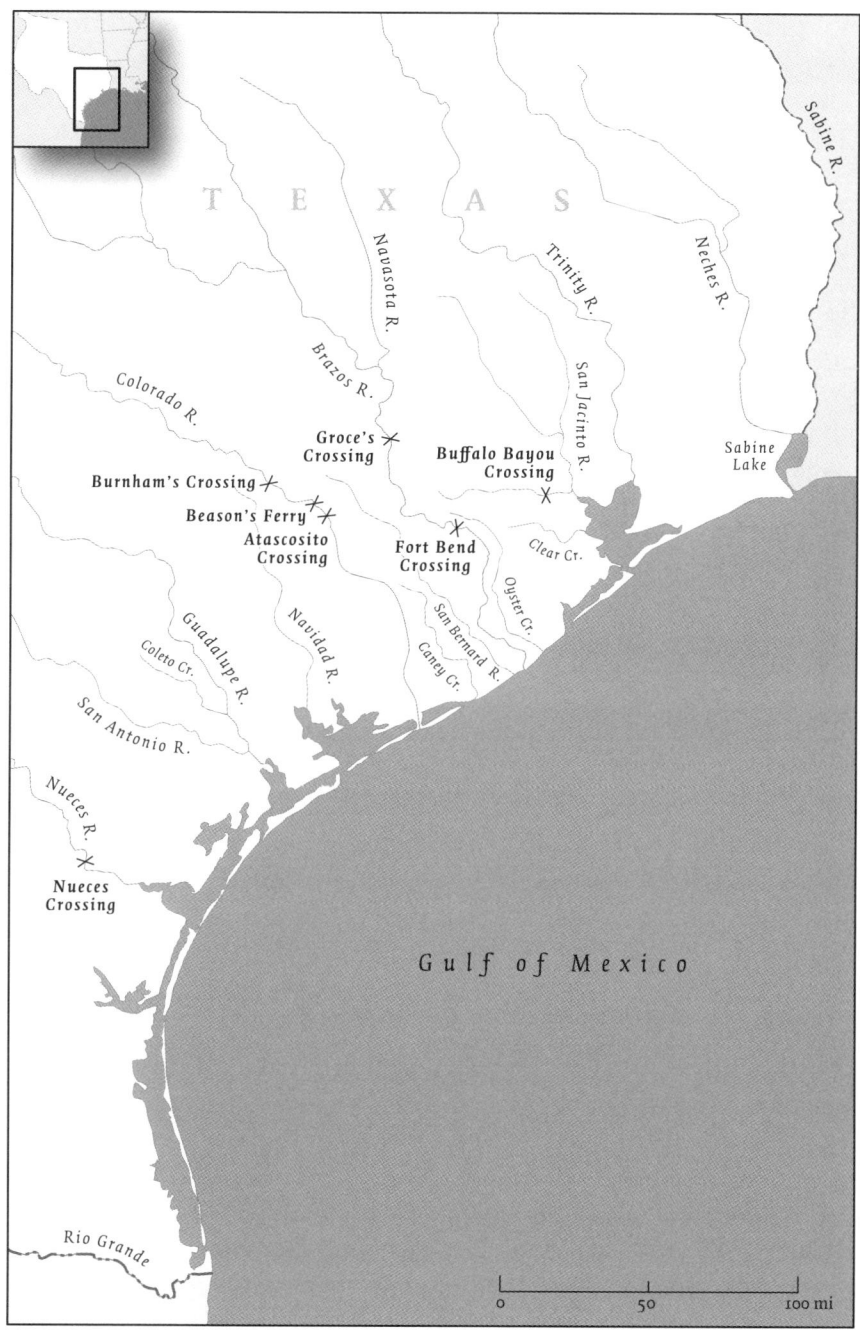

Figure 4. Map of Texas rivers, creeks, and crossings. *Courtesy of Erin Greb Cartography*

hundred families camped on the west bank of the Neches River waiting for the flood waters to recede, but the wet and muddy conditions created an epidemic of dysentery and disease. Dr. Nicholas Labardie, a surgeon for the Texas army, lost both of his sons to disease during the escape.[59] Dilue Rose Harris lost her little sister to sickness, noting that "Mother was sick, and we buried our dear sister at Liberty."[60] In her reminiscences, Mary Crownover Rabb also described the dangers all around, including sickness and the death of her newborn child, Lorenzy.[61] Such privations and personal loss no doubt contributed to Mary's larger critique of General Houston's war strategy and cowardice. From the perspective of hindsight, Mary asserted that "Old Sam was affraid [sic] and would not fight."[62]

The threat to newborn babies posed by disease and inclement weather prompted women to band together to protect the most vulnerable. Elizabeth Bullock Huling recalled the plight of one refugee, a mother who was weak in condition, traveling with a baby only nine days old: "While she was camping one night there came up a terrific storm; the other women of the camp held blankets over the sick woman for her protection from the elements."[63] Creed Taylor maintained that "there were no strangers or aliens encountered along this terrible journey. All were friends, comrades, and countrymen." As an example, he provided the story of a woman who gave birth to a fifth child just after crossing the Colorado River during the trek toward the safety of the Louisiana border. A family offered the woman space in their rickety open wagon, throwing out some of their belongings to make room for a woman they had never seen before: "and how during rains, by day or night, willing hands held blankets over the mother and babe to protect them from the downpours and chilling storms."[64] Such generosity, no doubt, saved the lives of many of the weak and less fortunate along the road.

Extreme conditions were one of many obstacles for the fleeing civilian population. As they hastily threw their belongings together to escape the threat of an advancing army, many retreating families had just enough provisions to deliver them to the safety of the Louisiana border. This included their pack animals. A threat to this especially important constituent of their escape was the needs of the Texas army, specifically the need to impress animals—horses and oxen—for the army. Public support was strong for the Texas forces, but the desire to escape the approaching Mexican army was equally strong. Creed Taylor relayed a story told to him by "an eyewitness," Capt. J. H. Greenwood, who held quasi-command at Fort Houston and assisted families from that area in their escape to the Sabine. Among the traveling party was a Mrs. Moss and her invalid husband who relied on an ox-drawn wagon to make their escape. The party intersected with a group of Tennessee volunteers headed to the Alamo, including the nephew of Davy Crockett, who were apparently in need of transportation animals and decided to impress the Moss's oxen. In defense of her animals, "the brave woman appeared on the scene and raising her pistol said: 'I will kill the first man that attempts to take my oxen.' One of the men made a step forward, when the plucky woman leveled her pistol and said, 'take another step and you die;' and she meant it."[65] The Tennessee volunteers relented, opting to fall back and ride away. Shortly thereafter, the traveling party heard cannon shots emanating from the town of San Augustine; unsure of what was at hand, the mystery was explained when men from the town came at full speed toward the group shouting, "Hurrah for Texas. Houston has taken Santa Anna and his army prisoners."[66]

In the end, Houston's military tactics prevailed. Not only did the Mexican forces suffer a massive defeat at San Jacinto on April 21, 1836, but their leader, General Santa Anna, was captured in the process. After the battle of San Jacinto, scores of Mexican corpses blanketed the property of Mrs. Margaret "Peggy" McCormick, who abandoned her property and joined the Runaway Scrape in April 1836 ahead of Santa Anna's approaching forces. When she returned, she found that most of her livestock had been consumed by both the Texas and Mexican armies. The landscape reeked with the decaying bodies of hundreds of Mexican soldiers. Peggy made her way to Houston's camp to demand that he remove the putrefied corpses from her land: "unmindful of the niceties of military protocol, [she] barged into the commander-in-chief's presence."[67] A heated exchanged ensued wherein Houston proclaimed: "Madam, your land will be famed in history as the classic spot upon which the glorious victory of San Jacinto was gained! Here was born, in the throes of revolution, and amid the strife of contending legions, the infant of Texas independence! Here that latest scourge of mankind, the arrogantly self-styled 'Napoleon of the West' met his fate!" Clearly unimpressed with Houston's legacy argument, Peggy replied, "To the *devil* with your glorious history! Take off your stinking Mexicans."[68] In the end, Houston refused the demand, and the task of burying the bodies was left to Peggy McCormick, her two sons, and her neighbors.

As treaty negotiations began, Houston's decision to spare Santa Anna's life garnered criticism from many—not surprising, given the heavy sacrifices incurred by both the military and civilian population. In exercising restraint rather than the instinct for revenge against a sworn enemy, Sam Houston once again drew fire from his female critics. Like numerous other women, including Elizabeth Hart, Rebecca Westover Jones lost her first husband, Capt. Ira Westover, at the Goliad massacre in March 1836. She deemed Santa Anna as the murderer of her husband and undeserving of mercy. For such women, the emotional toll of wartime weighed heavily, especially the recent scars of husbands and sons lost, so they viewed Houston's diplomatic approach to Santa Anna with disdain. Even many years after the fact, she exclaimed: "If the women whose husbands and sons he murdered could have reached him, he would not have lived long!"[69]

The brevity of the Texas Revolution prevented any significant structural changes or realignments of gendered power in antebellum Texas; any added legal or administrative responsibilities for women, for example, were extraordinarily short term. Even the longer military campaign of the Civil War, twenty-five years later, produced only marginal advances in gender dynamics for southern women. Indeed, southern gender conventions proved to be more fixed than fluid, especially in comparison to the experiences of their northern counterparts. However, the circumstances of the Runaway Scrape did provide some opportunities for women to challenge the judgment of the men who often traveled alongside them. Women might have to answer to husbands and fathers, to some extent, but that didn't mean they always agreed with them. The often-one-dimensional rendering in the standard lore and traditional history cast women in stoic yet noteworthy supporting roles in the larger drama of masculine sacrifice and triumph during the Texas Revolution. Writing in 1991, historian Fane Downs lamented the "suffocating Texas macho myth" that relegated women's experiences to the margins of Texas history.[70] Martial in nature, the Texas Revolution is typically regarded as a male event. And yet, whether it was within the family or at the military-strategy level, decisions being made by men deeply affected the women, children, and enslaved persons who took to the road to escape Santa Anna's forces. In some circumstances, these decisions meant life or death; consequently, a number of women found their voice, using it to question the character, authority, and judgment of not only the men who opted out of military service but also of the men leading the campaign.

3
DESERTERS, NONCOMBATANTS, AND CRIMINALS

The Fulfillment and Failures of Manly Obligations

> *Will any man, under these circumstances, longer refuse to turn out, because his interest requires his attention? Will any one dare to have the effrontery to say, that his interest must be attended to, when Texas is in danger of being overrun, and the women and children in cold blood massacred....*[1]
>
> —*Capt. Mosely Baker*

Desertion is a common feature of war; however, the reasons behind a man's decision to not to fight—to either flee the battlefield or avoid it altogether—can vary dramatically. During the brief military campaign of the Texas Revolution, the insurgent call to take up arms against the centralizing policies of Mexican president Gen. Antonio López de Santa Anna failed to galvanize all men in Texas. While some men were deeply inspired by the call to arms, believing passionately in the struggle for independence, other men left the frontlines because military decisions, implemented by those in the highest levels of command, placed them in an untenable position—protect their families or remain and fight. This dilemma created a crisis of sorts for scores of Texas men engaged in the war effort, forcing them to choose between two equally compelling, manly obligations. Interim President of the Republic of Texas, David G. Burnet, recognized their predicament, stating, "To provide for and protect our wives and children is a sacred duty, prompted by nature and sanctioned by every manly feeling." However, he cautioned against acting on such impulses and held that the better strategy was to reinforce and sustain the army, so that their wives and children would be secure from "the pollution" of the Mexican onslaught.[2] Not all Texas men were drawn into this wrenching predicament, however. Some men exploited the chaos of war to take advantage of the most vulnerable by engaging in criminal activity, prompting some to question not just their honor but their very claim to manhood.

The events that precipitated this dilemma for Texians began in the early months of 1836. After promising victories for the revolutionaries in the fall and early winter of 1835 (including the Battle of Gonzales, the Battle of Nueces Crossing, the Grass Fight, and the Siege of Bexar), circumstances turned dire for the Texas forces after two substantial setbacks delivered by Santa Anna's army beginning in early March: the fall of the Alamo and Colonel Fannin's surrender at Goliad. A critical decision ensued. If Gen. Sam Houston, commander of the Texas army, attacked the Mexican forces before they crossed the Colorado River, it could deal a decisive blow to their enemy, stemming its advance further into Texas. Houston's forces initially reached the Colorado River at Burnham's Crossing on March 17, 1836, where they were met by throngs of civilians fleeing the Mexican incursion. After assisting civilians across the flooded river, Houston marched his troops twenty-five miles south to the Beason's Ferry crossing on the Colorado, setting up camp on the east side of the river on March 20. This was a per-

Deserters, Noncombatants, and Criminals 65

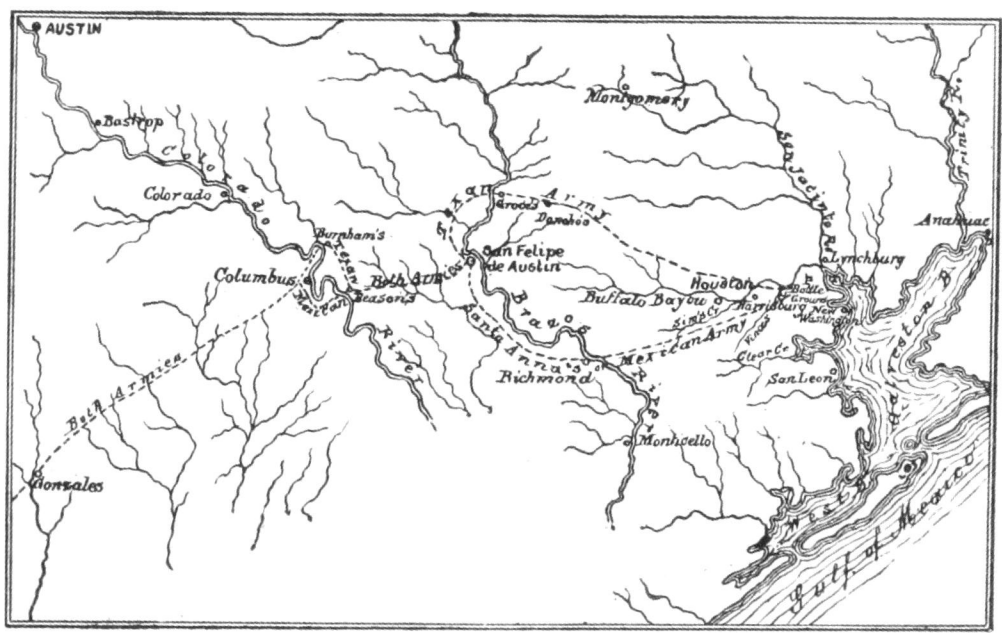

Figure 5. Map showing route of the Texas and Mexican forces from Gonzales to San Jacinto. Initially, General Houston intended to make the Colorado River his line of defense against the Mexican army; however, the plan changed. Houston's decision to retreat and fight another day contributed to the growing panic among the civilian population and the ensuing Runaway Scrape. *The Reading Room / Alamy Stock Photo*

ilous moment in the rebellion; every step taken by the Mexican army into the settled regions of Texas placed the women, children, and bondspeople left behind on farms and plantations at greater risk.

Records suggest that General Houston had every intention of confronting the Mexican forces at the Colorado, preventing them from crossing the river. In a letter dated March 24, 1836, Houston wrote: "All the troops that can be raised I wish placed at my disposal, as on the Colorado I make my stand, and it is deemed necessary to concentrate all the effective force at this point for the present."[3] Shortly after Houston's arrival at Beason's Ferry came word that a large Mexican force under Gen. Joaquín Ramírez y Sesma had reached the west bank of the river. Worse still, Houston learned of the defeat at Goliad and "fearing that his ill-trained set of volunteers might be good for but one decisive battle" (and it would not be at the Colorado), the Texas general opted to fall back and fight another day.[4] Serving in the

Texas ranks, Creed Taylor confirmed that Houston intended to attack the Mexican forces: "There is ample proof that the Texan commander planned to fall upon the enemy at the Colorado. But late in the evening of the 25th, word had come that Fannin and his entire force had surrendered, and this startling news threw the army into a state of excitement and confusion that amounted almost to open mutiny."[5] Houston's decision to retreat spurred the panicked exodus of the civilian population of Texas toward the Louisiana border. If the Texas army would not stand and fight, who would protect those left vulnerable to the Mexican assault? Would Houston continue retreating, or would he launch an attack on Santa Anna and halt the chase?

From the Colorado River onward, Houston's strategy to fall back prompted criticis—both positive and negative—from all sides. Mary Rabb, the Texas woman who lost a child while fleeing from Santa Anna's army during the Scrape and questioned General Houston's courage in writing, "Old Sam was affraid [sic] and would not fight," said her uncle warned Houston that if he did not stop the Mexicans from crossing the Colorado River, "he would loos half of his men that tha would leave him and go to ther fameleys [sic]."[6] When the Mexican army crossed the river the following day, Mary's uncle left Houston's army to move his family to safety. An officer under Houston's command saw it differently than Rabb. Houston was no coward, according to Col. John Milton Swisher; rather, he was a "brave and cool headed general." He argued: "There are times when it requires more courage to retreat than stand and fight, and this was the case at the Colorado . . . . To order a retreat under such circumstances, required a sublime moral courage that only Houston possessed." While praising Houston's principled stance, Swisher admitted, "The retreat was the signal to many men to quit the ranks, for the purpose of removing their families to a place of safety."[7]

The compulsion to protect their families from the Mexican advance was more than a gesture of compassion for Anglo Texans—it was a defining facet of their identity, specifically their southern identity. The "new men's history" that emerged in the 1990s differentiated representations of manhood by region.[8] Anthony Rotundo's groundbreaking *American Manhood: Transformations in Masculinity from the Revolution to the Modern Era* posited the self-made man as the dominant hegemonic ideal of the American North.[9] Southern historians countered with a model of masculinity focused on southern patriarchs. Nineteenth-century southern notions of masculinity were rooted in celebrations of honor, land independence, and patriarchal control of women, children, and enslaved laborers.[10] Manhood required an independent household, landownership, and submissive dependents—women, children, and persons held under bondage. Notions of honor and mastery were central to southern notions of masculinity. According to Lorri Glover and Craig Thompson, "Honor was externally presented for public consumption; mastery was internally realized for personal fulfillment." In the latter case, mastery was achieved by controlling households and commanding enslaved persons; in contrast to honor, mastery was "less scripted and more of a consequence to a man's self-identity."[11]

Many of those engaged in the hostilities of the 1830s were slaveholders who moved to Texas from the South in the late 1820s and early 1830s to take advantage of the optimal climate and vast territory available for cotton production. As Texas historian Randolph Campbell notes, "By 1830, the approximately ten thousand Anglo-Americans in Texas began to give the province an indelible imprint of the southern United States. Most of these colonists were natives of the American South."[12] However tenuous, these men predicated their status and identity on their exclusive membership in the class of men who embodied the southern slaveholding elite.[13] Historian Stephanie McCurry suggests that patriarchal masculinity provided southern men with "a virtually unlimited right of an independent man to mastery over his own household and property that lay within its boundaries."[14] In exerting and defining their manliness through their power over their households (including the defense of such households), southern men became "Masters of Small Worlds." The protection of the household from outside threats linked the interests of planter-elites and yeoman alike. Further, McCurry argues that it was through displays of martial manhood and the propagation of terms like "manly independence" and "womanly weakness" that southern men solidified their authority over their households and property.[15]

Houston's retreat and the very circumstances of the Runaway Scrape forced men to choose between two masculine compulsions: to protect their families or defeat their enemy on the battlefield. In *Manifest Manhood and the Antebellum American Empire,* Amy Greenberg identifies two dominant expressions of manhood practiced in both the North and South during the early to mid-nineteenth century: "restrained manhood" and "martial manhood."[16] Restrained men derived their manhood from being morally upright, reliable, and brave, while martial men eschewed the restraint of their male counterparts, believing that "the masculine qualities of strength, aggression, and even violence, better defined a true man."[17] Greenberg notes that not all men fell squarely into one category or the other; rather, there was much overlap. She positions her two models of manliness in the context of nineteenth-century American expansionism and growing sectional tensions, with martial manhood in the ascendency by midcentury—appropriate given the future fate of Texas. Preceding the belligerency of America's claim to Manifest Destiny by almost a decade, the Texas Revolution served as a precursor to the much broader militarism of mid-nineteenth-century America. Both expressions of nineteenth-century manhood—restrained and martial—implied some level of female protection, either through reliability and bravery or through their martial talents. David T. Moore adds another layer of complexity to southern notions of masculinity in his examination of southern Baptists and churchgoers more broadly. Moore carves out a model of southern manliness among evangelicals that engendered submission and humility, differentiating them from nonreligious white male southerners; however, he noted that during times of crisis, specifically wartime, the churched and the unchurched shared a resistant spirit to perceived threats, "the Baptists could marshal an honorable defense of liberty against tyranny with the same zeal and vigor that they mustered to combat sin and the devil. In these moments, especially, many evangelical and worldly men discovered an unexpected, mutual respect."[18]

Michael Kimmel argues that during the 1830s, with the ascendency of Andrew Jackson, the champion of the War of the 1812 and the Creek War, America ushered in a period of hypermasculinity—personified in the individual himself.[19] It was an age that heralded the military hero. The popularity of frontiersman and (later) Alamo-hero Davy Crockett in the early 1830s further exemplifies this point. On April 25, 1831, the play *The Lion of the West* opened in New York City; it was a thinly disguised and highly exaggerated dramatic retelling of Crockett's frontier experiences. Both President Jackson and Congressman Crockett parlayed their status as military heroes—a consequence of their military prowess during early nineteenth-century Indian wars—into positions of power in the American government. The Texas Revolution provided the forum for men to become heroes, but they would need to prove themselves on the battlefield. Thus, in the early months of 1836, enlisted men found themselves grappling between competing notions of nineteenth-century manliness. Was the more heroic move to stay and fight or to take leave and rescue their families?

From a policy perspective, it is unclear that military leaders granted Texas soldiers "official" permission to leave the ranks and move their fam-

Deserters, Noncombatants, and Criminals

ilies to safety. In fact, the opposite seems to be true. Creed Taylor disclosed that Houston reported to the Military Committee that only twenty men deserted the ranks to join their families. But, Taylor noted, "I have undisputed knowledge that more than one squad left on the morning of the 14th, and during the day there were more than fifty men who openly declared their intention of going to the relief of their threatened families, defying the authority of the Commander or anyone else and daring the officers to make any attempt to prevent their going."[20] For his part, Houston gave orders to arrest any man who attempted to leave camp without permission, intimating that the harshest penalty would befall those found guilty of desertion; in the course of weeks, the penalties escalated in severity. Of note, Taylor distinguished this group in his account as "so-called deserters," suggesting that he saw them otherwise. He noted that Houston's orders to arrest deserters "became a jest around the camp fires and on the march."[21] Consequently, desertions increased.

It is hard to gauge the number of men who left the front to go to their families, but one anecdote provides some insights on the frequency of the phenomenon. In an unsigned letter dated March 15, 1836, the author described recent encounters he experienced on the road while traveling back from Washington, Texas (also known as Washington-on-the-Brazos). He met two men who said they were from the army and were "on express" to let the people of "their section" know of the critical situation of the country and the need for more men to turn out. In other words, they were recruiting volunteers for the frontlines. The letter writer had not traveled far before meeting five others with the same mission. He wrote: "I remarked it took a great many to bear expresses in that direction." He surmised "that they were from the army, and was surprised that men would leave the field at this time to provide safety of property or families while our army was so far in advance." The anonymous writer concluded his letter by writing, "I give you this information that you may employ some means to remove the apprehensions of those so far distant from the seat of war, and when the services of men in the field are at the moment so much needed."[22] Written in mid-March, between the fall of the Alamo and the Goliad massacre and before Houston's retreat from the Colorado, the message conveyed in the letter is that desertions from the Texas army were underway, early and often. On Houston's efforts to arrest deserters and conscript those who avoided military service, Paul Lack notes, "These efforts failed to stem the tide—he lost hundreds to desertion during March and April."[23]

Houston's policy toward these so-called deserters was unclear not only to those inside the Texas ranks but also to onlookers in the civilian population. In his recollections of the Texas Revolution, Colonel Swisher wrote that "every family not only of our neighborhood but of the entire country" fled after hearing news of Houston's retreat from the Colorado. His father joined the army with a view of participating in the expected battle on the Colorado: "When General Houston made up his mind to retreat, he gave them permission to leave the army and seek a place of safety for their families."[24] At this point, his father and "many other families of the neighborhood" then commenced their "runaway scrape," joining the civilian population's flight to the Louisiana border. In a sketch of her experiences during the Runaway Scrape, Mrs. Anson Jones, wife of the former president of Texas, recalled that the fall of the Alamo and the "inhuman massacre of Fannin and his men at Goliad, showed to Texans the sort of foe with whom they had to deal with and caused a panic in even the bravest hearts." She continued, "Most of the colonists hastily prepared their families for flight to the eastern side of the Sabine river, and many of the men in the army now preparing to meet the enemy, were given leave to go home and see their families safe to the United States."[25] Taylor's, Swisher's, and Jones's accounts imply that witnesses to the events of 1836 perceived Houston's policy on leave was ambiguous at best and unserious at worst.

Letters and public proclamations in the early months of 1836 suggest that Houston's stance on deserters hardened over time, coinciding, not surprisingly, with the fortunes of the Texas army. As Creed Taylor noted, Houston reported to the chairman of the Military Committee that only twenty men deserted the army when he took his post at the Colorado. Taylor alleged, however, that the numbers of men leaving the ranks were much higher. In Houston's report, he stated: "I intend desertion shall not be frequent, and I regret to say that I am compelled to regard deserters all who have left camp without leave; to demand their apprehension; and that, whenever arrested, they be sent to me at headquarters for trial."[26] At this stage in the rebellion, in mid-March, Houston expressed regret that deserters would have to face trial for leaving the field. On March 21, 1836, Houston ordered the chairman of the Committee of Safety at San Felipe to take immediate measures "to arrest the deserts from the army—all persons leaving the country in a direction from the enemy, will be required to return, or their arms taken from them for the use of the army."[27] On April 4, Houston issued orders that "hereafter prisoners guilty of the crime of mutiny and desertion where sentenced by a Court Martial will suffer the penalty of the Law."[28] By April 13, roughly one month after expressing some regret for deserters' plight, Houston's orders were stark: "To Desert or Sleep on Post, will be death by Law."[29] From arrest to court martial to weapons confiscation to death, the escalation in the severity of penalty was clear. Indeed, the latter order of "death by Law" was concise in length and unforgiving in tone.

At the age of eighteen, James Monroe Hill joined the Texas forces with his father after the fall of the Alamo, joining William W. Hill's detachment at Columbus while his father, Asa Hill, served at army headquarters. After Houston's retreat from the Brazos River, Asa Hill was dispatched by Houston from the army to warn families that the Mexican army had crossed the Colorado. On his father's mission, James recalled: "He then came to me and showed me his furlough and detail to tell all the families that he could see, and send word to others, to cross the Brazos, that the enemy was crossing down at 'Tusky Seat' (Atascosito) [sic] crossing, on the Colorado, and to tell them that he, Houston, would keep between them and the enemy."[30] This was, of course, after Houston had fallen back from the Colorado despite initially pledging to stand firm. James's account provides insights on the mood of the Texas forces at this critical juncture and the flow of deserters. He wrote: "Here was a trying time to a great many. I suppose, as I then heard, and afterwards heard from good authority, that the night we camped at 'Old San Felipe' over five hundred men left without leave from the commanding General, some with good excuse, and others without any." James Hill's memory of events may have overestimated the number of deserters (in one evening) from Houston's army, but he clearly recalled that a great many left the ranks.

In her later reminiscences of the Runaway Scrape, Dilue Rose Harris expressed sympathy for the men who left the battlefield: "At the Trinity River men from the army began to join their families. I know they have been blamed for this, but what else could they have done? The Texas army was retreating and the Mexicans were crossing the Colorado."[31] Harris clearly recognized that there was criticism lodged at men who left the fighting, but her position was one of empathy given the enormity of their decision. Indeed, such issues did not escape the attention of the women who joined the exodus to the US border; Houston's strategy to retreat and fight another day affected everyone in Texas—men, women, and children. While Houston's stance on deserters hardened over time, he was unequivocal in his castigation of men in the war-torn state who chose to sit out of the fight and "idly observe the war." As early as mid-January, Houston wrote: "These, comrades, are for us the most dangerous, because he who is not with us is against us."³² One can imagine that Houston's opinion of noncombatants who casually sat on the sidelines while the war raged on did not improve after the demoralizing March defeats of the Texas army.

Because her husband was unable to leave Houston's forces to escort his family to safety, however temporarily, one wife expressed resentment toward two groups of Texas men: those who left the battlefield to secure the safety of their families—and never returned—and those who failed to join the fighting in the first place. Described as simply a pioneer woman by the *Dallas Morning News*, this Texas woman's record of her experience during the Runaway Scrape included a rather derisive account of the actions of men in her company who she described vaguely as "our neighbors."³³ With word that their advancing enemy was near, a group of neighbors that included men, women, children, and their enslaved people quickly gathered their personal items and set off for the west bank of the San Bernard River, so as to "get the San Bernard River between us and the enemy before night or we would all be prisoners." At the riverbank, the group began hiding their valuables in the thick mud and assembling a raft to cross the river to provisional safety. In this task, the pioneer woman was astonished to find that her male compatriots "would not lend a hand to help." Furthering her criticism, she wrote, "I suppose the reason of their conduct was that they did not want to get to Velasco too soon, for fear of being forced to fight or required to go and find the army. But no reason was given; they evidently did not expect to return or they would have felt some shame."³⁴ If the traveling party encountered army personnel at Velasco, the chronicler clearly believed these men would be deemed fit to fight and conscripted into service; in this woman's account, it is unclear what grounds allowed these "neighboring men" to avoid military service in the first place.

Indicative of her deep anguish with the circumstances, the pioneer wife cited in the newspaper article spent much of the Runaway Scrape worrying about whether her husband was dead or alive and whether she was now a widow. In her view, other families' situations proved less dire than her own, as she wrote, "All we could hear about our army was that all the men that had families had the privilege of taking them to a place of safety, which, of course, was out of the country. Finally, men would return and say they could not find the army."³⁵ Because her husband enjoyed no such privilege, this woman was clearly resentful of the other husbands who were able to lead their families to safety. On this, she was embittered to the point of hyperbole—as most enlisted men were neither leaving the army to escort their wives out of the country (deserting), nor was Houston cheerfully allowing for such a vast depletion of his forces. Although recounted long after the fact, the pioneer woman expressed frustration at both Houston's leave policy (which she deemed unequitable) as well as the lack of chivalry and courage exhibited by the "neighboring men" in her company.

For those committed to the Texas cause, who believed that all men in the state should enlist, the call to arms was frequently steeped in gendered terminology. Moseley Baker, a captain in the Texas forces, could not understand why any man would choose not to join the rebellion, especially after the fall of the Alamo. In a letter written on March 8, 1836, he wrote: "Will any man, under these circumstances, longer refuse to turn out, because his interest requires his attention. . . . When Texas is in danger of being overrun, and the women and children in cold blood massacred. . . ." Going further still, he opined, "Let all who remain without satisfactory reasons, be henceforth branded as a coward and a traitor, and an enemy to Texas."[36] The stark language of the "cold blood massacre" of women and children was meant to strike at the heart of nineteenth-century notions of chivalry and manhood. What kind of man could resist such a call? General Houston also relied on such language, proclaiming: "Protect your wives, your children, and your homes, by repairing to the field, where alone by discipline and concert of action, you can be effective."[37] Accentuating this point further, Houston noted, "Let the people not be any longer in dread of danger, if the men will turn out like men."[38] What is notable in such language, however, is how army operatives, like Baker and Houston, exploited the perceived Mexican threat to women and children as a recruitment tool for the Texas army.

In appeals to the civilian population, government officials also used similar gendered language to both mobilize volunteers and shame deserters. In his numerous proclamations to the people of Texas, interim President Burnet often relied on the threat to women and children to rally Anglo Texas men to join the fight: "Citizens of Texas! Your all is at stake. Your wives; your children, all that is dear and sacred to freemen summon you to the field."[39] For President Burnet, it was a man's sacred duty to protect wives and children.[40] Secretary of War Thomas Rusk also invoked women and children to both chastise and shame those not willing to fight. In an address to the public, Rusk wrote: "It pains me to say many, very many of you are flying before your enemy, a contemptible enemy, whom the people of Texas, if they would rally, could exterminate at one fell swoop from the face of the earth which they polute [sic] and disgrace." Further, he stated, "Will you continue to do so—will you permit the deaths of your murdered countrymen to go unavenged—will you abandon helpless women and children to their fate—will you desert the principles of liberty?"[41]

By tethering the need to "turn out" to the manly responsibility of protecting women and children, Texas military and government leaders posited deserters who failed to come to the defense of Texas families as lesser men. Even those who did not believe in the cause were subject to this character aspersion. After all, what kind of men would leave the women and children of Texas unprotected? As Mosely claimed, such men were cowards, traitors, and enemies to Texas. President Burnet pronounced, "If any man prove recreant, in this hour of his country's peril, let that man be marked, and the indignation of the people, the 'slow moving finger of scorn' will hold him in perpetual derision."[42] General Houston's assessment of deserters was equally harsh. For Houston, deserters threatened the larger war effort: "The man who abandons his post is more dangerous to the security of the army than twenty out of our lines."[43] And yet, with the fate of the revolution in jeopardy and the scorn of military leadership and their fellow citizens squarely upon them, some soldiers still found cause to desert.

If men who left the front to protect their families represented a somewhat gray area on the question of desertion, the same could not be said of men without families who chose to ignore the fight entirely. In his account of the Texas Revolution, Creed Taylor distinguished "so-called deserters," men with families who left the field, from a second, much less sympathetic, group. He stated, "It should be borne in mind that there were hundreds of men, mostly young fellows—adventurers we might call them—who had come from the states, and who had found shelter and temporary homes among the settlers." More specifically, he continued, "They had no families and could easily have joined Houston, thereby enabling him to repel the advance of the enemy, but instead, they sought their own safety by flight."[44] For Taylor, these unenlisted men were cowardly fugitives, acting only in their own self-interest. He maintained that scouts for the army regularly encountered carts and wagons with horses carrying only one small family but were accompanied by "from two to half dozen well-armed men, all fleeing from Santa Anna."[45]

Taylor lamented that these "cowardly fugitives" could not face military tribunal for deserting the ranks, because they never enlisted in the first place: "There was no law by which they could be forced into the ranks and made to fight the invaders." As Taylor understood, there was no official means to mete out punishment to those unwilling to fight for Texas. Yet, he divulged, "I am glad to say—and I speak as an eyewitness of more than one occasion—these 'skeedadlers' received the treatment their disloyalty merited. Ferry guards and scouts had orders to impress all the horses, arms, and ammunition, found in possession of these skulkers unencumbered with families."[46] In fact, the orders to impress the property of noncombatants came from the highest ranks of the Texas government. Interim President Burnet informed the citizens of Texas, and more specifically, the able-bodied men of Texas, that any man who refused service "shall forfeit his right of citizenship & all his lands in the Republic, and from hence forth treated as an alien and foreignor [sic]. Every name of those who defend the country shall be recorded, and those not on the list will be considered as abandoning his country."[47] Burnet advocated the policy of taking note of those who abandoned Texas in its hour of need so "that they shall not be able to return at a more propitious period, and claim an unjust participation in the rewards of our toils." He not only wanted to take names but also endorsed more immediate punitive measures. After recording names of persons attempting to cross the Sabine River, the Committee of Safety received orders by Burnet "to take from all such persons, horses and guns— The Constitution declares the forfeiture of their Lands and the necessity of the case requires that horses and guns, should not be removed from the Country at such a juncture."[48]

This escalation in rhetoric toward deserters reflected a growing concern about the overall success of the campaign. Not only did the call to service grow exponentially, but also officials intensified their threats toward noncombatants. The day after Burnet issued his orders to confiscate the property of men who refused to fight, Houston reiterated the threat. On April 8, 1836, Houston wrote the following orders to his army commanders: "And you are fully empowered to stop and arrest all deserters and to convey the same safety to the army, informing the inhabitants generally that those persons who refuse to assist [sic] in repelling the Enemy that their property will be confiscated for the use of the Government."[49] To be sure, the rhetoric of Houston and Burnet could not be clearer: deserters faced severe consequences. In the end, it proved difficult for military officers to invoke shame in these young noncombatants, in part, because they confounded nineteenth-century constructs of manhood. They neither exhibited the attributes of restrained manhood (namely, moral uprightness, concern, and responsibility) nor exercised the penchant for war associated with martial manhood.

According to Creed Taylor, the same ferry guards and scouts who busily engaged in confiscating the property of "skulkers unencumbered with families" applied a more lenient policy when it came to men with families: "Men with families were respected—often aided—and were allowed to retain their arms and a number of horses, but those without families and whose excuse was that they were along to guard the other fellow's family, were disarmed, dismounted, and, in many instances, set afoot on the water soaked prairie, and left to shift for themselves."[50] Taylor's language alone, referring to the men who left the ranks to bring their families to safety as "so-called deserters" and the latter group as "skeedadlers" and "skulkers unencumbered with families," indicates that he viewed these two groups of deserters very differently. The more benevolent dispersal of impressment policy toward men with families by guards and scouts in the Texas ranks suggests that many agreed with Taylor; by contrast, small favor was shown to men without families who chose not to fight. There was a hierarchy to desertion during the Texas Revolution, and men with families in danger occupied its highest rung.

Punitive efforts to impress horses from noncombatants did not come without risk, as S. F. Sparks discovered in the early months of 1836. Acting on orders from President Burnet, Sparks and his small company began the challenging task of impressing horses and guns for the army. The assignment, according to Sparks, led to "some very exciting times." His company's first opportunity for impressment came when two young men rode into the town of Lynchburg on "two good horses," prompting one of the soldiers in Sparks's company to opine that "they ought to be in the army." After being informed that their horses were being confiscated, one of the two young men "swore that he would press the man that had his horse." The moonlight revealed that the man clutched "a glistening bowie knife," which he pointed in Sparks's direction. He ordered Sparks to release his horse, stating, "Turn him loose, or I'll cut your head off." Sparks was also carrying a knife, which he jabbed at the assailant when the man got too close. The cut penetrated about an inch, but Sparks promised that he would run his straight knife through the man if he advanced further. The man cried, "You have cut me." To which Sparks replied, "You stand back now, or I'll cut you worse." The man stood down, saying, "If I thought my brother would get the horse, I would not mind it," thus ending the altercation. Sparks and his company took the horses and issued a receipt to their owners, a standard practice.[51] The young men were not described or reported by Sparks as deserters. As "young men," they were clearly eligible to fight and, as one of Sparks's associates complained, "ought to be in the army." Because they opted not to join their compatriots on the battlefield and were "unencumbered by family," the young men's horses were confiscated, and they were "set afoot and left to shift for themselves."

While Sparks and his company were officially authorized to press horses for the army, seamier types took advantage of the chaos to press horses and other goods from fleeing Texans to enrich their own coffers. Stories of the exploits of fake press gangs and robbers appear in multiple accounts of the Runaway Scrape, suggesting the practice occurred with at least some frequency. The criminal sort who exploited the vulnerable (especially women and children) failed to live up to early nineteenth-century masculine ideals that were steeped in notions of honor and restraint. In forging a new nation, the founders of the American republic proposed that the willingness to fight for one's liberty against the British and the exercise of self-restraint merited the honor and respect due to manhood and the rights of citizenship. Amy Greenberg situated the pursuit of "restrained manhood" well into the first decades of the nineteenth century. Lawlessness stripped men of their manliness. Men who engaged in licentious conduct deserved to be marginalized, stigmatized, ostracized, and even deprived of their liberty. The founders employed gendered language, "a grammar of manhood," that "drew on hegemonic notions of manhood to encourage disorderly men to conform to a standard of manly conduct conducive to individual self-restraint, good citizenship, and public order."[52] Historian Myra Glenn argues that in antebellum America men feared emasculation and enslavement, which led to the conviction that "a male was manly if he exerted agency, control, over his life and successfully defended his freedom."[53] Men who failed to live up to these lofty ideals—failures, criminals, exploiters—lacked any claim to the honor and respect esteemed to manhood.

The chaos in Texas in the early months of 1836 proved to be fertile ground for criminal activity. In March 1836, seventeen-year-old Guy Bryan, who accompanied his mother and other traveling families toward the safety of the Louisiana border before returning to join Houston's forces at San Jacinto, witnessed such activity. When his traveling party reached the crossing at the Trinity River where families were bottlenecked, Bryan relayed the following experience: "Here we were annoyed by a 'press gang' several men claiming to be authorized by government to press horses for the use of the army, we lost in that way two horses, which doubtless never reached the army, for these gangs often were horse thieves who adopted this method of stealing horses." Reflecting on the unfortunate event years later, he continued, "Mother and I had to submit to these and other impositions. My brothers and stepfather were in the army—I, a patriotic youth was easily deceived."[54] As a young man, inexperienced and vulnerable to the criminal element, Bryan lamented that he could not do more to protect his family from the encounter with the press gang. Had he been (like his brothers and stepfather) a man and not a youth, he would have properly fulfilled his manly obligations by challenging the horse thieves.

Properties left abandoned because of the Runaway Scrape were also susceptible to the criminally inclined who exploited the opportunity to steal and plunder. It was Texians, not the Mexican army, who posed the greater threat to Lydia Ann McHenry's property in Austin's colony, near the site of Bellville, Texas. Returning home from the journey eastward after reaching the Trinity River, McHenry registered her shock at the condition of the belongings that she left behind when the family took flight. In a July 17, 1836, letter to her brother, John Hardin McHenry, who resided in Kentucky, she described the state of her home when the family returned in mid-May: "My bed was destroyed & all my clothes stolen by plunderers, for the Mexicans were not in our neighborhood." Thankfully, they found all their cows and had enough to eat, "which was more than we expected."[55] Thus, the civilian population needed to worry not only about being robbed by fake press gangs along the road but also about their properties left vulnerable to opportunistic raiders.

Impressment abuses typically came in two forms. The first was private citizens posing as government representatives in an effort to steal property from their fellow countrymen. This was the abuse that Guy Bryan described in his account. The second was actual, legitimate members of the army impressing goods for their own financial gain, capitalizing on their position of trust.[56] In either case, the targets for exploitation were panicked civilians fleeing for their own safety. So great was the threat of fake press gangs confiscating civilian property that interim President Burnett and his neighbors were also victims of this method of duplicity: "scoundrels . . . on pretense of pressing for public service" stole the president's own pistols and his neighbors' horses.[57] Amid the turmoil, no one was fully safe from criminal activity, including the newly appointed president.

Racing ahead of the Mexican threat during the Runaway Scrape, Annie Fagan Teal traveled with a small child on her lap towards the Sabine River, "riding all day over the prairie, through woods or water." She described how her traveling party was met by a small band who took their guns from them. Of note, she did not identify this band as either soldiers or government officials. Further, she believed that the men mounted on fine horses, who warned the throngs of fleeing civilians to run for their lives and incited panic along the way, was part of a larger ploy: "The alarm given the settlers proved to be a plan concocted to rob and pillage the country, which was done on a magnificent scale; as of all the cattle owned by this colony, one cow only was left to them, she proved to refractory to drive." On returning to her home after the war, she observed, "The robbers were still at it; she saw load after load of elegant, richly carved Mahogany furniture taken from the deserted homes of rich Mexicans."[58] It is unclear what she thought of the looting of Tejano families' homes; however, she did make note of the occurrence and describe the perpetrators as robbers.

In his memoir of early Texas, Noah Smithwick, a soldier in the Texas forces, used much harsher terminology to describe the activity that Teal witnessed in her travels: "And, as if the arch fiend had broken loose, there were men—or devils, rather—bent on plunder, galloping up behind the fugitives, telling them the Mexicans were just behind, thus causing the hapless victims to abandon what few valuables they had tried to save."[59] Given the turmoil—Houston's retreat and Texas families fleeing for their lives—it is not surprising that criminals saw opportunity in the chaos, leading to an increase in lawlessness. Undoubtedly, there was less time to administer justice when the state was both at war and under invasion. Paul Lack described a band of criminals headed by James Boyce operating in Texas in the late months of 1835 and early 1836. One account tied the band to three murders and three serious assaults before Boyce was arrested and put on trial.[60] It is probably safe to assume that those engaged in plunder (or more severe crimes) did not suddenly abandon their exploits to fight for the Texas cause, choosing to confront Santa Anna's forces on the frontlines; such criminals were, in effect, noncombatants.

But what of the crime of disloyalty? In the waning weeks of the Revolution, Hervey Whiting, a physician from a small community southeast of Lynchburg, was accused by several witnesses of substantial crimes against the people of Texas, including robbing and pillaging his neighbors and, even worse, treason.[61] Witness testimonials alleged that Whiting was a Tory who aided and abetted the Mexicans in their efforts to chase down the Texas army; specifically, they believed that Whiting colluded with Col. Juan Almonte and General Santa Anna, himself. The fear of Toryism in Texas outstripped the actual prevalence of treasonous activity. As Paul Lack notes, "Tory behavior—defined strictly as giving aid and comfort to the centralist cause through military service or other voluntary support—characterized the response of a relatively small proportion of the total population."[62] In chronicling the mounting threats to the white civilian population as they raced to the American border, Dilue Rose Harris cited "wild Africans" among the slave contingents, large tribes of Indians, and "tories, both Mexicans and Americans, in the country."[63] She recalled that Deaf Smith told her he would be ashamed to be seen in a white shirt wherein he might be taken for a "tory or stay-at-home."[64] Harris's observations suggest that there was certainly talk of Tories among the populace, even if there were scant actual examples. Still, fears among Texans arose and accusations were lodged at specific individuals, both during and after hostilities subsided. Potential signs of disloyalty to the Texas cause included an unwillingness to take up arms against Santa Anna's forces (incapacity to fight required explanation and sometimes confirmation), staying in place when the Mexican army approached (rather than fleeing in panic), and engaging the Texians' enemy in direct communications. Whiting was guilty of all three.

The case of Hervey Whiting underscores both the suspicion of men who failed to enlist and the often-gendered defense these men invoked to justify avoiding service. At the outset, it is important to note that Whiting denied all charges. On May 3, 1836, he wrote a lengthy letter to Col. James Morgan rebutting the criminal accusations against him and providing context for his interactions with Santa Anna. He acknowledged in his letter that the allegations being leveled at him might be some of his "friends" seeing an opportunity to settle an old grudge. He described the charges as exaggerated tales: "First that I have turned tory & joined the Mexicans next that I have been robing & plundering all around the contry & concealing the property [sic]."[65] Whiting argued that he was not a Tory, but rather a patriot to the broader Texas cause. In his letter, he disputed all the charges against him, arguing the converse: that he was protecting the countryside from the criminal element at great personal risk to himself and his family.

According to Whiting, family obligations kept him from the battlefield. At the time of Santa Anna's arrival to the area, Whiting was cooped up "with the females of 3 family [sic] dependent on me for protection."[66] In his previous correspondence with Colonel Morgan, he explained that two of the three families were entirely dependent on him for support; therefore, he was unable to leave home or engage in any work to support the Texas forces without being derelict in his domestic obligations. Because he could not abandon his family, he sent a substitute, Gilbert Brooks (his future son-in-law), to serve the army in his stead.[67] In a deposition, Michael McCormick, a witness to the case, corroborated that Whiting oversaw a large family consisting mostly of females who were then in a "wretched state." More specifically, he testified that the Whiting family "was in a bad state of health in the spring of 1836." Although McCormick did not physically see the family, he had heard confirmations of their ill health. The witness posited that if he were in a similar situation to Whiting's he would not have enlisted, "considering his family would be much exposed."[68]

When Mexican forces reached the river crossing at Lynchburg, they "hoisted the Black flag," alerting locals of their much-dreaded arrival to the area. At the time, Whiting explained, he was in the process of securing the property of his neighbor, interim President Burnet. He was in fact protecting his neighbor's property, not plundering it. Upon hearing of Santa Anna's arrival, Whiting raced home to his family; while in transit, he saw people flying with the utmost speed away from the Mexican army. He noted "that every pass over the ferries were choked [sic] a strong wind precluded the possibility of leaving by water." They were stuck. He continued, "In family council it was concluded that the best & only chance was to remain where we were."[69] So the family's decision to stay put was based on prudence, not disloyalty, given the adverse travel conditions. As to his communications with General Santa Anna—probably the most hated man in Texas at the time—Whiting said he did so in service to his community. The Mexican general assured Whiting that his family and property would be safe from all violence and "requested me to communicate this information to my neighbors."[70] Santa Anna also informed Whiting that he might need to use his boat to cross the river, but he would get it back after his army crossed. Whiting presented his communications with Santa Anna not only as innocuous but also as a community service enterprise.

As to the charges of robbing and plundering, Whiting argued that the opposite was true. He was protecting his neighbors' property, specifically the property of the interim president of Texas, from a band of lawless plunderers who had been ransacking the neighborhood. He was personally insulted by this accusation, as "I have worked myself down without any prospect of remuneration to save the property of others and my life is now threatened for doing so." In a particularly bold move, Whiting charged his most ardent accuser, Lt. David Kokernot, of being the actual neighborhood plunderer: "He is desolating the homes of deserted families and grossly insulting women & children. This surely ought to be looked to—was he commissioned to do it?—at my house he shall not do it with impunity."[71] According to Whiting, Kokernot engaged in pillaging the abandoned homes of fellow Texans and insulting women and children along the way. In the end, Whiting's defense against charges of criminality and treason rested on his claims of protecting not only his family but also community homes and property.

Sensing that the fate of the uprising stood on the edge of a precipice, the leaders of the Texas Revolution deployed an all-encompassing strategy to compel men to join them on the battlefield. Hoping to exploit their martial tendencies, military and government officials exerted virtually every tactic at their disposal to rally men to the cause, including shame, alarm, and uncompromising threats. With confidence, Houston declared, "If the men will turn out like men," victory would soon follow.[72] Interim President Burnet assured that the day of vengeance was at hand: "Let the citizens of Texas do their duty manfully" by defeating Santa Anna's forces on the field.[73] And while Houston directed harsh criticism and threats toward deserters, he played a role in triggering the desertions under his command. It was *his* military strategy that placed the families of enlisted men in peril, prompting many of them to leave the army and secure their families to safety. Houston countered that the government fleeing in haste was an even greater source of alarm among the populace. Beginning at the Colorado, Houston's decisions to retreat and postpone the fighting to another day left the women and children on Texas farms and plantations at risk to an invading army.

Some observers to the events of 1836 sympathized with the plight of Texas men with families, both during and after hostilities ended. Decades after the fact, Dilue Rose Harris wrote, "At the Trinity River men from the army began to join their families. I know they have been blamed for this, but what else could they have done?" Harris argued that the men always planned to return to the fight: "It was the intention of our men to see their families across the Sabine River, and then return and fight the Mexicans."[74] That said, men without families who refused service garnered far less sympathy than their married counterparts. When it came to this group of noncombatants, it proved less effective for civilian and military officials to invoke shame for failing to come to the aid of Texas women and children; instead, they applied pressure through the threat of impressment (in the short term) and blacklisting (in the long term). Criminals who preyed on the vulnerability of a panicked population drew the highest level of scorn from their contemporaries. Not only did they fail to protect women and children, but they also exploited them; in doing so, they undermined the respect and honor conferred to manhood. Despite increasingly severe consequences, scores of men ignored their commanders' orders and left the ranks. Houston's military strategy created the predicament that compelled men to choose between their manly obligations to protect their families—indicative of restrained manhood—or stay in the fight, thus putting their martial manhood to the test. During the last weeks of the Revolution, Anglo Texas men grappled with appropriate expressions of their manliness—a microcosm of competing notions of manhood (sometimes overlapping, often in tension) acted out by men during the expansionist period of mid-nineteenth century America.

4

MANLINESS AND THE TEXAS ENEMY

The Dishonorable and the Depredators

Tell them the ruthless murderer is upon our soil—that all rights of freemen are disregarded—Tell them our women have been assaulted our virgins defiled and our men treated as devils, rather than Christians.[1]

—Brig. Gen. Thomas J. Green

In broadsides, speeches, and public declarations, Texas revolutionaries defended their cause as a revolt against tyranny. In his appeal to "The Friends of Liberty Throughout the World," Thomas J. Green, brigadier general of the Texian Army, implored sympathetic addressees to rally to their side "in the name of every tie which binds blood to blood, for means of prosecuting ou(r) [sic] war of Liberty, against a tyranny as despotic as the worst human passions can engender."[2] In a similarly toned address to the American public, Richard Ellis, president of the Texas Convention of 1836, stated their evidence confirmed "all that we have heretofore alledged [sic] of the barbarism of the arch fiend, who, after subverting the liberties of his own countrymen, has arrayed all of his forces to reduce us—the freeborn colonists of Texas—to the yoke of military and ecclesiastical despotism."[3] Theirs was a defense of liberty against a "cruel despot." Cloaking themselves in the language of liberty, they described themselves as freeborn men and aligned their cause with the Spirit of '76 and the revolutionaries who fought a similar campaign against the British decades earlier. They did so for both practical and ideological purposes. In the last months of the Revolution, Texians sought American support—money and volunteers—as their rebellion teetered on failure. At the same time, they increased their pleas for all Texas men to turn out and join Houston's forces on the battlefield. The pursuit of freedom, the resistance to tyranny, and the virtue of a noble and honorable fight were familiar tropes to the transplanted American men who migrated to Texas in the late 1820s and early 1830s.

The American founders interwove the concept of manhood with the language of liberty. In *A Republic of Men,* Mark Kann asserts that manhood modified liberty and, in doing so, injected an element of masculine merit into the vocabulary of the early Republic. One of the reasons for this linkage between manhood and liberty was to motivate men to join the fight against Great Britain. Men who suffused their fight in the defense of liberty and the eventual triumph over their enemies merited the honor and respect due to manhood.[4] In charge of raising and equipping an army of reserves from US volunteers, Thomas Chambers bound the Texas cause to the United States through blood and shared ideology: "The people of Texas, as was to be expected, faithful to the principles of that of liberty which they inherited as a birth right from their fathers and which was guaranteed to them by the constitution under which they were called a country, repelled the demand with a spirit of indignation becoming the sons of the heroes of '76."[5] Similarly, in a proclamation delivered at the end of March 1836, interim President Burnet appealed to Texas men to rally to the frontlines, asking his countrymen, "Is it possible that the free citizens of Texas, the descendants of the heroes of 76 can take panic at the approach of the paltry minions of a despot, who threaten to desolate our beautiful country?"[6] A week later, Burnet wrote: "The day of vengeance is at hand,—Let the citizens of Texas do their duty manfully and as becomes the name of Americans, and these minions of despotism will soon be annihilated."[7]

Texians met the masculine ideal that pervaded the antebellum period by positioning their cause under the banner of liberty. They were ready to take up arms for what they deemed a just cause. Historian Harry Laver argues that in the 1830s and 1840s, Texas independence (and later the Mexican War) presented a chance for another generation to join the militia, shoulder arms, and demonstrate their manliness.[8] Chapter 3, "Deserters, Noncombatants, and Criminals," focused on Texas men who faced derision for failing to meet their manly obligations to protect the women and children of Texas from an approaching threat. But what of the manliness of their perceived enemy? If manliness was linked to the fight for liberty, what can be said of men who fought on the side of tyranny?—those not engaged in an honorable and noble fight, but rather a war of extermination. For many Texans, there were *two* enemies that posed an imminent threat to the civilian population of the state: the invading Mexican army *and* indigenous tribes who launched raids on frontier settlements, which escalated in frequency during the 1836 rebellion, especially in East Texas. Military and civilian accounts rendered Mexican soldiers as dishonorable and Native Americans as depredators. In their own way, both of the enemies of Texians failed to live up to nineteenth-century American notions of manhood that celebrated coded principles such as sacrifice, duty, honor, moral turpitude, and restraint.

One strain of attack on the Mexican army lodged by military officials, who relied on reports from spies and captives, was that their troops lacked a genuine commitment to their cause. Anglo Texans characterized their invading foe not only as weak but also as unfree in condition—an army composed of convicts. For example, soldiers in the Mexican ranks were accused of lacking commitment, as they were "old convicts presd [sic] to fight," and, it was said, their officers had "to whip them to fight."[9] When employed by General Houston, this latter charge served the purpose of bolstering the case for the eventual triumph of the resolute Texas forces over their weaker, uncommitted enemy. Reporting to the chair of the Military

Committee, Houston opined that, on close examination, the army of Santa Anna was overrated and "the officers have to whip and slash the soldiers on the march."[10] In a later appeal to the "People East of the Brazos," Houston wrote: "The enemy cavalry are not numerous, as stated, and their infantry are men pressed into service, and convicts from prisons. Their army is encumbered with women and children." An effort clearly designed to reassure Texians that "if men will unite with the present force," then defeat of the opposing forces would quickly follow. He ended his letter by asserting: "We will whip them soon."[11] The charge of a convict soldiery was not completely without merit given that some local authorities in Mexico sent those found guilty of crimes (assault, robbery, or even murder) to the army in an effort to meet required military quotas.[12] They did not make up the majority of Mexican soldiers, however. Still, on this issue, Houston needed to draw a fine line between his characterization of an uncommitted and thus beatable foe and a dangerous, invading horde waging a war of extermination on the freeborn colonists of the state. The latter portrayal required that all Texas men needed to turn out—and turn out immediately.

The notion of a war of extermination instigated by Santa Anna and his army against all persons in Texas—civilians and soldiers—appeared with some frequency in personal letters and public dispatches from the state in the early months of 1836. For example, an ordinance outlining the provisions for organizing a militia for the Republic of Texas, signed by Richard Ellis, opened with the following ominous statement: "Whereas, the present exigencies of the country are such as imperiously demand the immediate organization of the physical force, for its prompt and energetic defence against a large invading army of merciless enemies, who are waging a war of extermination against all ages, sexes, and conditions...."[13] The Convention used the ordinance to compel "every man" to stand forth to protect the country against the invading army by enlisting in the newly formed militia. In a similar effort, after hearing of the fall of the Alamo and "the merciless and cruel murder of every man in the garrison," the citizens of Brazoria sounded the alarm to fellow Anglos, describing in stark terms their enemy's intentions: "the rapid advance of the enemy into the heart of Texas, with the avowed purpose of a general extermination of ourselves, our wives, our children, and all who inhabit this country."[14] Town residents implored all Brazoria men to come to the defense of the Texas uprising by volunteering for the army. Those unable to serve because of age, ill health, or "other casualties" needed to do their part in protecting the community on the home front—including providing every assistance to those in the field and rendering their enslaved persons to assist in building local fortifications.

Another charge leveled against the Mexican army was that it was made up of "hirelings;" men not committed to any aspirational cause besides their own personal profit. In the broader context of nineteenth-century perceptions of labor and the yeoman ideal, men who relied on wages were deemed not truly independent. This was especially true of the planter class in the American South who relied on the labor of enslaved people. This accusation also struck at the larger question of the virtuousness of the Mexican fight—whether it was grounded in something loftier than one's personal interest. In a letter relaying the tragic news of the loss of his brother at the Alamo to his family, Benjamin Goodrich, seething with contempt for his enemy, wrote, "We will meet him and teach the unprincipled scoundrel that freemen can never by conquered by the hirling [sic] soldiery of a military despot."[15] In his appeal for American support, Thomas Chambers asked, "Can it be believed that the Descendants of a Washington and a Franklin . . . will be left unaided to be exterminated by the murderous hirelings of tyranny and fanaticism in sight of a gallant and free people upon whom they call with the endearling [sic] names of fellow countrymen and brothers?"[16] In a further swipe at the adversary's character, interim President Burnet asserted that "the minions of despotism are as easily rallied as dispersed; they are equally servile and inefficient."[17]

Criticisms that the Mexican army lacked honor and commitment gave little credence to the idea that perhaps many in the Mexican forces believed in their cause and saw it as a defense of their nation against a rebellious uprising. Although his research focused on the Mexican-American War a decade later, Peter Guardino argues that Mexican men shared their American counterparts' notions of what it meant to be man, or "to have pants," a nineteenth-century idiom that translates in English as "stand up and act like a man." Part of acting like a man was to join the fight against threats to the nation (especially the American invasion of Mexico in 1846). Guardino notes that "Mexican men were repeatedly urged to defend not only their country and their religion, but also the honor of Mexican women."[18] This applies to the sexual threat of American men to the women of Mexico. Guardino differentiated citizen soldiers, or volunteers, from those who served in the regular army; the latter group were criticized for their failure to establish themselves in their local community, form families, and support them.[19] Citizen soldiers were the epitome of the masculine ideal.

They came to the rescue of their nation in a time of crisis but returned to their communities when the threat subsided. A citizen was supposed to act responsibly and provide for his family through honest work. Honor was an important component of Mexican masculinity as well. Guardino observes, "In Mexico, citizenship was a right of respectable men who worked to support their spouses, children, and aged parents. These were men who avoided promiscuity, heavy drinking, excessive domestic violence, immoderate gambling, and idleness. They were, in other words, honorable."[20] Indeed, Texians knew little about what constituted honor when it came to the culture of those they deemed their enemy.

With life, liberty, and property at stake, Anglo Texans did not hold back when it came to negatively branding their adversaries—Mexicans were "ruthless invaders," "bloodthirsty marauders," "ruffian tyrants," "a merciless horde," "audacious invaders," "murderers," "semicivilized and infuriate," and, as Burnet described, "minions of despotism."[21] In all, Texas insurgents charged that not only did Mexican troops lack the will to fight, but they added a myriad of smears admonishing their enemy's perceived propensity for ruthlessness and lack of humanity.[22] Emboldened with their declaration of independence adopted on March 2, 1836, Texas rebels cast Santa Anna and the Mexican army as "invaders" to a yet-to-be-realized nation, detaching and distancing them from their own country. However, in early March, as political officials debated and codified the aspirations of a new republic, much of the narrative of the Revolution had yet to play out.

Texas soldiers and civilians alike saved their strongest contempt for the leader of the Mexican forces, Gen. Antonio López de Santa Anna. Once again, there was a decidedly gendered tilt to the condemnations of the general. Santa Anna was described as a scoundrel, despot, arch fiend, ferocious tyrant, impotent invader, and ruthless murderer.[23] From the Texian perspective, the Mexican general lacked honor. Honor not only was one of the pillars of the southern masculine ideal but also played an important role in the rhetoric of the Revolution. Southern historian Edward Ayers argues that honor was an outward-facing attribute conferred upon you by your contemporaries rather than self-derived: "Southern men recognized the dictates of honor: a system of values within you have as much worth as others confer upon you."[24] For Southerners, honor was rooted in the defense of liberty and the supervision and security of those in their household: women, children, and enslaved laborers. "Manly independence" and "womanly weakness" solidified a man's control over his property and dependents.²⁵ Rather than serving as an honorable patriarch for the state, in the broader sense, it was General Santa Anna (and his forces) who posed a threat to the women and children of Texas. There was nothing honorable in that. In his argument for American support, Thomas Chambers claimed: "It is expected that the despot will attempt to advance immediately into the heart of the country to murder and butcher our families and devastate out homes."²⁶

Santa Anna's brutish reputation toward his enemies gained traction during the federalist rebellion in Zacatecas the previous year. In the wealthy mining town, Santa Anna quelled a nascent uprising against his centralist policies led by Francisco García Salinas in May 1835. After the defeat of García Salinas's forces, Santa Anna allowed his troops to sack and loot the city.²⁷ Based on this example, Texas rebels believed that he was a threat not only to soldiers on the frontlines but also to the women and children of the state, left vulnerable on the farms and plantations squarely in the sights of the Mexican advance. To drum up American support for the war, Brig. Gen. Thomas J. Green directed Adolphus T. McCall, an American traveling in Texas at the time of hostilities, to tell his countrymen upon his return that "the ruthless murderer is upon our soil—that all rights of freemen are disregarded—Tell them our women have been assaulted our virgins defiled and our men treated as devils, rather than Christians."²⁸ For Green, Santa Anna was not only a ruthless murderer who waged ignoble war against Texas soldiers but a pernicious sexual threat to Texas women. Green's comments came on the heels of the massacre of Colonel Fannin's troops at Goliad, where Texas soldiers were slaughtered as traitors rather than as legitimate wartime combatants. All the while, Santa Anna's forces marched closer to the most populated Texas settlements.²⁹

Although women are largely absent from historical retellings of military engagements during the Texas Revolution, one notable exception is the enduring fascination with Emily D. West, the "Yellow Rose of Texas," and her alleged role in the events immediately preceding the Battle of San Jacinto (in some accounts, Emily's last name is given as Morgan, denoting her contractual arrangement with plantation owner, Colonel Morgan).³⁰ Legend has it that the Yellow Rose kept General Santa Anna occupied in his tent before Sam Houston's army attacked the Mexican camp at San Jacinto on April 21, 1836. Why would Santa Anna allow himself to be distracted by a beautiful servant of mixed ancestry at this critical juncture in the war? Apparently, the general was notorious when it came to his antics with women. While it is doubtful that Texans living thousands of miles away from the capital would be fully aware of his scandalous reputation, in central Mexico, General Santa Anna was known as a compulsive womanizer, whose popularity in Mexico, according to one of his biographers, "appeared to benefit from the gossip generated by his sexual feats."[31] He was twice married to women under the age of fifteen (marital ages not uncommon among the affluent Mexican class) but attended neither ceremony. Despite these legal entanglements, Santa Anna was brazenly unfaithful, engaging in numerous extramarital affairs that often resulted in illegitimate children. On these affairs, his biographer notes, "Santa Anna's sexual appetite was well known at the time and there is no ostensible evidence that he cared for any of his mistresses."[32] According to Peter Guardino's study of Mexican masculinity and military service, hard drinking, macho, quick-to-anger, promiscuous men offered an alternative model of manhood to moral, responsible family men that had some credibility in Mexican popular culture.[33]

Because exercising restraint was one the dominating expressions of manhood in nineteenth-century America, Santa Anna's lack of self-discipline when it came to women, specifically his failings regarding Emily West (whether true or untrue), provided an opportunity for his critics, long after hostilities ended, to assail his character. From the perspective of American masculinity, restrained men derived their manhood from being morally upright, reliable, and brave.[34] Gail Bederman describes antebellum male identity as steeped in the middle-class virtues of a strong, "manly" character. She writes, "The middle class saw this ability to control powerful masculine passions through strong character and a powerful will as a primary source of men's strength and authority over both woman and the lower classes."[35] Self-mastery and restraint expressed and shaped middle-class identity. Santa Anna's inability to focus on the task at hand and control his sexual appetite defied such restraint. What might be perceived as machismo and strength in one model of manhood in Mexico did not translate to an American-centric culture that celebrated restraint and moral uprightness.

Regarding the Yellow Rose, anthropologist Holly Brear argues that the Emily West/Morgan legend (Brear uses the latter) draws on two dominant tropes of femininity in western mythologies. Brear situates the story of the Yellow Rose within a larger exploration of the Texas creation myth. In the first trope, Emily West assumes the role of temptress, luring General Santa

Anna away from the immediacy of his martial responsibilities. Women of color were especially susceptible to being cast as overtly sexual beings, serving to differentiate them from white women and justify their sexual exploitation by white men. Their inherent seductive qualities lured white men into sexual situations—whether they be Native American women during European contact, slave women on southern plantations, or raven-haired Mexican women in the Southwest. In stark contrast to the temptress is the second trope in western constructs—the pure, submissive white woman in need of protection by white men from the dangers of a dark-skinned invading army. Texas officials relied heavily on this second trope. Brear asserts that "women in Texas creation mythology are either purely sexual beings who tempt men and bring the downfall of those who become involved with them or they are faithful, asexual beings who believe in the eventual victory of the Anglo male and reserve themselves to be the valuable social wombs in the creation of a new Texas society."[36]

As to the peril of white women, in his seminal book *They Called Them Greasers,* Arnoldo de León cites several examples of prominent Anglo Texans who inserted the sexual threat of Mexican soldiers to white women into the rhetoric of war, focusing specifically on the writings of James W. Fannin, John W. Hall, and William Barret Travis.[37] Once again, the intent was a call to action designed to motivate Texan men to join the war effort. Writing in early February, few captured the alarmist tone more than Colonel Fannin who did not survive the Goliad massacre the following month. Fannin pondered how it could be possible that the freemen of Texas would not protect the honor of their mothers, wives, and daughters under threat by an "unprincipled Despot" and "Tyrant." He implored, "What can be expected for the *Fair daughters* of chaste *white* women, when their own country women are prostituted by a licensed soldiery, as the inducement to push forward into the colonies, where they may find *fairer* game?"[38] Despite the lurid warnings of Mexican rapists in early 1836, de León notes that no violations were reported, and the "rape theme practically disappeared." Indeed, after the Revolution, in periods of both peace and turmoil, Anglos "seldom saw Mexicans as a danger to white women."[39] A product of fear, urgency, and propaganda, the much-promoted sexual threat of Mexican soldiers against the white women of Texas, during their 1836 march northward, appears more rhetorical than realized. Yet such warnings served their purpose—they utilized gendered language and representations in an attempt to stoke fear and action on the part of Texas men, although it is unclear how persuasive such arguments were when it came to recruitment.

As General Santa Anna's army pressed northward, closing in on the farms and plantations in the settled regions of the state, rumors of Mexican atrocities toward women and children proliferated among the civilian population. Those in the line of fire clearly believed there was reason to be afraid. Both contemporary and later accounts of the Mexican advance included reports of brutal attacks on families. Perhaps, in a further effort to rally American support for the cause, a letter printed in the *Nashville Banner & Nashville Whig* included a firsthand account of events in Texas, dated March 28, reporting that "Santa Anna is now in Texas, with 8000 cavalry, with which he is scouring the country, committing the most horrid cruelties, putting to death every one he meets, without regard to age, sex, or condition. The females are usually given up to the brutal passions of the soldiers, and afterwards butchered."[40] In his diary chronicling his experiences of the Runaway Scrape, William Fairfax Gray wrote on April 12, 1836: "The bearer of the express states that the Mexicans were crossing the Brazos at Fort Bend. Other rumors speak of the murder of families of women and children by them on the Brazos."[41] Taken as a whole, the threat to white women and children rallied men to the cause, dissuaded them from deserting, and provided the rationale for American intervention into the Texas fight.

In her reminiscences of the Runaway Scrape, Jane Hallowell Hill recounted the tremendous anxiety among the civilian population that the Mexican army was targeting *all* in the state. She wrote, "In the year 1836, we were in the 'Runaway Scrape,' as it was then called, fleeing from Santa Anna's army. It was thought that they would overrun the whole country, sparing none." Hill's mother was so distressed by the fall of the Alamo and the advancing Mexican army that she brought only one trunk of belongings with her when she fled. Most of the family's belongings were ransacked and stolen during their absence. Hill recalled that the "Mexican army had camped within five miles of our house and burned the fence rails to make their fires. Whole families had been captured and killed not far from where we lived."[42] In her contemporaneous diary, Milly R. Gray, who was not in Texas at the time of the revolution, expressed delight at the news she received from Texas in May 1836 (from correspondence exchanged with her cousin) of the defeat of the Mexicans and the capture of Santa Anna.

Indeed, she leveled her harshest comments at the leader of the Mexican forces. Of Santa Anna, she wrote: "He had been such a ruthless tyrant and waged such a sanguinary war, even upon women & children, that all the friends of Humanity must rejoice that his career is checked—but we had a more personal interest. Mr. Gray having bought up lands in the country."[43] The Grays intended to make Texas their home, and peace was essential to that plan.

When families like the Grays purchased land in Texas, awaiting a victory by the Texas rebels so that they could establish a new home in a new land, they did so on contested terrain. As Americans migrated into the Mexican state of Texas in the 1820s and 1830s, they competed for land, food, and resources with indigenous tribes already in place—people who considered the land *their* home. Frontier attacks and violent confrontations with Native Americans were not limited to 1830s Texas; during the same period, the US government waged war against the Sauk and Meskwaki (Fox) tribes under the leadership of the Sauk war chief Black Hawk (1832), and the mid-1830s saw the outbreak of the Second Seminole War in Florida (1835–1842). In *The Threshold of Manifest Destiny,* Laura Clark Shire examines the expansion of the domestic sphere into Seminole lands in the 1820s and 1830s, focusing on the central role of white women in the settler colonizing process. Shire explores how sensationalist American press accounts of the Seminole wars in Florida concocted and promoted Indian depredation narratives in which white women and their children suffered injury or death and lost property when attacked by Seminoles.

Home and property were central to Shire's analysis. She asserts that the focus in depredation narratives on devasted homes and dead families "was a crucial part of the way these tales used gender and domesticity to reframe a war for Indian removal as a matter of domestic defense."[44] In the typical depredation narrative, white women fled their homes in haste, running away from their Indian attackers, only to return to the scene of the attack to witness the destruction of spaces they had exerted so much effort in creating and sustaining—the destruction of white domesticity. On land where Seminole homes once stood, authors of these narratives represented white women as innocents whose homes and families were tragically destroyed by vicious, barbaric Seminoles who ignored the sanctity of the home as a venerated space. Such stories of destruction reinforced racial and cultural differences between Native Americans and white colonizers, particularly in terms of family and domesticity.[45]

The threat to domesticity spaces was also an issue in Texas during the early months of 1836 as the revolt against Mexico intensified with the movement of Santa Anna's army into the state. For Noah Smithwick, the "ruthless invaders" from the south were by no means the only concern for Anglos Texans; rather, an equally dangerous threat to civilians were the frequent raids by Native American tribes on defenseless farms and plantations unleashed by the chaos of revolution. Smithwick served in a company of rangers, commanded by Capt. John Jackson Tumlinson Jr.—a unit charged with protecting the Bastrop area from Indian attack. As Santa Anna's forces marched northward, Smithwick, his fellow rangers, and every available man were called to Gonzales to plan for the state's defense, "thus leaving the frontier settlements exposed to both Mexicans and Indians."[46] During the early months of 1836, East Texas communities were especially vulnerable, as many Native American attacks emanated from the American side of the border. Both invading forces threatened the stability of frontier settlements in the state. In Smithwick's opinion, Indian raids were particularly insidious: "There was even more danger from Indians, who were hovering on the outskirts, than from Mexicans who would come by the highway."[47] Annie Fagan Teal affirmed the perceived Native American threat, recalling one man on horseback, racing alongside fleeing residents, shouting, "Run, run for your lives; Mexicans and Indians are coming, burning and killing as they come."[48]

While the fear of attack by indigenous tribes preceded the events of the Texas Revolution, once Texas men left for the front, their largely unguarded farms and plantations became even more vulnerable to raiding parties. In a May 18, 1836, letter to his brother, Samuel Allen described the volatility of the outlying settlements: "I lived immediately on the frontier where the Indians were very troublesome and was compelled when the Alamo was taken to remove my family to a place of safety both from Mexicans and Indians."[49] In remembering the frequent Indian raids on the Gonzales settlement, Ann Cardwell relayed that a full moon escalated the threat: "It was generally about the time of the full moon when the Indians would make their raids." She continued, "We had to be always on the alert, not knowing where the cruel creatures were lurking about the place watching for an opportunity to descend upon the family with murder, theft and burning rankling in their brutal hearts."[50] Cardwell was concerned not only with bodily harm but also with the theft of their property and the burning of their homes. Along the road during the Runaway Scrape, Ann Raney Coleman reported that her traveling party was forced to set up camp in late afternoon, rather than evening, because of rumors permeating among the group that Native Americans were killing families on their way to the Sabine.[51]

Worse than raids focused on stealing horses and cattle were those in which Texas colonists—particularly women and children—were taken captive by marauding tribes. According to her reminiscences, Ann Cardwell recalled the need for those in the Gonzales settlement to be constantly alert because "in the neighborhood they [Indians] would once in awhile steal a little child playing about the premises."[52] The threat of Indian capture was real.

Nomadic tribes such as the Comanche targeted women and children to replenish their numbers after deaths from disease and warfare depleted their population. Captive women could bear children and, importantly, serve as laborers, tanning bison hides for trade, while captured children assimilated more easily and were generally adopted as full tribal members.[53] Alternatively, tribes could also ransom their captives for much-needed goods; thus, there were a number of incentives for taking captives before and after the Revolution.

With the events of the Runaway Scrape swirling around them in the early months of 1836, Sarah Ann Horn's family decided to seek refuge in Matamoros, a destination much closer for them than the Louisiana border given their location near the Rio Grande in South Texas.[54] Using familiar language, Sarah described the setting of their travel: "At this time the bloody Santa Anna was ravaging the country, and was no less a terror to us than the Indians. He was carrying on a war of extermination against the Americans; and in order to keep out of his way, (he being now quite near us,) we took a circuitous route and went to San Patricio."[55] It is notable that Sarah described Santa Anna as waging war against "the Americans." On April 4, 1836, as the Horn family's traveling party made their way to San Patricio, the group was attacked by a band of Comanche Indians. During the melee, Sarah witnessed the execution of her husband, John Horn: "They instantly tore me and my children from my dear husband, when one of the savages struck him on the back of his head with a double barrel gun and he fell to the ground upon his face. I saw him draw his arms up under him, and raise his head once from the ground, when he uttered a deep sigh and the mortal agony was past him forever."[56] The Comanches took seven captives from the Horn's traveling party, including Sarah and her two sons. In September 1837, Sarah was purchased by American traders at a trading post near present-day Las Vegas, New Mexico. While in captivity, she was separated from her young sons; despite exhaustive efforts to negotiate a trade with the Indians after her release, Sarah never saw her sons again.[57]

By relaying the horrific details of the death of her husband, Sarah Horn's narrative fulfilled one of the most important goals of the captivity genre: highlighting the barbarity of her Indian capturers, especially when it came to families. In Shire's study of Indian depredation narratives in 1830s Florida, she notes that many white men were killed in an initial stage of an attack attempting to protect their families from "barbaric" Seminoles, while others (as the narratives divulge) were away fighting the war on other fronts,[58] a circumstance familiar to Texas families. In both depredation and captivity narratives from the period, women were cast as vulnerable onlookers, forlorn by the loss of their loved ones and property. Authors of Indian captivity and depredation narratives expected their audience to feel horror, fear, and sympathy with white victims of violence and employed sentimental language and domestic tropes to achieve this end.[59] In her examination of nineteenth-century captive narratives, June Namias distinguishes the emergence of the "frail flower" archetype in narratives published during the 1830s and 1840s, coinciding with the rise of the ideal of true womanhood and the mass marketing of sentimental fiction.[60] Appearing frequently in narratives from the period, the frail flower is "the poor, hapless woman who is taken unawares. She is shocked and distressed by her capture and by the deaths and dislocations that go with it."[61] In such narratives, women are portrayed as weak and despondent, while their Indian capturers are presented as brutish, sadomasochistic, and dirty.

As he patrolled the Bastrop region with his ranger company, protecting its settlements, Noah Smithwick did not hold back in his vituperation of Native Americans. While commenting on the size of the Texas forces in comparison to the much larger Mexican army, he noted that they were also outnumbered by Indians: "There were hordes of ruthless savages eagerly watching for an opportunity to swoop down on us and wipe us from the face of the earth and so regain their lost hunting grounds."[62] For Smithwick, too many of his fellow revolutionaries were focused exclusively on the Mexican threat, paying little attention to the risk of Indian attack. He wrote, cynically: "The Indians, taking advantage of the disturbed condition, were committing depredations, and the army, numbering not more than 500 or 600 men, rank and file, was preparing to invade Mexico and bring her rulers 'to a realizing sense of the situation,' having no time therefore for such trivial matters as the murdering of the citizens by the Indians."[63] Smithwick's use of the term *depredations* is worth noting. His perception of Native Americans was no doubt shaped by some of the atrocities he witnessed during his time as a ranger in Tumlinson's unit, including his account of a Comanche attack on the Hibbons traveling party. A band of Comanche warriors attacked the travelers, killing the two men in the party and taking the lone woman and her two small children hostage. The woman escaped, but not before having to witness her baby being snatched from her by an Indian who "bashed its brains out against a tree." Thankfully for the woman, Smithwick and his company were able to chase down the Comanches and rescue her three-year-old boy.[64]

Smithwick's negativity toward Native Americans not only derived from his personal experiences on the Texas frontier but also were rooted in the larger context of changing American policies towards Native Americans, as evidenced by the actions of President Andrew Jackson regarding Indian removal. Moving away from Thomas Jefferson's "noble savages" and a modest respect for honoring Indian culture and lands, Andrew Jackson ushered in an era of derision toward indigenous tribes, promulgating the idea that whites and indigenous peoples could not live together. To Jackson, Native Americans were like children who needed to be protected and separated from the white population. He argued that it was in their best interest to be removed from white settlers where they could escape "utter annihilation." In his Second Annual Message to Congress on Indian Removal, delivered on December 6, 1830, Jackson outlined the benefits for Native Americans: "It will separate the Indians from immediate contact with settlement of whites; free them from the power of the States; enable them to pursue happiness in their own way and under their own rude institutions; will retard the progress of decay, which is lessening their numbers." And gradually, he asserted, under the protection of the federal government and good counsel, removal would allow them "to cast off their savage habits and become an interesting, civilized, Christian community."[65] Converting such sentiments into law, Jackson signed the Indian Removal Act on May 28, 1830. Thus, as Americans moved in droves into the Mexican state of Coahuila y Texas in the late 1820s and early 1830s, they brought with them the notion that white Anglos and Native Americans were inherently at odds and should live apart.

Challenging the myth of race in American history, Jacqueline Jones's *A Dreadful Deceit* focuses on the contradictory and inconsistent fictions of "race" that various groups of people contrived for specific political purposes.[66] It is a good exercise to ask why race and racial difference is ascribed to a particular group of people at a particular time. Why cast people as a racial other? For Laurel Clark Shire's analysis of the Seminole wars in Florida, depictions of Indian barbarianism justified settler colonialism. Indian depredation narrators used racism and gender to manipulate readers: "They offered readers scenes of devastated domestic tranquility as sensational proof that the Seminoles had violated all of the family and domestic relationships held to be sacred and natural, just as stories of captivity had violated those same norms and elicited the accusation that indigenous warriors were 'indiscriminate' in their choice of victims."[67] Readers were expected to feel rage and horror at the "savages" who attacked families and destroyed homes. In this sense, racialized rhetoric on war and violence intersected with gendered constructions of the private home as the primary locus of women's experience, trauma, and authority. While a similar justification for retaliatory actions against Indian raids in Texas could also be made, an immediate goal of stoking fear by Texas officials, who accentuated the barbarity of Native Americans and the imminent threat to Texas homes, was to attract recruits and garner American intervention into the war.

As noted, the areas most concerned about Indian raids were the settlements in East Texas. Exacerbating these concerns were fears that local Tejanos, residing in and around the town of Nacogdoches, were conspiring with the invading Mexican army in an effort to establish an alliance with the Cherokees. According to rumors, the plan was that the Tejanos and the Cherokees would rise in rebellion against the white settlers once Santa Anna's forces arrived in the area. Suspicions surrounding the Tejanos of East Texas dated back to the earliest stages of the Revolution. When the local movement against Santa Anna's government grew in the summer of 1835, months before shots rang out at Gonzales, the approximately six hundred Tejanos living in Nacogdoches did not join the inchoate rebellion, opting to remain loyal to Mexico. For their part, the Tejanos had at least one well-placed official in power—the captain of the local militia was ex-alcalde Vicente Córdova, who was not interested in joining the rebellion. As Paul Lack notes, "The only question seemed to be whether the Tejanos would actually attempt to block the course of the revolution or would acquiesce in a kind of nervous neutrality."[68]

With the Mexican army hundreds of miles away, an uneasy stalemate between the factions arose: "In essence, Córdova agreed not to resist the

Revolution, whose leaders in turn did not insist on Tejano participation in the war against other Mexicans."[69] However, distrust of Nacogdoches Tejanos among the Anglo population reached a fever pitch once news of the Texas army's defeat at the Alamo and Goliad made its way to the settlement in mid-April. The increasingly real possibility that the Mexican army could reach the communities in East Texas prompted "a full-blown panic." While Lack argues that evidence of a conspiracy between the Nacogdoches Tejanos and Cherokees is decidedly weak, there can be no doubt of the impact of such rumors—Anglo residents were in a panic and directed their fears at the local Tejanos.[70] Armed conflict between the two groups seemed inevitable, but "prudence on both sides averted a major flareup."[71]

While the Nacogdoches community was nearly up in arms in the early months of 1836, Texas military officials were appealing to the United States to stop the threat of Indian attacks. On March 19, 1836, Henry Raguet, the chairman of the Committee of Vigilance and Safety in Nacogdoches, wrote in a letter to be delivered to the commanding officer at Fort Jesup in Louisiana: "We fully believe that we are in imminent danger of an attack from the various tribes of Indians who are daily arriving in our neighborhood from the territories of the United States."[72] Raguet implored the US government to take measures to stop the Indian incursions. Officials at San Augustine, another community in East Texas concerned with Indian attacks, sent emissaries to Fort Jesup to lobby for American assistance.[73] As the weeks passed, Raguet and other members on his committee, escalated the distressed tone of their appeals to the United States by underscoring the threat to women and children: "We hope that higher views govern the councils of a nation from which we derive our origin and principles; and from whom we must have a sympathy of itself sufficient to redeem our wives and children from savage barbarities."[74] On April 12, 1836, R. A. Irion, acting commander for the Nacogdoches municipality, wrote: "You know our condition. Comment is useless. Many women and children must fall victims to the merciless enemy."[75]

The growing fear of imminent attack prompted Nacogdoches residents—who were, by this point, disproportionately women and children—to abandon the town and retreat in haste to the Sabine. As the crisis unfolded, the citizens of Nacogdoches continued their appeal to the commanders of the US military stationed at Fort Jesup (approximately 90 miles away) to come to their aid. On the town's behalf, John Mason wrote to the Maj. Gen. Edmund P. Gaines, on April 13, 1836, encouraging him to intervene to protect vulnerable Anglo Texans: "The expectation is that, at this moment, Nacogdoches is occupied by the Indians and Mexicans; and, if they pursue the families on their flight, all must be massacred, without instantaneous relief." Mason called on General Gaines to dispatch five hundred men from the garrison to march into Texas territory to protect the fleeing residents from massacre, stating, "My object is singly to save the women and children."[76] Once again, invoking the specific threat to women and children was deemed the most effective strategy by Texas officials to garner desired outcomes, in this case, American intervention.

This appeal created quite a quandary for General Gaines, given that part of his mandate on the Louisiana border was to prevent US soldiers from intervening in the Texas Revolution.[77] However, based on the unsubstantiated rumors that thousands of Mexicans and Indians, working in tandem, were imminently plotting to slaughter the women and children of East Texas, the general was forced to act. And so, despite being directly ordered not to intervene in the rebellion in Texas, the perceived threat to white women and children fleeing from the community of Nacogdoches prompted General Gaines to send six hundred US troops to the Sabine to protect those on either side of the river.[78] In justifying his actions to the Secretary of War in Washington, Gaines provided evidentiary statements "reporting that the Indians, in part from our side of the supposed line between the United States and Mexico, were imbodied and deemed to be employed in driving many of the white families of Texas to the Sabine." Upon reaching the Sabine, Gaines reported that he "met several hundred Texian women and children, with some men, retiring under the influence of great panic."[79] In his correspondence, Gaines noted that although the actual hostilities in the region between whites and Indians seemed minimal, his troops would stand guard on the American side of the river.

As was the case in Nacogdoches, a claim that generated intense alarm among the populace was that internal enemies (such as Native American tribes) sought alliances with invading Mexican forces to exterminate the people of Texas. Although less common than the Indian threat, there were some in Texas concerned that enslaved people in the state would also join forces with their enemy and attack the predominantly white population. Upon hearing news of the fall of the Alamo and the advancement of the Mexican army, the citizens of Brazoria developed a set of resolutions to address the mounting danger, including resolutions on military service, community defense, and fortifications. D. C. Barrett, the chairman of the committee convened to deal with town safety, noted in his report that the avowed purpose of the invading army was "a general extermination of ourselves, our wives, our children, and all who inhabit this country." Further, Barrett wrote: "And we have moreover been appraised of the horrid purpose of our treacherous and bloody enemy, to unite in his ranks, and as instruments of his unholy and savage work, the negroes, whether slaves or free, thus lighting the torch of war, in the bosoms of our domestic circles." Again, the threat was presented as an attack on domestic tranquility. The committee resolved that families needed to be especially attentive to the threat of a potential enemy within their own households, "securing in a proper manner all negroes, against the means of doing injury to our families and placing all in a state of every possible safety."[80]

As much as Anglo Texans feared the Mexican army and Native American attacks in the early months of 1836, the threat of slave rebellion was an enduring concern. Enslaved people—men, women, and children—were literally in their midst. Further still, such laborers represented a significant investment for Texians, especially for those already overly extended from the costs of breaking ground on potentially lucrative farms and plantations; rebellion and/or flight represented not only a possible physical threat but also significant financial risk. In his history of slavery in Texas, Andrew Torget describes how Anglo authorities along the Brazos River plantations, fearing a planned insurrection among their enslaved persons, rounded up nearly one hundred of their enslaved persons in the fall of 1835 "who were either 'whipd nearly to death' or hung for their supposed conspiracy."[81] Despite the severe punishments meted out in this episode, fears of insurrection continued as Texas military fortunes waned in the spring of 1836. Torget also highlights the very legitimate fear among Texian slaveholders that Santa Anna planned to liberate those enslaved as he marched through the state, citing letters that Santa Anna wrote to Mexico City seeking permission to free the enslaved in Texas as part of the effort to quash the rebellion. Torget wrote: "Santa Anna's vision for redeeming northeastern Mexico would mean the end of chattel slavery in Texas, and likely colonization along with it."[82]

The news of demoralizing spring defeats for the Texas army and Houston's decision to fall back generated intense panic among the Texian civilian population, escalating their fears of advancing Mexicans and invading Indian tribes. To be sure, some of these threats were real. However, the preponderance of rumors and heightened alarm that the Mexican army was attempting to recruit Native Americans or enslaved people to their side of the fight exaggerated the number of actual instances of collusion. Rumors abounded among the fleeing colonists. As noted, Ann Raney Coleman reported traveling parties fleeing the fighting set up camps in the early afternoon rather than the evening because of the fear of nighttime Indian attack.[83] As the rebellion faltered, Texas officials intensified their effort to attract volunteers and rally American support. In their appeals, they often emphasized the threat to white women and children as the chief justification for intervention, no doubt expecting that men—both inside and outside of Texas—would feel obligated to fulfill their manly obligations to protect women and children.

Texans articulated their cause for revolution as a fight for liberty against a "cruel despot." They enveloped their rebellion against Mexico in the Spirit of '76, with Santa Anna displacing King George III as their merciless oppressor. They did not shroud their fight against Native Americans in the language of liberty; rather, this fight was against an adversary who posed a threat to the households—perceived sites of domestic tranquility—that southern patriarchs were obligated to protect. From the perspective of the masculine ideal, both Santa Anna's army and Native Americans waged a dishonorable war against the women and children of the state. The leader of the Mexican forces was described variously as a scoundrel, despot, arch fiend, ferocious tyrant, impotent invader, and ruthless murderer.[84] Branding their enemy as "ruthless invaders" engaged in a "war of extermination" against not only men on the battlefield but defenseless women and children, military and government officials employed a rhetorical strategy designed to mobilize troops and secure American support. In the latter case, the strategy worked, however temporarily, when General Gaines sent six hundred American troops to the Sabine to protect fleeing Texas women and children from attack. For the Texas revolutionaries, their enemy lacked the claim to a noble cause and the honor bestowed upon men who protected the most vulnerable. They paid little heed to any sense of honor and manliness on the opponent's part. The assault on Texas families and their homes might come from the Mexican army's advance or through Indian depredations. While the persistent risk of Indian captivity intensified during the chaos of war, the fervent language of Mexicans and Natives Americans scheming to defile and destroy the white women and children of Texas appears to be a calculated gamble.

5

GENDERED HEROISM

Pamelia Mann and Sam Houston

We had a yoke of oxen pressed that belonged to a Mrs. Mann. She was said to be a notorious woman . . . this woman rode up to General Houston and said: "General, I have come for my oxen and I'm going to have them." Houston said: "Madam don't irritate me."[1]

—S. F. Sparks

Most heroes remembered during times of war are men. Their names appear on public buildings and busy thoroughfares often decades, even centuries, after their glory in combat, an honor bestowed not only to soldiers who proved victorious in battle but often to those slain in the effort. Men were expected to meet the moment. While countless women have contributed to military efforts in every theater of war, a precious few are singled out and memorialized; the Texas Revolution is no different in this regard. Despite the brevity of the military campaign, the rebellion produced its fair share of heroic men, including James Bowie, William Barret Travis, Davy Crockett (all felled at the Alamo), and the hero of San Jacinto, Gen. Sam Houston. To this day, there is immense interest in the much-vaunted male heroes of the Revolution who are immortalized in books, television, and film. Facing seemingly insurmountable odds, the commander of the Texas army quickly became legendary. Houston parlayed his victory over Santa Anna's forces on April 21, 1836, into a storied career in Texas politics. Grateful civilians and soldiers under his command celebrated his triumph on the battlefield. Ranger Noah Smithwick wrote of his first encounter with General Houston: "At the Cibola, Sam Houston came up with us. It was my first sight of the man who more than all others was destined to win enduring fame from the struggle we were inaugurating."[2] Waxing reflectively on his experiences as a soldier during the Revolution, Col. John Milton Swisher asserted that the commander proved himself to be "a brave and cool headed general" who possessed "sublime moral courage."[3] Creed Taylor proclaimed that "Houston was undoubtedly the best equipped and ablest man from a military standpoint in Texas at the time."[4]

In the spring of 1836, events on the ground belie this exalted portrayal of Houston, however. As noted in previous chapters, the general drew sharp criticism from a range of critics who questioned his nerve and, by extension, his manliness after his decisions to retreat from the Colorado River and not engage the Mexican army. He was cast by some as a coward who refused to fight. His quick defeat of Santa Anna's forces at San Jacinto quelled much of this initial criticism regarding his war strategy. After this decisive victory, others criticized his willingness to negotiate an armistice with Santa Anna, forcing him to sign over Texas to the revolutionaries rather than execute him as a war criminal. The subject of whether Houston exploited his success on the battlefield for personal gain also became a point of contention. In the spring and early summer of 1836, the cacophony of Texans second guessing the commander of the Texas army was long and

Figure 6. Illustration of General Sam Houston, who served as commander-in-chief of the Army of Texas. His victory over the Mexican forces at San Jacinto cemented his status as a war hero and led to his election as the first president of the Republic of Texas. *Ivy Close Images / Alamy Stock Photo*

strong. And yet, as the axiom says, To the victor, go the spoils, including the prize of washing away any doubts of Houston's courage in the public imagination while he was under duress in the weeks following the fall of the Alamo and massacre at Goliad. In the end, most Texans remembered Sam Houston as the hero of San Jacinto and first president of the Republic; questions that arose during and immediately after the rebellion regarding his character and manhood steadily subsided.

Few women are remembered for their contributions to the revolt against Mexico that began in the fall of 1835 and concluded at San Jacinto on April 21, 1836. Indeed, the scarce number of females who managed to break through the largely male cast of historical actors involved in the rebellion can be counted on one hand. They include Susanna Dickinson, wife of Capt. Almaron Dickinson, who survived the battle of the Alamo along with her infant daughter, Angelina; the servant of mixed racial ancestry, Emily West (the Yellow Rose of Texas), who supposedly visited Santa Anna in his tent before San Jacinto; and Pamelia Mann, a widow known for a notorious confrontation she had with General Houston during the Runaway Scrape.[5] The latter joined the small but significant cadre of women who felt compelled to draw weapons on men who threatened both their property and their escape to safety. During the panicked exodus of 1836, confrontations arose between women who felt obliged to question the authority and even manliness of some of the men they met on their escape to the Louisiana border, prompting some to resort to threats of violence. Generally, women's roles during the Texas Revolution tend to be minimized and relegated to the last weeks of the campaign, specifically their involvement—as featured participants—in the Runaway Scrape.

In the latter instance, the discordant episode between Pamelia Mann and General Houston and her oxen found its way into soldiers' memoirs of the Revolution, including S. F. Sparks and Robert Hancock Hunter,[6] as well as later accounts. Two short articles, published more than seventy years ago, retell the story and provide further biographical information on Mann: William Ransom Hogan's "Pamelia Mann: Texas Frontierswoman" (1935) and Andrew Forest Muir's "In Defense of Mrs. Mann" (1946).[7] Her encounter with Houston during the Runaway Scrape is also referenced in more contemporary histories of the Texas Revolution, including in works by Paul Lack, Fane Downs, James Haley, and Mary Scheer.[8] While the story is amusing in itself, there is a larger question as to why Mann's antics with Houston warranted such attention and continued retelling. According to Hogan, "Veterans of the Texas army, relating the story of the San Jacinto campaign after the lapse of a quarter of a century, still remembered Mrs. Mann and her oxen."[9] Why was Pamelia Mann so compelling? Were her actions deemed heroic by these veterans in a manner analogous to her male counterparts?

At its root, the confrontation between Houston and Mann centered on the issue of impressment. To keep his forces amply supplied, Houston pressed into service crops, livestock, and other necessities from civilian farms and retreating caravans. This effort did not always go smoothly. Recall from Chapter 2, for example, the incident where Mrs. Moss, traveling with her invalid husband, pulled a pistol on a group of Tennessee Volunteers (which included Davy Crockett's nephew) who attempted to impress her oxen.[10] On another such occasion, the effort to impress provisions from an older widow who lived on a farm on the Brazos River proved especially challenging for Houston and his men. Finding themselves bogged down by especially rainy conditions and bad roads, Houston's men relied on a yoke of oxen "borrowed" from Mrs. Pamelia Mann to help pull one of their cannons along the route. According to Texas soldier Hunter's firsthand account of events, Mann stipulated to General Houston that "if you are going on the Nacogdoches road you can have my oxen, but if you go the other to Harrisburg you cant [sic] have them, I want them myself." Houston replied that "well I am going the Nacogdoches road."[11] With that response, Houston procured Mann's oxen. However, according to Hunter, Houston didn't specify to Mann exactly how far he was going on the Nacogdoches road. The army went about six miles up the road to where it forked with the Harrisburg road. There, they turned onto the Harrisburg road and proceeded along it for another ten to twelve miles before "Mrs. Mann overtook us." She rode up to General Houston and said, "General you tole [sic] me a dm lie, you said that was going on the Nacogdoches road sir I want my oxen." Houston told Mann that he could not spare the oxen because they needed them to pull the cannon. Mann responded, "I don't care a dm for your cannon I want my oxen." Donning two holster pistols and a "very large knife," Mann jumped down from her horse, turned around to the oxen, and proceeded to cut the rawhide tug with her knife, releasing the oxen to her control; all the while, "no body [sic] said a word."[12] Next, Mann jumped back on her horse and, with whip in hand, steered her oxen away from the astonished army.

Houston's need for the oxen remained, however. Consequently, Houston directed his wagon master, Captain Rohrer [Rover, in this record], to retrieve the oxen from the departing woman, warning his officer: "Capt Rover that woman will fite [sic]." Several hours later, Captain Rohrer returned to Houston's camp emptyhanded. According to Hunter's account, the boys hollered out to Captain Rover, "Hai [sic] Capt where is your oxen, she would not let me have them, how come your shirt tore so, & some of the Boys would say Mrs. Mann tore it [off] of him what was that for, she wanted [it] for baby rags."[13] When he returned emptyhanded with a badly torn shirt, he justified his failure to recover the oxen by stating, "She was a *man* after all."[14] In this go-round with Houston and his wagon master, the strong-willed widow clearly emerged the victor. Paul Lack succinctly summed up the episode by noting that Mann retrieved her oxen "in a scene full of indelicate language, threats, and brandishing of pistols."[15]

S. F. Sparks, another soldier under Houston's command responsible for acquiring provisions for the army, relayed the following account of what he witnessed: "We had a yoke of oxen pressed that belonged to a Mrs. Mann. She was said to be a notorious woman . . . this woman rode up to General Houston and said 'General, I have come for my oxen and I'm going to have them.' Houston said: 'Madam don't irritate me.'" The term *notorious* is doing a lot of heavy lifting in this quote. It denotes, at once, notoriety and scandal. Apparently, Mann was not amused with Houston's response. She responded, "Irritate the devil. I'm going to have my oxen." Sparks noted that she drew a pistol and pulled upside the team and said "Wo!" which prompted the team to stop. Houston ordered the driver to keeping moving. Sparks claimed the driver fell in the water and said, "Oh Lord, I'm shot." Next, Mann unhitched the oxen and drove off. Sparks concluded his description of the event by stating: "We called this Houston's defeat."[16]

Then and now, Pamelia Mann is admired for her pluck—her willingness to challenge the leader of the Texas forces to protect her property after General Houston reneged on their initial agreement to take the Nacogdoches road. In no rendition of the Mann–Houston confrontation is Mann presented as a shrinking violet or, perhaps more aptly, a Texas bluebonnet. It is precisely her show of strength and "unladylike" exploits that registered amusement with both those who witnessed the event and later commentators. Similar to other women who challenged men during their flight to Louisiana (at times, wielding pistols), Mann applied an appropriate—and admired—display of nerve toward Houston and his men on that April day in the spring of 1836. To a certain degree, the exigencies of the war and the panicked exodus of the civilian population jumbled social norms and gendered expectations. Toward the end of the Revolution, accusations abounded of men acting like women (i.e., cowardly and unmanly) and women acting like men (i.e., brazen and authoritative). *Brazen* seems a particularly apt term for Pamelia Mann. As her biographer, William Ransom Hogan wrote: "In an age in which self-effacement behind a family front was held to be a high female virtue, the self-reliance of her kind adds bold and welcome strokes to a cross-section picture of the womanhood of her time."[17]

Mann garnered respect from her contemporaries for stepping outside the boundaries of nineteenth-century prescribed gender roles during a time of crisis. The sentiment proved fleeting. Her fortunes in the years that followed the Revolution were marred by controversy, character aspersions, and legal peril. From the years 1836 to 1840, when lawsuits over property and land proliferated Texas courts, Pamelia Mann was entangled in "more litigation and was prosecuted for more different crimes than any man of her time," according to Hogan.[18] In this short span of time, she was plaintiff in seven civil cases and defendant in eleven.[19] During the early years of the Republic, Mann was indicted for crimes that included counterfeiting, forgery, larceny, assault with intent to kill, and fornication. Although charged with many offenses, she was convicted only once. The elevated status she enjoyed for her bold exploits during the Revolution faded after she sustained a barrage of scandals and expensive court actions that impugned her reputation and diminished her wealth.

From the Mann family's earliest days in Texas, beginning in 1834, Pamelia Mann played an important role in shaping the family's fortunes. Shortly after their arrival, the family purchased land and established a farm in the vicinity of San Felipe. One unpublished reminiscence from 1835 described a near-fatal encounter between Pamelia, her son, Flournoy, and a traveling party led by a teamster who attempted to tear down a fence on Mann's property, which impeded his preferred route (rather than opting to detour around the property). The writer recounted: "The premises belonged to Mrs. Mann, who though a woman, had the reputation of being able to take care of herself, and ready, on short notice to redress her grievances." When the teamster approached the fence, a young man appeared with a gun prepared to defend the property against vandalism. The account continued, "At this juncture, Mrs. Mann, standing in the doorway of the house near by, cried out to the young man in strong angry tones: 'Shoot him down, Nimrod! Shoot him down! Blow his brains out! ["Nimrod" was Flournoy Hunt, her son]."[20] Thankfully, her son hesitated before pulling the trigger, giving the traveling party time to prudently alter their route around the Mann property and avoid possible bloodshed.

Mann knew General Houston before their fabled encounter. She served as a courier for the cause, delivering a package of letters from Governor Smith to Houston in early February 1836. In her letter that accompanied the package, she disclosed that she feared for her life after some men in San Felipe witnessed her receiving the correspondence. She wrote: "Sum gentle men in San Fellippee saw me receive and offered me one hundred dollars to let them intercept them but I cannot be bought by munney [sic]."[21] She promised to point out the men to General Houston the next time she was in his company. Her actions and letter suggest that Mann clearly favored the uprising. She noted that her precinct "went the hole [sic] hog" in support of independence and hoped that Houston would forgive her bad spelling. During the period of the Constitution Convention in early March 1836, Pamelia and her husband, Marshall, opened a boarding house in Washington-on-the-Brazos that catered to convention delegates and interested onlookers, including diarist William Fairfax Grey.[22] After the convention adjourned, Mann returned to her property near San Felipe. According to one of her biographers, Pamelia Mann enjoyed a cordial relationship with General Houston before their dispute over the impressed oxen. Survivors who escaped the massacre at Goliad apparently witnessed Houston lying in his tent with his head in Pamelia's lap as she combed his hair.[23] Muir contends that this rather intimate episode occurred shortly before Mann and General Houston had their falling out.

Following the Mexican defeat at San Jacinto, Mann moved to Harrisburg where she suffered her first judicial defeat; on September 6, 1836, she was sued by Antonio Scounton and was ordered to pay him $487.17. In the months that followed, the Mann family moved from Harrisburg to Houston, establishing themselves as one of the earliest families of the new capital. In early March, records indicate that Pamelia Mann purchased two lots on the northeast corner of Congress and Milam streets—a central location where she would open a hotel, in May 1837, named the Mansion House. For the period of the early Republic, this new two-story property located across from the city square was tastefully appointed with a parlor and spacious dining room for guests. The tables were adorned with china dishes and German silver cutlery, while coffee was dispersed through urns, tea from Britannia pots, and an assortment of hard liquor and wine from decanters.[24] It was a modest, though stylish, oasis for visitors to the new capital where official government operations had commenced only one month earlier, on April 19, 1837.[25] Government officials, diplomats, clerks, army officers, and prospective businessmen boarded at the newly opened Mansion House in central Houston. While men of all sorts frequented the hotel, the cost was not cheap. Patrons were charged nine dollars a week to stay at her establishment.[26]

The makeshift capital of Houston grew up overnight. Dilue Rose Harris noted that interest in the site prompted some of the young men from her neighborhood, including her brother, to check out the newly minted "city of Houston." It was apparently an effort. After returning from a prolonged absence, the group reported that it was hard work to find the city in the pine woods. They described the surveyed site plotted for the new capital as a "dugout canoe, a bottle gourd of whiskey, and a surveyor's chain and compass" used by "four men with an ordinary camping outfit."[27] From a handful of settlers, the town boasted a population of 2,009 months after it opened for business. It was rustic, however. There were a few unfinished frame houses and a few brick ones, but most of the dwellings were built of logs. When it rained, the site became a sea of mud, directly related to the marshy terrain on which the town was founded. In an article on early Texas inns, Ellen Garwood described the coarse condition of the town, adding, "The atmosphere of Houston, even during the evidences of reform, must have been a perfect backdrop for the rugged character of Mrs. Pamelia Mann."[28] In its early months, many bloody brawls occurred in the streets, saloons, and bordellos of frontier Houston.[29] Businesses adapted to the crude environs. On Mann's career as an innkeeper, Garwood wrote, "[She] was characterized less by steadfast bravery than by a tempestuous and gaudy daring."[30] For Garwood, audaciousness in the early Republic could be both qualified and quantified.

Mann did not limit herself to the profits gleaned from her hotel; she opened a livery across from her hotel and sold cords of wood to the navy. In the three years that she resided in Houston, her wealth tripled: "In 1837, she owned eight lots, four slaves, three horses, 40 head of cattle, five buildings, and furniture, all assessed at $15,370. Three years later she owned 2250 acres, ten lots, thirteen slaves, four horses, and ten head of cattle, all assessed at $42,530."[31] While the new republic struggled under the weight of inflation and debt, Mann did very well for herself—capitalizing on new business ventures and expanding ongoing investments. In addition to assisting his wife with her businesses, particularly managing the livery, Marshall Mann served as doorkeeper to the Congress (when it was in session), where he received seven dollars a day for his services to the Senate and five dollars a day when he served the House of Representatives.[32] Unfortunately, Mr. Mann battled a lingering illness that took his life in October 1838. Pamelia Mann's good fortune took a significant blow with the death of her husband, but that was only one of many calamities she faced in the last months of 1838.

Mann's troubles with the law began with a larceny charge for which she was indicted on December 7, 1838, stemming from an incident in which she confiscated the contents of a trunk that was on her property but not belonging to her, containing a handsome sum of money and other valuables. The scenario was contrived by a group of men who, based on a previous incident involving a local doctor's trunk, wanted to see if Mann would take the bait—which she did. When the authorities attempted to retrieve the doctor's trunk from Mann (during the initial episode), they met a formidable adversary: "The Madam seemed to have committed to memory the whole vocabulary of Billingsgate, which she in no measured terms dealt out; called to her aid a band of renegades which she retains in her service, and emphatically declared that her house should inherit the fame of Goliad if the invading army did not immediately beat a retreat."[33] Mired by postponements and witnesses who failed to appear, the larceny case never reached legal resolution with the last continuance filed in May 1840.[34] Unfortunately for Mann, another charge arose on the same day and posed a much bigger threat, both legally and temporally, for the charismatic hotel owner.

On December 7, 1838, the grand jury indicted Pamelia Mann for forgery. For Texans, the stakes were especially high for those found guilty of this crime; in the first year of the new Republic, Sam Houston signed an act that mandated the death penalty to those convicted of forgery. The alleged forgery took place on March 1, 1836, days before the fall of the Alamo and weeks before Mann's oxen dispute with General Houston and his men during the Runaway Scrape. Mann was charged with forging the signature of Mrs. Mary Hardy on a receipt acknowledging the payment of a $998 debt contracted on March 1, 1836. According to a later published account, Pamelia Mann borrowed one thousand dollars from Hardy, and when she came to collect the debt, Mann produced a receipt that included not only Hardy's signature but also William Barret Travis's signature (who allegedly witnessed the transaction). It bears repeating that the date of the receipt exchange between Mann and Hardy was March 1, 1836. Andrew Muir noted, "If these curious statements are true, Pamelia in this instance demonstrated a stupidity alien to her usual canniness."[35] On March 1, 1836, William Barret Travis was holed up at the Alamo, along with approximately more than 180 other Texas revolutionaries,[36] under siege by Santa Anna and at least eighteen hundred Mexican troops. Given that Mann opened a boarding house for members of the Constitutional Convention, who likely engaged in discussing the state of the rebellion as they boarded at Mansion House, is it possible that Mann did not know of Travis's whereabouts at the time? At any rate, Travis lost his life, along with so many others, in the futile defense of the Alamo on March 6, 1836, and clearly did not witness the transaction on March 1.

Beginning with the indictment issued on December 7, 1838, and continuing for the next five months, Mann found herself imprisoned in the Harris County jail with the prospect of a death sentence looming dangerously over her head. The Harris County jail was rudimentary in condition—small cells, poor ventilation, miserable sanitation, with little to no privacy. As to the ambiance of the facility, William Ransom Hogan writes: "A continuous foul stench rose to high heaven as a reminder of the vindicatory justice of early

Harrisburg County and as evidence of the difficult jail-housing problem of a newly settled town on the frontier."[37] As dire as the situation appeared, Mann was at least able to attain a strong legal defense; she was represented by the law firm of Houston and Birdsall (composed of Sam Houston and John Birdsall). Because Houston conducted none of the business of the firm, her defense fell on the shoulders of John Birdsall, the former attorney general of the Republic during Houston's first administration.[38]

On May 8, 1839, Pamelia Mann appeared in court and pled not guilty to the crime of forgery. The trial date was set for May 17, 1839. After the selection of jurors, the introduction of evidence, and arguments by counsel (for and against), jury deliberations on Mann's fate began three days after the start of the trial.[39] Unfortunately for the accused, mounting a persuasive defense of his client's innocence proved to be an impossible task for John Birdsall. Apparently, it was not an easy deliberation for the all-male jury, although one holdout viewed the evidence against Mann as largely circumstantial. The final verdict found her guilty of forgery, but the jury included a recommendation of leniency directed at the court and President Mirabeau Buonaparte Lamar. While there was little doubt as to whether Mann committed the forgery, there was a growing consensus among both the jurors and the wider public that the penalty in this instance did not fit the crime. The editor of the Houston-based *Morning Star* argued that capital punishment for forgery was excessive and that very few offenses merited such a harsh sentence, proposing that either the law be stripped of its cruel finality or that Mann be rendered a pardon.[40]

Gender roles also played a role in the jurors' recommendation for mercy. In their petition to President Lamar, they stated: "That considering the peculiar situation of the accused, being a female, a mother, and a widow, and an older settler of the country; and more especially seeing the punishment of Forgery is Capital, and therefore in the estimation of the jury, severe and bordering on vindictive justice."[41] Before President Lamar could act on the matter, the court delivered its ruling. On May 24, 1839, the judge in the trial remanded Mann back to her jail cell for a three-day period (until May 27, 1839), after which she would be taken to the place of her execution and "then and there between the hours of twelve and two o'clock of said day she be hanged by the neck till she is *dead*, and may the *Lord* have mercy on her Soul."[42] In what must have seemed like the longest twenty-four hours of her life, Mann's torment was alleviated the following day when President Lamar issued a pardon and ordered her release from custody. She escaped a death sentence—her most serious indictment—but other charges emerged during this same period that put Mann in further legal jeopardy.

Two indictments against Mann arose in early May 1839, concurrent with the period of her forgery case. On May 7, 1839, Pamelia Mann, Tandy Brown, and Flournoy Hunt were indicted for assault with intent to kill. The case faced two continuances in 1839 and 1840 but was never brought to trial.[43] Her fellow defendant in this case, Tandy Brown, would become Mann's fourth husband, but not before their relationship was mired in scandal. On May 8, 1839, the grand jury indicted Pamelia Mann and Tandy Brown for fornication. This is the lone charge in Mann's history that was sexual in nature. As a reminder, Mann's third husband, Marshall Mann, died in October 1838. At some point over the course of 1838, she began a relationship with Tandy Brown, a younger man closer in age to her son than to herself (he was six years older than Flournoy). While Mann faced a slew of legal challenges during this tumultuous period, the fornication charge went furthest in undermining her reputation and character. There is some question to the legitimacy of the charge. Garwood points out that the fornication charge was partly refuted by evidence that the widow was following the custom of informal marriage (based on Mexican law) wherein marriages could be entered into but not sanctioned until blessed by an itinerant priest.[44] The couple formalized their nuptials on August 4, 1839. Tellingly, their marriage contract stipulated that Mann would control her property and business interests as if she was feme sole.[45]

When she squared off with General Houston over the impressment of her oxen during the Runaway Scrape, she was a married woman free of legal scandal. Three years later, Mann faced charges of forgery, assault, and fornication for an illicit union outside of marriage. Scandal and legal entanglements continued to plague her the following year, ending abruptly with her death on November 4, 1840. Mann's independence and pluck were celebrated attributes in the harried last months of the rebellion—she stood up in defense of her property against no less than the commander of the Texas army. In the period that followed the Texas Revolution, gender expectations contracted; women were largely expected to stay in their prescribed lanes (to the extent they could in the rough-and-tumble environment of frontier Texas). While rudimentary aspects of frontier life in 1830s Texas blunted sharply defined notions of separate spheres—where men operated in the public sphere (i.e., business and politics) and women focused their efforts on the private sphere (i.e., home and family), divergent sex roles persevered. As Mary Scheer notes, "While the harsh and dangerous conditions of living on a frontier often mitigated the model of separate spheres for the sexes, requiring women to perform typically male duties, the family circle, centered on the home and family, remained the locus of the female world."[46]

The independent-minded Pamelia Mann challenged such prescriptions. Her "masculine" propensities unsettled authorities in the newly formed Republic of Texas. This new nation, steeped in the most progressive democratic ideals of the day, fell short when it came to making significant alterations to the political and social fabric.[47] As her biographer mused, "She was rough and crude and sometimes violent, to be sure, but the community in which she lived and her male associates were likewise rough and crude and violent. She acted and probably thought as a man; her peccadilloes were masculine." Muir continued, "Despite her masculinity she had feminine charm and was attractive to men. She did not wait for law or custom to emancipate her; she tore from herself the shackles of tradition."[48]

Circumstances influenced gender expectations. As the situation turned dire in the early months of 1836 and the Revolution hovered on an edge, Texians celebrated nerve, spirit, and spontaneity among both civilians and soldiers. Pamelia Mann evinced such traits. Cowards faced disdain. Men were expected to be brave, which, in the context of the last weeks of the Texas Revolution, entailed neither deserting nor retreating. Men who refused the call to arms faced opprobrium for deserting the rebellion in its time of need. Worse still, gender-based queries asked what kind of men would not come to the protection of the state's vulnerable women and children who were in the crosshairs of an approaching army. Sam Houston, whose military strategy contributed to the vulnerability of Texas' civilian population (in his decision to fall back), also confronted questions from contemporaries regarding his courage and manliness. Mary Rabb claimed that Houston was "affraid [sic] and would not fight."[49] The rebuke from the interim president of the Republic, David Burnet, was especially harsh: "The enemy are laughing you to scorn. You must fight them. You must retreat no farther. The country expects you to fight."[50] A soldier under Houston's command, J. W. Robinson later wrote: "The man that has fear in his bosom may fancy that he sees it in every eye that meets his own—if it was not fear that made the Major General tuck his tail and run from the Colorado, from half his own number and from the Brazos, it was total want of military capacity."[51]

Houston's cautious, deliberative approach to war strategy and his ultimate success on the battlefield echoes the tensions between Greenberg's two models of nineteenth-century masculine ideals: restrained manhood and martial manhood. Despite his critics, Houston exercised restraint in his decision making at the Colorado (as opposed to running headlong and unprepared into the fight). When the outcome of the rebellion seemed most dire, hyperbole and fear escalated among military and political officials who saw themselves as waging a war against tyranny. Having migrated to Texas from the United States in the 1820s and 1830s, the southern men who swelled the ranks of the Texas military were well versed in the linkages between manhood and the fight for freedom. As Mark Kann notes, "Manhood modified liberty and thereby injected an element of masculine merit into the rhetoric of early American citizenship."[52] The crisis of wartime and the threat to liberty invoked a martial, unifying response in southern men, even among evangelicals.[53] When faced with the threat to one's liberty, cowardice, indifference, and/or the general inability to meet the moment was a hallmark of failed manhood.

Initially, it was thought that Houston's forces would stand their ground and prevent the Mexican army from crossing the Colorado River; however, the general, upon hearing news of the Goliad massacre and that the Mexican army across the river had received reinforcements, decided to retreat from the Colorado, allowing more time to better stock and train his army.[54] Mixed messages emanated from Houston's camp. Before his family joined the Runaway Scrape, Guy Bryan recalled the arrival of an emissary from Houston, Lieutenant Sharp, who was tasked, based on Houston's authority, with assuring the civilian population that there was no cause for alarm, they should not leave their homes, and that his army would never retreat from the Colorado. However, Sharp, at the same time, delivered a confidential letter from Colonel Somervell to Mr. Perry (Bryan's stepfather) that advised him to leave his home immediately with his family and bondspeople and go eastwards "for the country would soon be in possession of the enemy, as he was satisfied that Houston did not intend to fight but retreat from the Colorado."[55] One messenger, contradictory messages. Consequently, the Perry family took to the road and the safety of the Louisiana border.

In a scenario that resembled the altercation between Mann and Houston, Creed Tayler described an incident that took place after the army retreated from the Colorado and before it reached Harrisburg. One night during the retreat, Houston's forces came across a small farm owned by an enlisted man whose family remained at home after he joined the fighting, "the brave wife and mother refusing to join in the great exodus known as the 'Runaway Scrape.'"[56] As Houston's men approached the farm, they began tearing down the fence posts for firewood. The woman pleaded with General Houston to leave her fence intact, but Houston rebuffed her request, explaining the army's dire need for fires to cook their rations. He promised that once he whipped "old Santa Anna," he would return and have his men repair the damages. With a withering scowl and shaking her finger defiantly, she retorted, "You big, cowardly, nasty, old rascal! You'll never come back this way, and you know it; you are running now, like a cur dog, from a gang of thieving Mexicans, and you'll not stop running until you get out of Texas. When you whip Santa Anna! Huh!"[57] A fellow soldier under Houston's command, Capt. W. P. Zuber, reiterated the sentiment, noting that after Houston's decision to fallback, "the general belief was that the commander intended to continue his retreat to the Sabine river, disband, the army, and abandon the country."[58] While Zuber's observation is likely overstated, there were clearly some in the ranks and the civilian population who doubted Houston's commitment.

Serving under Houston's command at the time, Colonel Swisher addressed the lingering questions surrounding Houston's strategy. He wrote: "Much fault was found with General Houston for not giving battle to Sesma's division on the Colorado; and for years after it was the fruitful theme of discussion between his friends and enemies."[59] But noting that there were times that require more courage to retreat than to fight, he championed Houston's astute decision making at this critical stage in the rebellion. He argued that even if Houston was able to gain victory over Sesma's forces, it would be the cause of concentrating several divisions of the Mexican army, which could happen in a matter of days, and any chance of victory would have been squandered. Swisher surmised: "As the entire responsibility rested on General Houston, he preferred to be charged with cowardice for falling back in the face of an inferior force rather than risk an injury to the cause of his country."[60] Swisher viewed Houston as "a brave and cool headed general" who saw the big picture when it came to military strategy, not a coward who balked under pressure.

The pace of events did not allow muttered suspicions of Houston's courage and competence to fester. As the army moved south, it came to a crossroads where it could have turned toward Nacogdoches and, by extension, the Louisiana border or continue south to Harrisburg, the seat of the government. Critics of Houston's retreat claimed that it was his men who forced his hand to turn toward Harrisburg, against the commander's will. However, as Randolph Campbell notes, evidence of this claim comes from men who despised Houston from personal spite or jealousy or from men who deemed his earlier retreats from the Mexican army as indicative of cowardice.[61] At any rate, Houston's army reached Harrisburg (intact) on April 18, 1836, only to find that the Mexican army had reached the town three days earlier in a failed attempt to catch the government personnel who had already fled to the coast. The following day, Houston's scouts captured three Mexican couriers carrying correspondence revealing not only that the Mexican army was nearby, albeit with a reduced force as the rest of the Mexican army was still west of the Brazos, but also that it was under the command of Santa Anna himself. No longer in retreat, the Texas army went on the offensive.

Relieving his forces of men who were too sick to travel—some 250 men—and extra baggage, Houston gathered his forces and headed eastward, crossing Buffalo Bayou to place his forces in front of the Mexican army as it turned north. On the night of April 19, the commander drove his men to the point of exhaustion so that they would reach Lynch's Ferry on the San Jacinto River ahead of the Mexican army.[62] By midafternoon on April 20, the Texas army was in the sights of Santa Anna's scouts. The Mexican commander withdrew his forces three quarters of a mile south of the Texas army and made camp. Both sides took advantage of the respite to obtain some much-needed rest; unfortunately for Houston's army, at approximately nine o'clock in the morning, General Cos reached the Mexican camp with more than five hundred reinforcements, further advantaging their numbers over the Texian force. The stage was set for the pivotal moment in the Texas Revolution. At three o'clock on the afternoon of April 21, Houston ordered his troops into battle formation. Shortly thereafter, the Texas army began its advance. As the Texans closed in, the Mexican army lobbed volleys at the advancing forces, but most missed their targets. One soldier's eyewitness account described the barrage of the Texas assault: "Then each man took cool and steady aim, and seven hundred rifles and muskets rent the welkin. It was our first and last volley; charging without a halt, we were in another moment in possession of the woodland and the enemy's breastwork, the remaining veterans of Santa Anna, mostly in disorder, endeavoring by flight to save their lives."[63] In less than twenty minutes, the Texas army

Figure 7. Painting of the decisive battle of the Texas Revolution: the Battle of San Jacinto, April 21, 1836. Houston's forces overwhelmed the Mexican army led by General Santa Anna (who was captured at the battle and forced to sign the Treaty of Velasco recognizing Texas independence from Mexico). *World History Archive / Alamy Stock Photo*

gained complete possession of the Mexican camp. The Texians' defeat of the Mexican army was swift and decisive; one of the spoils of their victory was the capture of the leader of the Mexican forces and president of Mexico, General Santa Anna.

With little time to bask in the glory of his victory, Houston faced another difficult decision: What should be done with his notorious captive? He, along with Secretary of War Thomas Rusk, chose to negotiate a battlefield armistice on the terms of surrender with Santa Anna, securing the independence of Texas and retreat of Mexican forces in exchange for the safe return of the captive Mexican commander. Houston's actions in this regard once again garnered sharp criticism. The commander of the Texas forces wasn't shirking from a fight but rather thwarting the public's thirst for revenge against their hated enemy; thus, the criticism was less about Houston's lack of courage (and propensity for retreat) and more about his lack of conviction. In his decision to not engage the Mexican army at the Colorado and not to execute the Mexican president, Houston demonstrated restraint and tactical thinking as to what would most benefit the Texas cause—both on the battlefield and in the political sphere. Such decisions required him to once again navigate the bumpy waters of competing notions of restrained manhood and martial manhood.[64] Even after his heroic victory at San Jacinto, questions of Houston's character remained.

Interim President Burnet had little choice but to defend the measures taken by Houston and Rusk in their efforts to secure the peace.[65] Because Burnet supported the armistice, he was subject not only to public scorn but also to physical threat. At issue in the formal peace treaty, the Treaty of Velasco (signed on May 14), was Article 5, a secret provision that allowed for Santa Anna's release contingent on his following through on issues of prisoner exchanges and the return of captured property, and most important, official recognition of Texas independence. Article 5 stipulated: "The prompt return of Genl. Santa Anna to Vera Cruz being indispensable for the purpose of effecting his solemn engagements, the Government of Texas will provide for his immediate embarkation for said port."[66] Burnet acknowledged that the decision to spare General Santa Anna's life was unpopular with a civilian population freshly reeling from the depredations of war, receiving "an almost universal disapprobation from the people of Texas" and that "a wild and intractable spirit of revenge is abroad among the people."[67]

Critics of the secret treaty provision to return Santa Anna to Mexico expressed their concerns in various forums, including private correspondence, letters to their elected officials, and locally adopted resolutions. Writing to his brother, Caleb Allen, in May 1836, Samuel Allen expressed his opposition to the policy of freeing the commander of the Mexican army. Though enlisted, Samuel Allen did not fight at San Jacinto because he left the ranks to secure the safety of his family from the Mexican advance during the Runaway Scrape. On the policy, he wrote: "The tyrant is now in our power—he richly deserves death and we ought to inflict it on him to avenge the brave and gallant spirits [illegible] who have been inhumanely murdered by his order." He noted that "it was him not us who made a choise [sic] of the mode of warfare which he has been carrying on and so let him abide by the consequences." As to how "the tyrant should die," Allen recommended "a public tribunal should pass the sentence of death upon him to intima date [sic] others who might attempt the same course."[68]

Similarly, in a June 3, 1836, letter addressed to interim President Burnet and members of his cabinet, Memucan Hunt provided his assessment of the mood of the Texas populace on the subject of the removal of General Santa Anna: "Depend upon my assurance, that this act will produce civil excitement, to an extent that will not stop of violence upon your honorable body, and I feel fully justified in the remark from my intercourse, that nine tenths yea nineteen twentieths seem to demand that the Government, shall comply with the wishes of so large a majority." Hunt's specific demand was that General Santa Anna "had better be executed twenty times if that could be done that often."[69] A citizens' assembly from the townships of Austin and Harrisburg warned public officials that it would be "Hazerdious [sic] for the government to act against the known wishes of their constituents" on the matter.[70]

For so many, the issue was personal. Rebecca Westover Jones, who lost her husband, Capt. Ira Westover, at the Goliad massacre in March 1836, wrote on the nonexecution of Santa Anna: "If the women whose husbands and sons he murdered could have reached him, he would not have lived long!"[71] Lydia Ann McHenry expressed utter disgust for Texas officials who failed to hold Santa Anna accountable. With the exceptions of Gen. Lorenzo de Zavala and Gen. Mirabeau Lamar, she proclaimed that the Cabinet was "perhaps the most imbecile body that ever sat in judgment on the fate of a nation. Weak, corrupt, & orderlous [sic], they were with difficulty prevented from setting Santa An[n]a at liberty, not withstanding all his crimes, upon the bare word that he would pay the expenses of the War." To McHenry's liking, Lamar protested the measure and voted against it. However, she wrote: "Our President [Burnet] was so determined on having the gold that he had him [Santa Anna] conveyed on board in the night."[72] McHenry described how the citizens of Velasco demanded that Santa Anna be returned on shore and face the consequences of his actions. Backing up the citizens' demands was Gen. Thomas Green who arrived from the United States with seven hundred troops. One of the "affrightened Cabinet" members was able to negotiate a settlement whereby Santa Anna was brought to shore but remained under the protection of the Cabinet (specifically, placed under guard at the home of Sam Williams). Green continued his demand that Santa Anna be turned over to him and his men and surrounded Williams's house. Recognizing the mounting threat to the Mexican general, Houston intervened. McHenry wrote: "Genl. Houston has ordered him to be brought to the eastern part of Texas, where *he* is still confined with his wound, afraid either that the Cabinet will set him [Santa Anna] free, or the citizens assassinate him."[73] For Houston's critics, his role in negotiating terms with Santa Anna, sparing his life, and protecting him from the mob, was further evidence of his failed leadership and poor decision making.

With the Revolution behind them, the next step for Texans was to form a new government for their inchoate republic and elect its first president. The hero of San Jacinto did not initially seek a nomination for the presidency, preferring to return to the army. Despite his views on the matter, many of Houston's supporters favored his nomination over the other well-known candidates for the position, specifically Henry Smith, the first American governor of Texas (provisional state government established by the Consultation in 1835) and Stephen F. Austin, regarded as the father of Texas. Once Houston succumbed to pleas for him to accept the nomination, Henry Smith dropped out of the contest and supported Houston's candidacy. Houston's critics focused on what they perceived as his character flaws. Clarinda Pevehouse Kegans, who was a child at the time of the Runaway Scrape, noted that her grandfather, Alexander Hodge, didn't like Sam Houston; their family appreciated his leadership on winning the battle of San Jacinto but did not support him for president. She wrote: "He had a reputation for drinking too much and he had not bothered to do anything worth a hill of beans for Texas since he came. Even after the war Grandpa was suspicious he would try to use his new fame to get elected president of Texas. Grandpa thought Mr. Austin deserved to be. So you see Grandpa was right as usual."[74]

Company commander Jesse Billingsley, who fought at San Jacinto, emerged as a critic of Sam Houston after the war. He took issue with the perception of Houston's inflated role—both public and personal—in defeating Santa Anna's forces during the terminal battle, attributing the victory instead to the Texian forces. Further, he, along with other detractors, bristled at any attempt by Houston to politically capitalize on this exaggerated role. Historian Stephen Hardin contends that "many—indeed most—of those who had served under him during the 1836 campaign insisted that Houston exaggerated his contributions to advance his political ambitions."[75] Billingsley asserted: "The thief and the murderer I can guard against, but the liar I cannot. Therefore I must say that Houston is the basest of all men, as he has, by willfully lying, attempted to rob that little band of men of their well earned honors on the battlefield of San Jacinto. He has assumed to himself credit that was due to others."[76] This was a scathing rebuke from a fellow soldier who contested Houston's spotless character and charged the commander not only with deceit but with spreading falsehoods at the expense of his men.

Adopting a similar attack, former interim President Burnet, who sparred with Houston over his decision to fall back from the Mexican advance, declared that "Gen H. has long and habitually acted on the Spanish proverb, that 'a lie that can gain belief for one hour, is worth the telling.' . . . Gen. Houston knows how to appreciate and to profit by the old Spanish proverb, and he knows that his furtive laurels will wilt and wither into utter loathsomeness, under the full light of truth!"[77] As to the appropriate response to his battlefield victory, Houston found himself in the crosshairs of the delicate balance between chivalry and conceit. Obviously, his enemies leaned on the latter characterization. Heroes did not capitalize on their achievements. The model response to martial triumph was best reflected by the actions of the celebrated hero of the American Revolution—the American Cincinnatus, Gen. George Washington.[78] After his victory on the battlefield over the British, Washington retired to private life on his farm, eschewing the limelight. Only after numerous entreaties did General Washington agree to be drafted into political office, reluctantly acquiescing to serve his country as its first elected president (voted unanimously by sixty-nine electors); once again, he did so out of a sense of duty, not ambition.

Despite his initial desire to serve the new republic in a military, not political, capacity, Houston acquiesced to demands that he run for office. Consequently, his enemies cast him as deceptive, self-serving, and callous. While those who served in the military met the era's veneration of martial manhood, other occupations allowed men to validate their manly bona fides. Anthony Rotundo argues that politics offered such an opportunity. In the nineteenth century, the political sphere was perceived as a masculine space. Rotundo notes that Americans viewed some professions as more manly than others, clarifying that "politics, for instance, was seen, even by its detractors, as a masculine pursuit. Aggression, deceit, competition, and a spirit of self-interest—all traits that middleclass culture associated with men—were vital in the quest for the manly goal of power."[79] The art, perhaps, was to not look like you were seeking power but rather to fulfill the much more honorable pursuit of public service. In this undertaking, Houston needed to strike a delicate balance. While his critics may have questioned his ambition and willingness to capitalize on his success on the battlefield, Houston's transition to politics allowed him to position himself as a hero of another sort—one who excelled in the lofty, yet decidedly manly, political aspirations of the new Republic.

During and immediately after the 1836 military campaign, Houston faced questions regarding his courage and integrity. At the peak of hostilities, his critics claimed that he failed to display a sufficient level of martial acumen, shirking from the Mexican forces in retreat. After the fall of the Alamo and the Goliad massacre, an elevated sense of anxiety swelled among both enlisted men and the civilian population in the state. As the rebellion teetered on a precipice, there was simply no room for cowardice; gendered expectations held by the populace insisted that men needed to act like men—not retreat nor desert. Even after his decisive victory over the Mexican army, criticisms of his decision making initially persisted. In the end, things worked out fine for Sam Houston. The denunciations of his military strategy and lack of integrity waned as his political fortunes grew. He won the Republic of Texas' first presidential election in 1836. The questions that arose regarding Houston's manhood during the last months of the Revolution faded with time. Past and present, his legacy reflects his military and political achievements: the hero of San Jacinto, first (and third) president of the Republic of Texas, and senator and governor of the state of Texas after annexation.[80]

The plucky antics and spirited demeanor of Pamelia Mann, who challenged Houston and his men when they tried to impress her oxen during the Runaway Scrape, fared less well in the post-Revolution period. It was amusing for some of her contemporaries, veterans of the Texas army,[81] for Mann to act like a man in the chaos of war and the ensuing Runaway Scrape. As her biographer noted, "Her peccadilloes were masculine,"[82] while a contemporary of hers commented, "She was a *man* after all."[83] In the early years of the Republic, Mann faced charges of forgery, assault, fornication, and countless lawsuits. Hers was a mixed legacy. Indeed, nineteenth-century boundaries of female assertiveness were narrow. Amy Greenberg reminds us that both martial and restrained masculinities eschewed female intrusions into the public sphere.[84] In this same chaotic atmosphere, a desperate civilian populace, government officials, and an anxious military corps expected Sam Houston to exude bravery and tenaciousness in his military strategy—hallmarks of nineteenth-century martial manhood. In the aftermath of San Jacinto, the presumption among the populace was that the general needed to appear principled and selfless in his countenance—attributes associated with restrained manhood. For his critics, he failed on both fronts. As Texas settled into a peacetime Republic, the supposition was that men and women should settle into their expected roles. This was difficult for Pamelia Mann. By contrast, serving as the Republic's first president, Houston did not challenge the status quo by unsettling gender dynamics or nineteenth-century societal norms; ultimately, his presumed failures in manhood and character receded from memory. His was a legacy of bravery and conviction, hers, scandal and disrepute.

CONCLUSION

Remembering the Last Months of the Texas Revolution

Uncle Tommys wife onley lived one day after tha got home thare was many births and deths on that road while we was running from the mexicans [sic].[1]

—*Mary Crownover Rabb*

When women penned their own stories or relayed to family members their experiences during the last months of the Texas Revolution, they did more than provide interesting anecdotes; indeed, they filled in the storyline. Through a historical lens, military campaigns are typically presented as male-centric events—both heroes and foes alike tend to be men who proved their valor on the battlefield or died trying. For the most part, women are marginal figures in these venerated tales of warfare. However, in the last months of the 1836 campaign, two critical losses to the Mexican forces and Sam Houston's decision to fall back at the Colorado River changed the dynamic and created "great excitement" among the civilian population.[2] The Mexican advance posed a threat to the farms and plantations in south and central Texas; further, the instability created opportunities for Indian raids and threats to life and property in East Texas, bringing the whole of Texas into the firing line. Women and children were not only actively engaged in the perilous retreat to Louisiana, but threats to their safety—the *fair daughters* of chaste *white* women[3]—formed the basis of heated rhetoric employed by government and military officials hoping to recruit converts to the Texas cause.

Reminiscences by women such as Dilue Rose Harris, Ann Raney Coleman, Clarinda Pevehouse Kegans, and Rosa Kleberg not only inserted women and families into the narrative of the Texas Revolution but also conveyed nineteenth-century notions of gender norms and expectations, with stories predicated on how women and men responded to a period of crisis. Harris and Kegans were children at the time of the Runaway Scrape; however, because of her incorporation of her father's journal of the events and her detailed account, Harris is the most cited source on the Runaway Scrape. Historians that have included her account (and similar reminiscences) include Mary Scheer, Angela Boswell, Light Townsend Cummins, Faye Downs, and Stephen Hardin. Almost all scholarship on the Runaway Scrape references Harris's three submissions to the *Quarterly to the Texas State Historical Association* published around the turn of the twentieth century. One of the most enlightening sources of the period is Coleman's memoir. At the time of the Runaway Scrape, Coleman was an adult mother who kept a diary of events and began writing her memoirs in her late sixties. In recounting the Runaway Scrape, these women not only presented stories that celebrated heroism but also revealed episodes where individuals and groups failed to rise to the challenges of the times—where words and deeds disappointed.

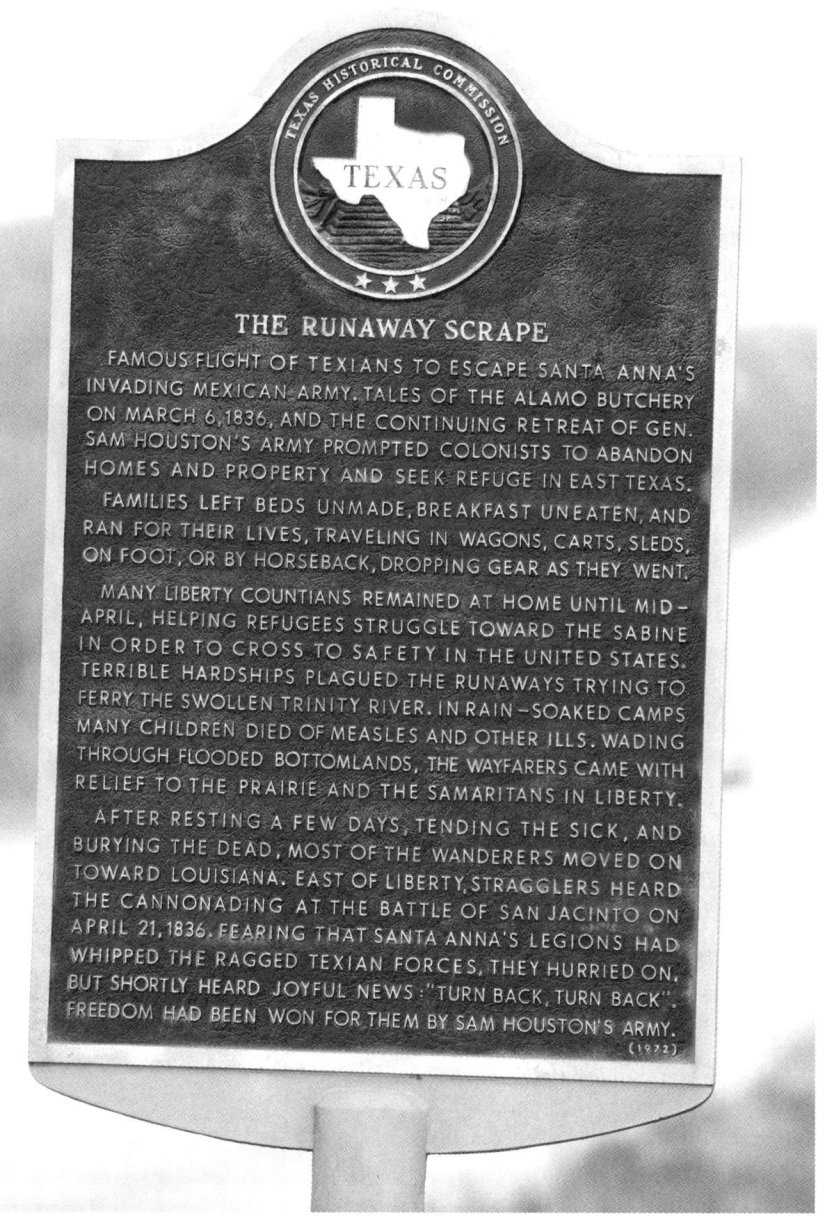

Historical marker of the Runaway Scrape located in Dayton, Texas, in Liberty County, on US Highway 90 (on the right when traveling east). *Courtesy of the Liberty County Historical Commission*

Memoirs afforded their authors the opportunity to weigh in on the past—not just chronicle historical events but offer their opinions on those events. In this sense, reminiscences tend to be subjective, not objective, mediums. Even with such caveats, they still provide an important vector to historical understanding. As Paula Fass notes, "Indeed, for historians the memoir is an important historical tool, and for social historians especially, it provides the appealing voice too often otherwise missing as we try to reconstruct the lives of ordinary people."[4] While there are ample sources detailing the actions and correspondence of military leaders and government officials during the Texas Revolution, the personal accounts from ordinary men and *women* fill in a much-needed perspective of events on the ground. No historian would rely solely on memoirs, which often contain deep biases, to understand and evaluate a larger historical subject—like a revolution, for example—but rather, personal stories provide unique perspectives on commonly depicted historical experiences. As Fass states, "No, the memoir is not a substitute for systemic historical reconstruction, and the personal is never the same as the social . . . the memoir illuminates subjectivity, how the social and political are processed." In attempting to gain perspectives on nineteenth-century notions of gender, personal observations—even those articulated late in life—are constructive sources, perhaps essential, for addressing this specific category of analysis. Memoirs are not autobiographies, or full life stories, but usually record a significant life period, a particular aspect of the writer's life, or a collection of memories.[5] Despite its flaws, which can include misremembering, self-aggrandizement, and whitewashing, the memoir provides an important window into personal perceptions of the past, reflecting established and provisional social dynamics.

Many of the memoirs of the Runaway Scrape were published in the late nineteenth and early twentieth centuries. Looking backward was a hallmark of this period. These publications overlapped with the rise of the Lost Cause, which grew in popularity among southerners in the 1890s and reached its apex in the years before the outbreak of war in Europe. The Lost Cause honored soldiers of the Confederacy and celebrated the southern way of life, all the while ignoring slavery's role as a contributing factor to the Civil War. In Texas, more than half of the sixty-eight Civil War monuments created to honor the heroes of the war were erected between the years 1900 and 1915. Kelly McMichael argues that the creation of collective memory, like war memorials, is not just a simple act of recalling the past, but an intricately contrived means of forming a particular social identity based on a largely invented story.⁶ The Lost Cause venerated a period long past, reaffirming traditional values and white supremacy in the face of modernizing trends such as immigration, urbanization, and industrialization. Women were pivotal to the Lost Cause movement, raising money to fund Confederate monuments and commemorative celebrations. In asserting themselves in the movement, early twentieth-century women became purveyors of a past that was largely militaristic in nature and male-centered in scope.

In the post–Lost Cause era, Texans reinterpreted their past once again. At once, they situated Texas history into the story of nineteenth-century American expansion westward and the celebration of a triumphant military campaign: the Texas Revolution. Wanting to move past slavery and Confederate defeat, Texans focused on the successful 1830s rebellion against Santa Anna's forces. Intentionally and increasingly, Texas became a part of the American West and less a part of the American South. The focus on the Texas Revolution allowed Texans to draw historical distinctions from other Confederate states. As Texas historian Walter Buenger points out, "Northeast Texans abandoned the limited possibilities implicit in the Lost Cause and adopted the mantle of progress of the Texas Revolution."⁷ As the fight for independence from Mexico became the defining historical moment for many Texans' identity, survivors of the 1836 campaign—both men and women—wrote their stories into the history of this celebrated event.

The turmoil of war and civilian flight demanded that participants adopt unfamiliar and, at times, confrontational stances against fellow countrymen and women, including pitting wives against their husbands. In disclosing a tense situation wherein two men threatened to take possession of a ten-year-old enslaved girl who was bonded to her family and traveled with them during the Runaway Scrape, for example, Ann Raney Coleman offered an interesting framing of her response to the crisis and her husband's failure. The men claimed that her husband still owed them fifty dollars for the little girl, who served as her son's nurse, and if he didn't pay the balance, they would take the girl as security. To Coleman's chagrin, her husband agreed to let them take the girl, prompting Coleman to threaten the men with a pistol and declare that if they tried to take the girl, they would have to kill her first. Her husband managed to procure the pistol from her grasp, averting any bloodshed. As the men left with the young girl in tow, Coleman noted that one of the men said to her, "Madam, you ought to be the man such times as these. You could defend yourself and property well if you had no husband."[8] Several decades after the fact, she felt compelled to include such comments in her memoir, underscoring her then-husband's perceived weakness as a man. One of the tenets of nineteenth-century manhood was that men were expected to protect their family and property; in this instance, it was she who acted the man.

Some women used their later reminiscences to critique the cowardice of men, both acquaintances and strangers, who failed to rise to the challenges of the crisis. Deserters were prime targets for opprobrium. While her husband and brother bolstered the Texas cause by serving on the battlefield, Rosa Kleberg had little time for those not willing to fight. She noted, "Deserters were constantly passing us on foot and on horseback. The old men with the families laughed at them and called to them, 'Run! Run! Santa Anna is behind you!'"[9] Men who ran from combat were mocked. Recounting her experiences in 1820s and 1830s Texas to her descendants, Mary Crownover Rabb used the opportunity of her memoirs to describe the harrowing escape and criticize the commander of the Texas forces. Rabb accused Houston of cowardice and charged that he was afraid to face the Mexican army. Rabb claimed her uncle warned Houston that if he did not stop the Mexicans from crossing the Colorado River, "he would loos half of his men that the would leave him and go to ther fameleys [sic]."[10] Rabb lost her infant child, Lorenzo, during the Runaway Scrape, so she was painfully aware of the personal sacrifices that resulted from the decision to revolt against Mexico and the invasion that followed. She wrote, "Thare was many births and deths on that road while we was running from the mexicans [sic]."[11] The Runaway Scrape upended any sense of domestic security for Texas families, generating a sense of trauma and loss for Texas women in particular. For women living through the tumultuous last weeks of the Texas Revolution, it was not only structures and material goods that were at risk but also the very notion of the family home as a space for safety and sanctity. When Rabb wrote her reminiscences in 1875, Sam Houston had twice been elected president of the Republic of Texas, represented the state in Congress as a senator, and served as governor before his contentious removal in 1861. However, the hero of San Jacinto did not evade Rabb's blunt characterization of him as a coward and poor strategist when it came to his decision to retreat at the Colorado.

Several men also chronicled their experiences of the Texas Revolution in memoirs and reminiscences late in life. In doing so, they cemented into the historical record events that they deemed meaningful for future generations. Creed Taylor, a soldier who served under Houston's command, used the opportunity of his memoirs to distinguish between men who left the fighting to secure the safety of their family from those who chose to never fight in the first place. In his account of the 1836 campaign, Taylor differentiated "so-called deserters," men with families who left the field, from a second, much less sympathetic, group. He stated, "It should be borne in mind that there were hundreds of men, mostly young fellows—adventurers we might call them—who had come from the states, and who had found shelter and temporary homes among the settlers." More explicitly, he continued, "They had no families and could easily have joined Houston, thereby enabling him to repel the advance of the enemy, but instead, they sought their own safety by flight."[12] For Taylor, by acting merely in their own self-interest, these were lesser men—cowards who showed no interest in either the lofty notions of independence or in protecting vulnerable families from the perceived enemy threat. Taylor lamented, "Unfortunately there was no authority for the arrest of these cowardly fugitives, there was no law by which they could be forced into the ranks and made to fight the invaders." For the unenlisted, there was no official means to mete out punishment to those unwilling to fight for Texas. According to Taylor, they paid for their disloyalty—ferry guards and scouts had orders to impress all horses and arms from "skeedadlers" and "skulkers," from men, unencumbered with families, who refused to join the frontlines.[13]

Another soldier from the Texas ranks, John Milton Swisher, used his reminiscences to defend General Houston from attacks that raised doubts about his courage and decision making. Through his own story, he sought to resuscitate Houston's reputation from both contemporary and later attacks on his manliness. Swisher asserted: "As the entire responsibility rested on General Houston, he preferred to be charged with cowardice for falling back in the face of an inferior force rather than risk an injury to the cause of his country."[14] Swisher viewed Houston as "a brave and cool headed general" who saw the big picture when it came to military strategy, not a coward who balked under pressure. He argued: "There are times when it requires more courage to retreat than stand and fight, and this was the case at the Colorado. . . . To order a retreat under such circumstances, required a sublime moral courage that only Houston possessed."[15] Cowardice was an affront to celebrated displays of martial masculinity, a particularly rampant strain of manliness in 1830s and 1840s America that applauded qualities of strength, aggression, and even violence.[16] Historian Michael Kimmel argues that during the 1830s, concurrent with the presidency of Andrew Jackson, America experienced a period of hypermasculinity—personified in the individual himself.[17] It was an age that heralded the military hero, leaving little room for men who chose to fight another day (Houston) or not at all (deserters as well as men who refused to enlist in the first place).

Noah Smithwick reserved space in his memoir to fulminate on the ruthlessness of two perceived enemies: "Mexicans and Indians." He called the Mexican army "ruthless invaders, who were said to be waging a war of extermination."[18] The Mexican army was cast as invaders to their own nation. As Santa Anna's forces marched northward, Smithwick and his fellow rangers were summoned to Gonzales to plan for the state's defense, "thus leaving the frontier settlements exposed to both Mexicans and Indians."[19] After demoralizing spring losses on the battlefield, Texas authorities employed fervent language to cast their enemies as a threat to the white women of Texas, thus, reiterating the need for men to enlist. The assault might come from the Mexican army's advance or from an attack from indigenous tribes, or both. Smithwick's vituperation went furthest when it came to Native Americans, whom he saw as a more insidious threat to Texas settlements. He wrote, cynically, "The Indians, taking advantage of the disturbed condition, were committing depredations, and the army, numbering not more than 500 or 600 men, rank and file, was preparing to invade Mexico and bring her rulers 'to a realizing sense of the situation;' having no time therefore for such trivial matters as the murdering of the citizens by the Indians."[20] Despite defining their cause as a fight for liberty against a "cruel tyrant," Texians did not cloak their fight against Native Americans in the language of liberty; rather, this fight was against a dangerous adversary who presented a threat to Texas households—sites of safety and domestic tranquility—that southern patriarchs were obligated to protect. From the perspective of the masculine ideal, both Santa Anna's army and Native Americans waged a dishonorable war against the women and children of the state. Branding the military adversaries as "ruthless invaders" and depredators against not only men on the battlefield but defenseless women and children, military and government officials employed a rhetorical strategy designed to mobilize troops and secure American support. For the Texas revolutionaries, their enemy lacked the claim to a noble cause and the honor bestowed upon men who protected the most vulnerable.

One soldier under Houston's command, S. F. Sparks, who was a teenager serving in the Texas army during the rebellion, used his recollections to convey more than one instance of female audaciousness. He was one of the sources who relayed the encounter between Pamelia Mann and Sam Houston regarding the impressment of her oxen, referring to Mann as a "notorious woman" and the confrontation between the two as "Houston's defeat."[21] Sparks also recalled his encounter with a family who lived a few miles from Washington-on-the-Brazos and had joined the throngs of civilians fleeing the Mexican advance. Consistent with virtually all accounts of the spring months of 1836, Sparks described the Runaway Scrape as "a complete panic." He came across a couple and their small children who were struggling with the logistics of keeping their belongings together while driving ten or twelve head of cattle east. The man's wife and youngest child rode a pony alongside. Fellow travelers passed them and urged them to go as fast as they could because the Mexicans were close behind. Apparently, the news was more than the man could handle. Referring sardonically to the husband as a "heroic man," Sparks explained that the man told his wife that it would be better for one of them to escape than for all to be killed, so he decided it should be him. He took her and the child off the horse and left them on the side of the road as he crossed the river without them.[22]

Driving the cattle, the wife and her children continued along the route and came across her husband an hour later as he sat under a tree. She told him, "Now you get behind this breastwork of cotton bales and fight." He hopelessly replied that it wasn't worth fighting and they would all be killed. She replied, "Well, I will. If I can get a gun, I'll be durned [sic] if I don't go behind that breastwork and fight with those men."[23] A fellow soldier in Sparks's company gave the woman an old musket, and she remained half the night behind the makeshift fortifications, ready to take on the Mexicans alongside the Texas forces. It's an interesting anecdote, but it also underscores Sparks's desire to relay an instance that upended gender performances. The episode clearly highlights the husband's failure to fulfill his manly obligations by not stepping up to the fight—a failure observed not only by his wife but also by passing soldiers. Worse still, he left his dependents behind with no protection from the advancing army (and no pony). Courage eluded the man but not his wife. This story as well as the Mann and Houston incident point to examples of women acting outside of expected gender roles during the chaos of the last months of the 1836 campaign. By including them in his memoirs, Sparks imbued these examples of gender inversion as meaningful to the larger historic moment.

The pressures of war created new spaces for women to exert discernable levels of agency and brashness when it came to their male counterparts.

And yet, there were limitations to such attitudes. Toward the end of the Revolution, accusations abounded of men acting like women (i.e., weak and unmanly) and women acting like men (i.e., brazen and authoritative). On the surface, gendered expectations appeared in flux, or possibly in transition. However, a closer examination of the heated gendered rhetoric exchanged during this period indicates that it was delivered with a goal in mind. Criticisms lobbed at men who chose not to fight, for example, were intended to provoke shame and invoke action, specifically enlistment to the army. References to manly obligations and the threat to women and children proved to be useful rhetorical flourishes in recruiting converts to the cause. As related to gender, any shifting of attitudes and expectations proved short lived. While contemporaries may have found it interesting for women such as Pamelia Mann to act like men in the chaos of war and the ensuing Runaway Scrape, as Texas settled into a peacetime Republic, the expectation that followed was that men and women should also settle into their assumed roles.

The trials and tribulations Mann endured reflect the rigidity of nineteenth-century social conventions regarding female brazenness. The tensions that arose during the Runaway Scrape provide an important window into seemingly shifting gender dynamics in revolutionary Texas. The threat of an invading army unmoored discretion and unleashed alarm among not only the heavily outnumbered Texas army but also the vulnerable civilian population. For the men, women, and children who took to the road hoping to survive the Mexican advance, the ensuing escape to the Louisiana border created stresses and strains *for* participants and *between* participants. During the last months of the Revolution, fear of defeat prompted larger questions of what it meant to be a man or to be woman in a period of war and retreat. Post-rebellion peace realigned the gender landscape, underscoring the liminality of revolutionary change when it came to issues of gender. In his biography of Pamelia Mann, William Ransom Hogan wrote: "In an age in which self-effacement behind a family front was held to be a high female virtue, the self-reliance of her kind adds bold and welcome strokes to a cross-section picture of the womanhood of her time."[24] The larger question remains as to how welcome a woman with Mann's self-reliance and boldness was in post-Revolution Texas. After all, the harried times of the spring of 1836 had seemingly settled down.

Notes

Introduction

1. David G. Burnet to the Citizens of Texas, proclamation, March 18, 1836, in *The Papers of the Texas Revolution,* ed. John H. Jenkins, vol. 5, *1835–1836,* (Austin: Presidial Press, 1973), 126–27.

2. Rosa Kleberg, "Some of My Early Experiences in Texas," *Quarterly of the Texas State Historical Association* 1, no. 4 (April 1898): 300. Dilue Rose Harris used similar terminology to describe the atmosphere before the fall of the Alamo: "The people had been in a state of excitement during the winter." Dilue Rose Harris, "Reminiscences of Mrs. Dilue Harris, II," *Quarterly of the Texas State Historical Association* 4, no. 3 (January 1901): 160.

3. Crystal Sasse Ragsdale, ed., "Rosa von Roeder Kleberg (1813–1907)," in *The Golden Free Land: The Reminiscences and Letters of Women on an American Frontier* (Austin: Landmark Press, 1976), 35n26. Ragsdale incorporated not only Rudolph Kleberg's original manuscript in her account but also other unpublished Kleberg and von Roeder materials provided by the family.

4. Kleberg, "Some of My Early Experiences," 300.

5. Ragsdale, "Rosa von Roeder Kleberg," 35n25; 27.

6. Kleberg, "Some of My Early Experiences," 301.

7. Late nineteenth-century accounts commonly used the phrase "Runaway Scrape" to describe events; however, the term was employed much earlier. One of the earliest usages of the phrase appears a Houston newspaper's republication of a letter from a Texas soldier traveling with Houston's army. The letter is dated March 15, 1836, less than two weeks after the fall of the Alamo. The soldier writes, "Tongue cannot tell the terrors of this wild rout of Texas' population, which has been dubbed the 'Runaway Scrape.'" Ed Kilman, "Texas Heartbeat: The March Day When Texas Reached Its Lowest Ebb and 'Died A-Borning,' As a Soldier Eye Witness Feared," *Houston Post,* March 15, 1959.

8. In the mid-1830s, newly arrived Anglo American colonists to Texas commonly referred to themselves as Texians. The term became closely associated with the revolutionary period and the revolutionaries themselves, despite that Tejanos (Texas residents of Mexican descent) were also participants in the rebellion. In the period of the early Republic of Texas, the term evinced a heightened sense of nationalism, which was fostered by the second president of the Republic of Texas, Mirabeau B. Lamar. The term's usage faded with annexation and statehood in 1845, after which residents of the state commonly referred to themselves as Texans. Herbert Fletcher, "Texian," *Handbook of Texas Online*, updated July 30, 2022, https://www.tshaonline.org/handbook/entries/texian. In an effort to incorporate the common usages of the day, both *Texians* and *Texans* are used throughout the book to refer to the Anglo-American colonists who migrated to the Mexican state in the early 1830s and fought against the Mexican army during the Texas Revolution.

9. James T. DeShields, ed., *Tall Men with Long Rifles: The Glamorous Story of the Texas Revolution, As Told by Captain Creed Taylor, Who Fought in That Heroic Struggle from Gonzales to San Jacinto* (San Antonio: Naylor Company, 1935), 125.

10. Initial Mexican units crossed the Rio Grande in mid-January, but the bulk of Mexican forces were still making their way through the cold temperatures of northern Mexico with Santa Anna.

11. Lt. Colonel William Barret Travis to "The People of Texas & all Americans in the world," February 24, 1836, in *The Papers of the Texas Revolution,* ed. John H. Jenkins, vol. 4, *1835–1836,* (Austin: Presidial Press, 1973), 423.

12. The number of soldiers killed at the Alamo is estimated at 182 or 183. A small handful of persons were spared to relay the story of what happened to the people of Gonzales, including Susannah Dickinson, wife of Captain Almaron Dickson (killed during the battle), her infant daughter, Angelina, and Lt. Colonel William Barret Travis' enslaved person, Joe.

13. Mrs. T. C. Allan and Mrs. Thomas O'Connor, comps. and eds., "Reminiscences of Mrs. Annie Fagan Teal," *Southwestern Historical Quarterly* 34, no. 4 (April 1931): 325.

14. Joan W. Scott, "Gender: A Useful Category of Historical Analysis," *American Historical Review* 91, no. 5 (December 1986): 1056.

15. Scott, 1067.

16. Scott, 1068.

17. Victoria Robinson and Diane Richardson, *Introducing Gender & Women's Studies,* 4th ed. (London: Palgrave, 2015), 10.

18. Jeanne Boydston, "Gender as a Question of Historical Analysis," *Gender & History* 20, no. 3 (November 2008): 576.

19. Margaret Jacobs, "Western History: What's Gender Got to Do with It?" *Western Historical Quarterly* 42, no. 3 (Autumn 2011): 303.

20. Thomas J. Rusk, Secretary of War, to the People of Texas, April 13, 1836, in Jenkins, *Papers of the Texas Revolution*, vol. 5, 461.

21. Burnet to the Citizens of Texas, March 18, 1836, in Jenkins, vol. 5, 126–27.

22. Mary S. Helm, *Scraps of Early Texas History: By Mary S. Helm, who, with her first husband, Elias R. Wightman, founded the city of Matagorda, in 1828–29* (Austin: B. R. Warner & Co., 1884), 89.

23. Light Townsend Cummins, "'Up Buck! Up Ball! Do Your Duty!': Women and the Runaway Scrape," in *Women and the Texas Revolution*, ed. Mary L. Scheer (Denton: University of North Texas Press, 2012), 157.

24. In her influential 1966 article "The Cult of True Womanhood, 1820–1860," Barbara Welter explored the notion of separate spheres and "the cult of domesticity." Welter examined notions of womanhood that were relayed largely through prescriptive literature from the period. Tropes of separate spheres and domestic ideology, however, represented an ideal rather than most women's reality; indeed, the separately gendered private and public spheres represented only a small (often class-driven) minority of women experiences in the nineteenth century. Rustic frontier conditions blurred gendered labor divisions; defined spheres that confined women's labor and decision-making responsibilities to the household were further complicated during times of war. Barbara Welter, "The Cult of True Womanhood, 1820–1860," *American Quarterly* 18 (Summer 1966): 151–75; Elizabeth Jameson, "Women as Workers, Women as Civilizers; True Womanhood in the American West," in *The Women's West*, eds. Susan Armitage and Elizabeth Jameson (Norman: University of Oklahoma Press, 1987), 145–64; Julie Roy Jeffrey, "Permeable Boundaries: Abolitionist Women and Separate Spheres," *Journal of the Early Republic* 21, no. 1 (2001): 79–93; Elizabeth York Enstam, *Women and the Creation of Urban Life: Dallas, Texas, 1843–1920* (College Station: Texas A&M University Press, 1998); Angela Boswell, *Her Act and Deed: Women's Lives in a Rural Southern County, 1837–1873* (College Station: Texas A&M University Press, 2001); Mark M. Carroll, *Homesteads Ungovernable: Families, Sex, Race, and the Law in Frontier Texas, 1823–1860* (Austin: University of Texas Press, 2001). For challenges to "true womanhood" arguments, see Jameson and Jeffrey. For Texas examples, see Enstam, Boswell, and Carroll.

25. Paul D. Lack, *The Texas Revolutionary Experience: A Political and Social History, 1835–1836* (College Station: Texas A&M University Press, 1992), 259.

26. Houston examples include Randolph B. Campbell, *Sam Houston and the American Southwest* (New York: Pearson Longman, 2007); James L. Haley, *Sam Houston* (Norman: University of Oklahoma Press, 2004); John Hoyt Williams, *Sam Houston: The Life and Times of the Liberator of Texas, an Authentic American Hero* (New York: Simon & Schuster, 1993); Crockett examples include James E. Crisp, *Sleuthing the Alamo: Davy Crockett's Last Stand and Other Mysteries of the Texas Revolution* (New York: Oxford University Press, 2005); Sarah Ann

McGill, *Davy Crockett* (Toledo, OH: Great Neck Publishing, 2005); Michael A. Lofaro, *Davy Crockett: The Man, The Legend, the Legacy, 1786–1986* (Knoxville: University of Tennessee Press, 1985); Jim Donovan, *The Blood of Heroes: The 13-Day Struggle for the Alamo—and the Sacrifice That Forged a Nation* (New York: Little, Brown, 2012). These are just a recent sampling of biographies of Texas revolutionary soldiers.

27. Angela Boswell, *Women in Texas History* (College Station: Texas A&M University Press, 2018), xi.

28. Light Townsend Cummins and Mary L. Scheer, Introduction to *Texas Identities: Moving Beyond Myth, Memory, and Fallacy in Texas History* (Denton: University of North Texas Press, 2016), 7.

29. Jacobs, "Western History," 298. Jacobs's essay was a response to an article published in 2010, which chastised western historians for their neglect of women and gender history in their scholarship; see Susan Lee Johnson, "Nail This to Your Door: A Disputation on the Power, Efficacy, and Indulgent Delusion of Western Scholarship That Neglects the Challenge of Gender and Women's History," *Pacific Historical Review* 79, no. 4 (November 2010): 605–17.

30. Caroline von Hinueber, "Life of German Pioneers in Early Pioneers," *Quarterly of the Texas State Historical Association* 2, no. 3 (January 1899): 227–32; republished by Ragsdale, "Caroline Ernst von Roeder von Hinueber," in *The Golden Free Land*, 10–18.

31. Dilue Rose Harris, "Reminiscences of Mrs. Dilue Harris," pts. I, II, and III, *Quarterly of the Texas State Historical Association* 4, no. 2 (October 1900): 85–127; 4 no. 3 (January 1901): 155–89; 7, no. 3 (January 1904): 214–22.

32. Marguerite Starr Crain, *Two Glass Buttons: A Story of the Runaway Scrape* (Midland, TX: Nita Stewart Haley Memorial Library, 1988).

33. C. Richard King, ed., *Victorian Lady on the Texas Frontier: The Journal of Ann Raney Coleman* (Norman: University of Oklahoma Press, 1971); Helm, *Scraps of Early Texas History*; Mary Crownover Rabb, *Travels and Adventures in Texas in the 1820s: Being the Reminiscences of Mary Crownover Rabb* (Waco, TX: W. M. Morrison, 1962).

34. King, *Victorian Lady*, xviii–xix.

35. Harriet A. Ames, "The History of Harriet A. Ames During the Early Days of Texas," Box 2Q403 vertical files, Dolph Briscoe Center for American History, University of Texas at Austin; Mrs. Mary A. Baylor, "Reminiscences of Mrs. Mary A. Baylor," Box 2Q430 vertical files, Dolph Briscoe Center for American History, University of Texas at Austin; Rosalie B. Hart Priour, "The Adventures of a Family of Emigrants Who Emigrated to Texas in 1834: An Autobiography by Rosalie B. Hart Priour," Box 2R154 vertical files, Dolph Briscoe Center for American History, University of Texas at Austin.

36. DeShields, *Tall Men;* Noah Smithwick, *The Evolution of a State or Recollections of Old Texas Days* (Austin: Steck Company, 1935).

37. Smithwick, *Evolution of a State,* x.

38. Paul Lack, ed., *The Diary of William Fairfax Gray: From Virginia to Texas, 1835–1837* (Dallas: De Golyer Library & William P. Clements Center, 1997).

39. S. F. Sparks, "Recollections of S. F. Sparks," *Quarterly of the State Historical Association* 12, no. 2 (July 1908): 61–79; Beulah Gayle Green, ed., *Narrative of Robert Hancock Hunter, 1813–1902, from His Arrival in Texas, 1822, through the Battle of San Jacinto, 1836* (Austin: Cook Printing Company, 1936).

40. John Milton Swisher, *Early Days in Texas: Reminiscences of Colonel Swisher,* photocopy of transcript, A976.4 SW, Austin History Center, Austin, Texas.

41. George P. Garrison, "Guy Morrison Bryan," *Quarterly of the Texas State Historical Association* 5, no. 2 (October 1901): 121–36; Guy M. Bryan to Kate S. Terrell, August 15, 1895, Guy Morrison Bryan Papers, file #2N247, folder #8, Dolph Briscoe Center for American History, University of Texas at Austin.

42. A recent publication details some of the notoriety of John Holmes Jenkins III, specifically his salacious history of forgery, arson, and gambling. See Michael Vinson, *Bluffing Texas Style: The Arsons, Forgeries, and High-Stakes Poker Capers of Rare Book Dealer Johnny Jenkins* (Norman: University of Oklahoma Press, 2020).

43. See Stephen L. Hardin, "'A Hard Lot': Texas Women in the Runaway Scrape," *East Texas Historical Journal* 29, no. 1 (1991): 35–45; Fane Downs, "'Tryels and Trubbles': Women in Early Nineteenth-Century Texas," *Southwestern Historical Quarterly* 90, no. 1 (July 1986): 35–56; Cummins, "'Up Buck!'" 153–78. While not singularly focused on the Runaway Scrape, Lack's *Texas Revolutionary Experience* provides one of the most detailed accounts of the crisis. Also see Adrienne Caughfield, *True Women and Westward Expansion* (College Station: Texas A&M University Press, 2005). An important effort at filling the gender gap in the historical record is the 2012 publication *Women and the Texas Revolution,* edited by Mary Scheer. This collection of short essays not only provides overviews of Anglo-American women's experiences during the Revolution but also explores those of Native, Tejana, and African American women.

44. Carolyn Callaway, "The Runaway Scrape: An Episode of the Texas Revolution," master's thesis, University of Texas at Austin, 1942.

45. Kate Scurry Terrell, "The 'Runaway Scrape,' 1836," in *A Comprehensive History of Texas, 1685–1897,* ed. Dudley Wooten (Dallas: William G. Scarff, 1898), 669–71. Indicating his own commitment to documenting the revolutionary period, Guy M. Bryan submitted several chapters to this two-volume collection.

46. Randolph B. Campbell, *Gone to Texas: A History of the Lone Star State* (New York: Oxford University Press, 2003), 110.

47. Andrew J. Torget, *Seeds of Empire: Cotton, Slavery, and the Transformation of the Texas Borderlands, 1800–1850* (Chapel Hill: University of North Carolina Press, 2015), 148; Randolph B. Campbell, *An Empire for Slavery: The Peculiar Institution in Texas, 1821–1865* (Baton Rouge: Louisiana State Press, 1991).

Chapter 1

1. James T. DeShields, ed., *Tall Men with Long Rifles: The Glamorous Story of the Texas Revolution, as Told by Captain Creed Taylor, Who Fought in That Heroic Struggle from Gonzales to San Jacinto* (San Antonio: Naylor Company, 1935), 106.

2. C. Richard King, ed., *Victorian Lady on the Texas Frontier: The Journal of Ann Raney Coleman* (Norman: University of Oklahoma Press, 1971), 84.

3. King, 87.

4. Anne Firor Scott, *The Southern Lady: From Pedestal to Politics, 1830 to 1930*, 25th anniversary ed. (Charlottesville: University of Virginia Press, 1995).

5. Lydia Howard Sigourney, *Letters to Young Ladies,* 2nd ed. (Hartford, CT: William Watson, 1835), 27.

6. Mrs. Mary S. Helm, *Scraps of Early Texas History: By Mary S. Helm, who, with her first husband, Elias R. Wightman, founded the city of Matagorda, in 1828–29* (Austin: B. R. Warner & Co., 1884), 89.

7. Adrienne Caughfield, *True Women and Western Expansion* (College Station: Texas A&M University Press, 2005), 8.

8. Laura Clark Shire, *The Threshold of Manifest Destiny: Gender and National Expansion in Florida* (Philadelphia: University of Pennsylvania Press, 2016), 56.

9. Shire, 57–58.

10. DeShields, *Tall Men,* 103–4.

11. DeShields, 106.

12. Angela Boswell, *Women in Texas History* (College Station: Texas A&M University Press, 2018), 36.

13. Shire, *Threshold of Manifest Destiny,* 81.

14. Edward E. Baptist, *Creating an Old South: Middle Florida's Plantation Frontier before the Civil War* (Chapel Hill: University of North Carolina Press, 2002), 48.

15. Jo Ella Powell Exley, ed., "Mary Sherwood Wightman Helm," in *Texas Tears and Texas Sunshine: Voices of Frontier Women* (College Station: Texas A&M University Press, 1985), 23.

16. Exley, 19–20.

17. Helm, *Scraps of Early Texas History,* 56.

18. King, *Victorian Lady,* 26.

19. King, 26.

20. Colgate D'Eve Donaldson to Lawson Moore, May 31, 1836, William Moore Papers, 2F58, Dolph Briscoe Center for American History, University of Texas at Austin, Texas.

21. Donaldson to Lawson Moore, May 31, 1836.

22. Donaldson to Lawson Moore, May 31, 1836.

23. Donaldson to Lawson Moore, May 31, 1836.

24. Donaldson to Lawson Moore, May 31, 1836.

25. Moore-Morse Family Papers, Creator Sketch, MC091; Albert and Ethel Herzstein Library, San Jacinto Museum, La Porte, TX.

26. Moore-Morse Family Papers.

27. Mark M. Carroll, *Homesteads Ungovernable: Families, Sex, Race, and the Law in Frontier Texas, 1823–1860* (Austin: University of Texas Press, 2001), 82.

28. Carroll, 83.

29. Allan C. Jones, *Texas Roots: Agriculture and Rural Life before the Civil War* (College Station: Texas A&M University Press, 2005), 107–10.

30. Crystal Sasse Ragsdale, ed., "Caroline Ernst von Roeder von Hinueber," in *The Golden Free Land: The Reminiscences and Letters of Women on an American Frontier* (Austin: Landmark Press, 1976), 12.

31. Harriet A. Ames, "The History of Harriet A. Ames during the Early Days of Texas," Ames (Harriet A.) Reminiscences, 2Q403, Dolph Briscoe Center for American History, University of Texas at Austin, 11.

32. Ames, 11.

33. Ames, 7.

34. Ames, 12.

35. Ames, 12.

36. While Potter initially proved the hero for Harriet and her two children during the Runaway Scrape, their relationship took an unexpected turn in the period that followed. Potter beseeched Harriet to marry him, claiming that her current marriage was invalid because it had not been solemnized by a priest. She acquiesced, and the couple were married, again by bond. Although Potter assured Harriet that their marriage was valid and that he had introduced a law in Congress pursuing such codification, when he died, his will referred to Harriet as Mrs. Harriet Page, seemingly omitting any recognition of his own marriage to Harriet. A strange case, indeed. Carroll, *Homesteads Ungovernable,* xi–xii; Judith N. McArthur, "Harriet A. Moore Page Potter Ames (1810–1902)," *Handbook of Texas Online,* updated August 2, 2017, https://www.tshaonline.org/handbook/entries/ames-harriet-a-moore-page-potter.

37. Jane Hallowell Hill, "Recollections of Jane Hallowell Hill," Thompson Family Papers Texas, 1832–1998, folder 1, MS288, Fondren Library, Rice University, Houston, Texas, 54.

38. Mary A. Baylor, "Reminiscences of Mrs. Mary A. Baylor," 2Q430, Dolph Briscoe Center for American History, University of Texas at Austin, 8.

39. For an in-depth account of this exchange, see Linda English's "'That Very Trying Time': Guy Morrison Bryan Recalls the Runaway Scrape," *Central Texas Studies: Journal of the Central Texas Historical Association,* vol. 3 (December 2018): 67–79.

40. Guy M. Bryan to Kate S. Terrell, August 15, 1895, Guy Morrison Bryan Papers, file #2N247, folder #8, Dolph Briscoe Center for American History, University of Texas at Austin.

41. Bryan to Kate S. Terrell.

42. Bryan to Kate S. Terrell.

43. Rosalie B. Hart Priour, "The Adventures of a Family of Emigrants Who Emigrated to Texas in 1834: An Autobiography by Rosalie B. Hart Priour," Box 2R154 vertical files, Dolph Briscoe Center for American History, University of Texas at Austin, 41.

44. Winnie Allen, "While Houston Battled at San Jacinto: Pioneer Women Left Record of Panic That Spread over Texas when Mexican Invasion Was On," *Dallas Morning News,* April 24, 1927.

45. Linda English, *By All Accounts: General Stores and Community Life in Texas and Indian Territory* (Norman: University of Oklahoma Press, 2013), 159–60. The Adelsverein was a society of German princes who organized a mass emigration of Germans to Texas.

46. Ragsdale, "Caroline Ernst von Roeder von Hinueber," 13–14.

47. Ragsdale, 14.

48. M. Jourdan Atkinson, "Maria Bachman Atkinson, 1801–1863; Harriet Bachman Jourdan, 1815–1881," in *Women in Early Texas,* ed. Evelyn, M. Carrington (Austin: Texas State Historical Association, 1994), 25. In records, Groce's Landing is also known as Groce's Ferry. For a brief history of Seth Thomas mantel clocks and their popularity in the nineteenth century, see Seth Thomas History, accessed December 23, 2020, https://clockhistory.com/sethThomas/company.

49. Atkinson, 25.

50. Atkinson, 26.

51. Marguerite Starr Crain, *Two Glass Buttons: A Story of the Runaway Scrape* (Midland, TX: Nita Stewart Haley Memorial Library, 1988), 127. The author is Clarinda's great-great-granddaughter and it is telling that she named her book after the two glass buttons. She provides full excerpts from the undated and unbound memoirs of Clarinda Pevehouse Kegans in her "Notes" section.

52. Crain, 126, 127.

53. Crain, 133.

54. Crain, 133.

55. Gary S. Zaboly, *Baltimore Gazette and Daily Advertiser,* April 30, 1836, in *An Alter for Their Sons: The Alamo and the Texas Revolution in Contemporary Newspaper Accounts* (Buffalo Gap: State House Press, 2011), 299.

56. See Michael Rugeley Moore, State Archives Resources Contribute to the Rediscovery of San Felipe de Austin, November 7, 2018, https://www.tsl.texas.gov/outofthestacks/state-archives-resources-contribute-to-the-rediscovery-of-san-felipe-de-austin. "San Felipe in ashes" is referenced in Sam Houston to James Collingsworth, March 17, 1836, *The Papers of the Texas Revolution,* ed. John H. Jenkins, vol. 5, *1835–1836* (Austin: Presidial Press, 1973), 123. Also see Stephen Moore, *Eighteen Minutes: The Battle of San Jacinto and the Texas Independence Campaign* (Austin: Republic of Texas Press, 2004), 140–41. In his reminiscences, Moses Austin Bryan challenges Houston's assertion that he did not order the burning of San Felipe. Bryan asserted that he was initially ordered by Captain Moseley Baker to burn the town, but he asked to be excused from the assignment because "I did not wish to destroy the first town laid off by my uncle in the wilderness of Texas." He then ordered Edward O. Pettus to burn the town "at Houston's command." According to Bryan, many of the men disapproved of the burning of the town because the Mexican forces had not yet arrived. When the news came that Houston denied giving the command, Baker wrote to Houston seeking confirmation of Houston's denial. Houston responded to Baker's letter (which Bryan witnessed) that "he was perfectly satisfied with everything which Captain Baker had done while in command at that post, without saying whether he had ordered him to burn the town or not." Moses A. Bryan, "Reminiscences of M. A. Bryan," Moses Austin Bryan Papers, MC 060, folder 91–31, Albert and Ethel Herzstein Library, San Jacinto Museum of History, La Porte, Texas, 18–19.

57. Ed Kilman, "Texas Heartbeat: The March Day when Texas Reached Its Lowest Ebb and 'Died A-Borning,' as a Soldier Eye Witness Feared," *Houston Post,* March 15, 1959.

58. Samuel Rogers quoted in Anne H. Sutherland, *The Robertsons, the Sutherlands, and the Making of Texas* (College Station: Texas A&M University Press, 2006), 100.

59. Joaquím Ramírez y Sesma to General Antonio Lopez de Santa Anna, March 15, 1836, published in *Daily National Intelligencer,* May 1836, in Zaboly, *An Alter for Their Sons,* 294.

60. Shire, *Threshold of Manifest Destiny,* 65.

61. Shire, 85.

62. Dilue Rose Harris, "Reminiscences of Mrs. Dilue Harris, II," *Quarterly of the Texas State Historical Association* 4, no. 3 (January 1901): 165; Light Townsend Cummins, "'Up Buck! Up Ball! Do Your Duty!': Women and the Runaway Scrape,"

in *Women and the Texas Revolution*, ed. Mary L. Scheer (Denton: University of North Texas Press, 2012), 156.

63. Mrs. [Frances] George Sutherland to Sister, June 5, 1836, Sutherland (George) Papers, Box 2K328 vertical files, Dolph Briscoe Center for American History, University of Texas at Austin.

64. Priour, "Adventures of a Family of Emigrants," 31.

65. Priour, 34.

66. Mary Crownover Rabb, *Travels and Adventures in Texas in the 1820s: Being the Reminiscences of Mary Crownover Rabb* (Waco, TX: W. M. Morrison, 1962), 14.

67. Rabb, 14–15.

68. Marguerite Starr Crain, "Hodge, Alexander Hodge (1760–1836)," updated October 30, 2019, https://www.tshaonline.org/handbook/entries/hodge-alexander.

69. Helm, *Scraps of Early Texas History*, 60.

70. Paul D. Lack, *The Texas Revolutionary Experience: A Political and Social History, 1835–1836* (College Station: Texas A&M University Press, 1992), 12.

71. Fane Downs, "'Tryels and Trubbles': Women in Early Nineteenth-Century Texas," *Southwestern Historical Quarterly* 90, no. 1 (July 1986): 43–45.

72. Lack, *Texas Revolutionary Experience*, 12. Mary Sherwood Wightman Helm's husband taught Sunday school classes in Texas. Helm, *Scraps of Early Texas History*, 47.

73. George R. Nielson, "Lydia Ann McHenry and Revolutionary Texas," *Southwestern Historical Quarterly* 74, no. 3 (January 1971): 393.

74. Donaldson to Lawson Moore, May 31, 1836.

75. Sutherland to Sister, June 5, 1836.

76. Rosa Kleberg, "Early Experiences in Texas II," *Quarterly of the Texas State Historical Association*, vol. 2 (July 1898–April 1899): 170.

Chapter 2

1. C. Richard King, ed., *Victorian Lady on the Texas Frontier: The Journal of Ann Raney Coleman* (Norman: University of Oklahoma Press, 1971), 92–93.

2. James T. DeShields, ed., foreword to *Tall Men with Long Rifles: The Glamorous Story of the Texas Revolution, As Told by Captain Creed Taylor, Who Fought in That Heroic Struggle from Gonzales to San Jacinto* (San Antonio: Naylor Company, 1935), ix.

3. DeShields, 102.

4. DeShields, 107.

5. DeShields, 110.

6. Mary L. Scheer, ed., "'Joys and Sorrows of Those Dear Old Times': Anglo-American Women during the Era of the Texas Revolution," in *Women and the Texas Revolution* (Denton: University of North Texas Press, 2012), 82.

7. Charles L. Martin, "Women and Old Men's Retreat before Mexican Invaders Big Page in the History of Texas," unidentified newspaper clipping, VF-General File, Texas Revolution, 1835–1836, Runaway Scrape, Daughters of the Republic of Texas Library, San Antonio, Texas.

8. Kate Scurry Terrell, "The 'Runaway Scrape,' 1836," in *A Comprehensive History of Texas, 1685–1897*, ed. Dudley Wooten (Dallas: William G. Scarff, 1898), 669.

9. Dilue Rose Harris, "The Reminiscences of Mrs. Dilue Harris, II," *Quarterly of the Texas State Historical Association* 4, no. 3 (January 1901): 165–66. According to Harris, Uncle Ned was part of a delegation of some "twenty to thirty negroes from Stafford's Plantation" (p. 163).

10. Harris, 164.

11. Mary S. Helm, *Scraps of Early Texas History: By Mary S. Helm, who, with her first husband, Elias R. Wightman, founded the city of Matagorda, in 1828–29* (Austin: B. R. Warner & Co., 1884), 12.

12. Helm, 16.

13. Uncle Jeff Parsons, interview with the *Galveston News*, Sons of DeWitt Colony Texas, accessed July 24, 2020, https://www.sonsofdewittcolony.org/muster-gon2.htm.

14. Harris, "Reminiscences, II," 160.

15. Harris, "Reminiscences of Mrs. Dilue Harris, I," *Quarterly of the Texas State Historical Association* 4, no. 2 (October 1900): 93. Peterson, Dorothy Burns, ed., *Daughters of the Republic of Texas, Patriot Ancestor Album*, vol. 1 (Nashville, TN: Turner Publishing, 1995), 122.

16. David G. Burnet, proclamation, March 25, 1836, in *The Papers of the Texas Revolution*, ed. John H. Jenkins, vol. 5, *1835–1836* (Austin: Presidial Press, 1973), 188.

17. Harris, "Reminiscences, I," 85.

18. Marguerite Starr Crain, *Two Glass Buttons: A Story of the Runaway Scrape* (Midland, TX: Nita Stewart Haley Memorial Library, 1988), 130. The author is Clarinda's great-great-granddaughter. She provides full excerpts from the undated and unbound memoirs of Clarinda Pevehouse Kegans in her "Notes" section.

19. Crain, 134.

20. Angela Boswell, "Traveling the Wrong Way Down Freedom's Trail: Black Women and the Texas Revolution," in Scheer, *Women and the Texas Revolution*, 109–11. Boswell briefly addresses some of the experiences of African Americans during the Runaway Scrape.

21. King, *Victorian Lady*, 82.

22. King, viii, 53–54n6. Ann was born on November 5, 1810.

23. King, 57.

24. King, 36, 57.

25. Paul D. Lack, *The Texas Revolutionary Experience: A Political and Social History, 1835–1836* (College Station: Texas A&M University Press, 1992), 213–14.

26. Aurelia Hadley Mohl, "Mrs. Thomas J. Rusk," Women of the Texas Republic and Revolution Papers, Box 2R119 vertical files, Dolph Briscoe Center for American History, University of Texas at Austin, 18–19.

27. Mohl, 19.

28. Mohl, 19.

29. Lack, *Texas Revolutionary Experience*, 215.

30. Lack, 218.

31. Lack, 219.

32. Lack, 219.

33. For an example, see King, *Victorian Lady*, 82. Hervey Whiting also claimed to have sent a substitute to serve in his stead. Hervey Whiting to Colonel James Morgan, May 3, 1836, in Jenkins, *Papers of the Texas Revolution*, vol. 5, 157.

34. Sam Houston to Thomas J. Rusk, Secretary of War, March 29, 1836, in Jenkins, vol. 5, 234. On the blame game, also see in this volume, Houston to Carson, 307; Burnet to Rusk, 444; Houston to Raguet, 504.

35. Paul Lack, ed., *The Diary of William Fairfax Gray: From Virginia to Texas, 1835–1837* (Dallas: De Golyer Library & William P. Clements Center, 1997), 158–59.

36. Lack, 159.

37. Lack, *Texas Revolutionary Experience*, 287n19.

38. S. F. Sparks, "Recollections of S. F. Sparks," *Quarterly of the State Historical Association* 12, no. 2 (July 1908): 63.

39. Sparks, 63.

40. Rosalie B. Hart Priour, "The Adventures of a Family of Emigrants Who Emigrated to Texas in 1834: An Autobiography by Rosalie B. Hart Priour," Box 2R154 vertical files, Dolph Briscoe Center for American History, University of Texas at Austin, 31.

41. Priour, 37, 39, 44.

42. Hobart Huson, "James, John (1788–1836)," *Handbook of Texas Online*, updated December 3, 2020, https://www.tshaonline.org/handbook/entries/james-john.

43. Priour, "Adventures of a Family of Emigrants," 43–44.

44. Priour, 51.

45. See Van Winkle, Irene, "The Priour Family Has Long History," *West Kerr Current*, May 18, 2006, http://wkcurrent.com/priour-family-has-long-history-p838-71.htm.

46. King, *Victorian Lady*, 88–90.

47. King, 90.

48. King, 91.

49. King, 92–93.

50. King, 93–94. Ann and her husband moved to Louisiana and later purchased a new plantation in Pointe Coupee Parish. Unfortunately, misfortune plagued Ann and her family in Louisiana. She lost not only her two sons but also her husband,

John Thomas, to disease (her husband succumbed to an attack of inflammatory rheumatism in 1847). Her second marriage was to John Coleman, whom she later sued for divorce (pp. xiv, xv, 104, 105, 112, 122).

51. At times, this control extended to sexual violence against black women who were under their charge. See Edward E. Baptist, "'Cuffy,' 'Fancy Maids,' and 'One-Eyed Men': Rape, Commodification, and the Domestic Slave Trade in the United States," *American Historical Review* 106, no. 5 (December 2001): 1619–50, and Walter Johnson, *Soul by Soul: Live Inside the Antebellum Slave Market* (Cambridge: Harvard University Press, 1999).

52. Stephanie McCurry, *Masters of Small Worlds: Yeoman Households, Gender Relations, & the Political Culture of the Antebellum South Carolina Low Country* (New York: Oxford University Press, 1995), 6.

53. Anne Firor Scott, *The Southern Lady: From Pedestal to Politics, 1830 to 1930*, 25th anniversary ed. (Charlottesville: University of Virginia Press, 1995). For opposing views, see Drew Gilpin Faust, *Mothers of Invention: Women of the Slaveholding South in the American Civil War* (Chapel Hill: University of North Carolina Press, 1996), 256; LeeAnn Whites, *The Civil War as a Crisis in Gender, Augusta, Georgia, 1860–1890* (Athens: University of Georgia Press, 1995), 94; George C. Rable, *Civil Wars: Women and the Crisis of Southern Nationalism* (Urbana: University of Illinois Press, 1991).

54. Rable, *Civil Wars*, 112.

55. LeeAnn Whites and Alecia P. Long, eds., *Occupied Women: Gender, Military Occupation, and the American Civil War* (Baton Rouge: Louisiana State University Press, 2009), 6.

56. Harris, "Reminiscences, II," 163.

57. After marriage, her name became Caroline von Roeder von Hinueber. Crystal Sasse Ragsdale, ed., "Caroline Ernst von Roeder von Hinueber," in *The Golden Free Land: The Reminiscences and Letters of Women on an American Frontier* (Austin: Landmark Press, 1976), 14.

58. Harris, "Reminiscences, II," 165; Cummins, "Up Buck!" 156.

59. Stephen L. Hardin, "'A Hard Lot': Texas Women in the Runaway Scrape," *East Texas Historical Journal* 29, no. 1 (1991): 39.

60. Harris, "Reminiscences, II," 166–67.

61. Mary Crownover Rabb, *Travels and Adventures in Texas in the 1820s: Being the Reminiscences of Mary Crownover Rabb* (Waco, TX: W. M. Morrison, 1962), 14.

62. Rabb, 14.

63. Adèle B. Looscan, "Elizabeth Bullock Huling: A Texas Pioneer," *Quarterly of the Texas State Historical Association* 11, no. 1 (July 1907): 67.

64. DeShields, *Tall Men*, 108.

65. DeShields, *Tall Men*, 109–10. A similar confrontation is detailed in Chapter 5 between Pamelia Mann and Sam Houston.

66. DeShields, *Tall Men*, 109–10.

67. Andrew Forest Muir, "The Lady Was for Burning," *Southwest Review* 44, no. 2 (Spring 1959): 167.

68. John J. Linn, *Reminiscences of Fifty Years in Texas* (Austin: Steck Company, 1935; facsimile reproduction), 264. On Peggy McCormick's fate, Jeffrey D. Dunn notes that Peggy lived on the battleground until the late 1850s when her home burned and she was found dead inside—arson was suspected. Jeffrey D. Dunn, "To the *Devil* with Your Glorious History," in Scheer, *Women and the Texas Revolution*, 187. Also see Margaret Swett Henson, "McCormick, Margaret (ca. 1788–1859)," *Handbook of Texas Online*, updated June 25, 2015, https://www.tshaonline.org/handbook/entries/mccormick-margaret.

69. Adèle B. Looscan, "Sketch of the Life of Oliver Jones, and of his Wife, Rebecca Jones," *Quarterly of the Texas State Historical Association* 10, no. 2 (Oct. 1906): 177–78.

70. Fane Downs, "Texas Women: History at the Edges," in *Texas Through Time: Evolving Interpretations*, eds. Walter L. Buenger and Robert A. Calvert (College Station: Texas A&M University Press, 1991), 100.

Chapter 3

1. Moseley Baker to Jones, et al., March 8, 1836, *The Papers of the Texas Revolution*, ed. John H. Jenkins, vol. 5, *1835–1836* (Austin: Presidial Press, 1973), 5, 22–23.

2. David G. Burnet to the Citizens of Texas, proclamation, March 18, 1836, in Jenkins, 126–27.

3. Houston to R. R. Royall, chairman of the committee at Matagorda, March 24, 1836, in Jenkins, 180.

4. Paul D. Lack, *The Texas Revolutionary Experience: A Political and Social History, 1835–1836* (College Station: Texas A&M University Press, 1992), 98.

5. James T. DeShields, ed., *Tall Men with Long Rifles: The Glamorous Story of the Texas Revolution, As Told by Captain Creed Taylor, Who Fought in That Heroic Struggle from Gonzales to San Jacinto* (San Antonio: Naylor Company, 1935), 121.

6. Mary Crownover Rabb, *Travels and Adventures in Texas in the 1820s: Being the Reminiscences of Mary Crownover Rabb* (Waco, TX: W. M. Morrison, 1962), 14.

7. John Milton Swisher, *Early Days in Texas: Reminiscences of Colonel Swisher*, photocopy of transcript, A976.4 SW, Austin History Center, Austin, Texas, 18.

8. See Brian C. Rindfleisch's overview of southern masculinity and sexual violence, "'What It Means to Be a Man': Contested Masculinity in the Early Republic and Antebellum America," *History Compass* 10, no. 11 (November 2012): 789–878.

9. Anthony Rotundo, *American Manhood: Transformations in Masculinity from the Revolution to the Modern Era* (New York: Basic Books, 1994).

10. At times, this control extended to sexual violence against black women who were under their charge. See Edward E. Baptist, "'Cuffy,' 'Fancy Maids,' and 'One-

Eyed Men': Rape, Commodification, and the Domestic Slave Trade in the United States," *American Historical Review* 106, no. 5 (December 2001): 1619–50, and Walter Johnson, *Soul by Soul: Live Inside the Antebellum Slave Market* (Cambridge: Harvard University Press, 1999). In her work on lynching, Ida B. Wells emphasized the hypocrisy inherent in a system that focused on the threat of black men raping white women rather than on factual accounts of white men raping their female slave dependents. See Ida B. Wells, *Southern Horrors and Other Writings: The Anti-Lynching Campaign of Ida B. Wells, 1892–1900*, Bedford Series in History and Culture (Boston: Bedford/St. Martin's, 1997). Also see Crystal N. Feimster, *Southern Horrors: Women and the Politics of Rape and Lynching* (Cambridge: Harvard University Press, 2011).

11. Craig Thompson Friend and Lorri Glover, eds., "Rethinking Southern Masculinity: An Introduction," in *Southern Manhood: Perspectives on Masculinity in the Old South* (Athens: University of Georgia Press, 2004), x.

12. Randolph B. Campbell, *Gone to Texas: A History of the Lone Star State* (New York: Oxford University Press, 2003), 96.

13. Lorri Glover, *Southern Sons: Becoming Men in the Nation* (Baltimore: John Hopkins University Press, 2007); Friend and Glover, *Southern Manhood*; Lorri Glover, "An Education in Southern Masculinity: The Ball Family of South Carolina in the New Republic," *Journal of Southern History* 69, no. 1 (February 2003): 39–70; James Oakes, *The Ruling Race: A History of American Slaveholders* (New York: Knopf, 1982); also see numerous publications on the topic by Elizabeth Fox-Genovese and Eugene D. Genovese.

14. Stephanie McCurry, *Masters of Small Worlds: Yeoman Households, Gender Relations, & the Political Culture of the Antebellum South Carolina Low Country* (New York: Oxford University Press, 1995), 6.

15. McCurry, 261.

16. Amy S. Greenberg, *Manifest Manhood and the Antebellum American Empire* (New York: Cambridge University Press, 2005), 12.

17. Greenberg, 12. Furthering the notion of restrained manhood, Gail Bederman describes antebellum male identity as steeped in the middle-class virtues of a strong, "manly" character. She writes, "The middle class saw this ability to control powerful masculine passions through strong character and a powerful will as a primary source of men's strength and authority over both woman and the lower classes." Self-mastery and restraint expressed and shaped middle-class identity. Gail Bederman, *Manliness & Civilization: A Cultural History of Gender and Race in the United States, 1880–1917* (Chicago: University of Chicago Press, 1995), 11–12.

18. David T. Moore, "Southern Baptists and Southern Men: Evangelical Perceptions of Manhood in Nineteenth-Century Georgia," *Journal of Southern History* 81, no. 3 (August 2015): 569.

19. Michael S. Kimmel, *Manhood in America: A Cultural History*, 2nd ed. (New York: Oxford University Press, 2006), 23–24.

20. DeShields, *Tall Men,* 120
21. DeShields, 120.
22. Letter to the Editors, March 15, 1836, in Jenkins, *Papers of the Texas Revolution,* vol. 5, 87.
23. Lack, *Texas Revolutionary Experience,* 143.
24. Swisher, *Early Days in Texas,* 34.
25. Aurelia Hadley Mohl, "Mrs. Anson Jones," Women of the Texas Republic and Revolution Papers, Box 2R119 vertical files, Dolph Briscoe Center for American History, University of Texas at Austin, 13.
26. Houston to James Collinsworth, Chairman of the Military Committee, dated March 15, 1836, in Jenkins, *Papers of the Texas Revolution,* vol. 5, 83.
27. Houston Army Orders, March 21, 1836, in Jenkins, 154.
28. Houston Army Orders, April 4, 1836, in Jenkins, 321.
29. Houston Army Orders, April 13, 1836, in Jenkins, 458.
30. James Monroe Hill, "Recollections of James Monroe Hill," Thomson Family Papers, 1832–1905, MS 288, folder 1, Fondren Library, Woodson Research Center, Rice University, Houston, Texas, 32–33.
31. Dilue Rose Harris, "Reminiscences of Mrs. Dilue Harris, II," *Quarterly of the Texas State Historical Association* 4, no. 3 (January 1901): 164.
32. Sam Houston to Soldiers and Citizens, January 15, 1836, in *The Papers of the Texas Revolution,* ed. John H. Jenkins, vol. 4, *1835–1836,* (Austin: Presidial Press, 1973), 29.
33. Winnie Allen, "While Houston Battled at San Jacinto: Pioneer Woman Left Record of Panic That Spread over Texas when Mexican Invasion Was On," *Dallas Morning News,* April 24, 1927.
34. Allen.
35. Allen.
36. Baker to Jones, March 8, 1836, in Jenkins, *Papers of the Texas Revolution,* vol. 5, 22–23.
37. Sam Houston to Citizens of Texas, April 13, 1836, in Jenkins, 453.
38. Sam Houston to the People East of the Brazos, March 31, 1836, in Jenkins, 253.
39. Burnet to the Citizens of Texas, proclamation, March 1836, in Jenkins, 259.
40. Burnet to the Citizens of Texas, March 18, 1836, in Jenkins, 126–27.
41. Thomas J. Rusk to the Citizens of Texas, April 13, 1836, in Jenkins, 461.
42. Burnet to the Citizens of Texas, proclamation, undated, in Jenkins, 227.
43. Sam Houston to Col. John A. Wharton re Private A. Scales Court Martial, April 2, 1836, in Jenkins, 297–301.
44. DeShields, *Tall Men,* 122.
45. DeShields, 122.
46. DeShields, 122

47. Burnet to the Citizens of Texas, proclamation, April 6, 1836, in Jenkins, *Papers of the Texas Revolution*, vol. 5, 341.

48. Burnet to Henry Raguet, April 7, 1836, in Jenkins, 355.

49. Houston to Col. Bowen and Capt. Black, April 8, 1836, in Jenkins, 381. On confiscation and citizenship, also see Houston Army Orders, April 5, 1836, in Jenkins, 332.

50. DeShields, *Tall Men*, 122–23.

51. S. F. Sparks, "Recollections of S. F. Sparks," *Quarterly of the State Historical Association* 12, no. 2 (July 1908): 63–64.

52. Mark E. Kann, *A Republic of Men: The American Founders, Gendered Language, and Patriarchal Politics* (New York: New York University Press, 1998), 31.

53. Myra C. Glenn, "Troubled Men in the Early Republic: The Life and Autobiography of Sailor Horace Lane," *Journal of the Early Republic* 26, no. 1 (Spring 2006): 70.

54. Guy M. Bryan to Kate S. Terrell, August 15, 1895, Guy Morrison Bryan Papers, file #2N247, folder #8, Dolph Briscoe Center for American History, University of Texas at Austin.

55. George R. Nielson, "Lydia Ann McHenry and Revolutionary Texas," *Southwestern Historical Quarterly* 74, no. 3 (January 1971): 402.

56. Lack, *Texas Revolutionary Experience*, 232. Lack provides an impressive inventory of people subject to shady property confiscation, see 308n52.

57. David G. Burnet to J. W. Moore and De Witt Clinton Harris, August 13, 1836, in *The Papers of the Texas Revolution*, ed. John H. Jenkins, vol. 8, *1835–1836*, (Austin: Presidial Press, 1973), 220.

58. Mrs. T. C. Allen and Mrs. Thomas O'Connor, comps. and eds., "Reminiscences of Mrs. Annie Fagan Teal," *Southwestern Historical Quarterly* 34, no. 4 (April 1931): 325, 326.

59. Noah Smithwick, *The Evolution of a State or Recollections of Old Texas Days* (Austin: Steck Company, 1935), 129.

60. Lack, *Texas Revolutionary Experience*, 213.

61. Some sources identify Whiting's first name as Hervey (Paul Lack), while others list it as Harvey (Andrew Forest Muir). I have chosen to use the former.

62. Lack, *Texas Revolutionary Experience*, 156.

63. Harris, "Reminiscences, II" 164

64. Harris, 174–75.

65. Hervey Whiting to Colonel James Morgan, May 3, 1836, in *The Papers of the Texas Revolution*, ed. John H. Jenkins, vol. 6, *1835–1836*, (Austin: Presidial Press, 1973), 158.

66. Whiting to Colonel James Morgan, 157.

67. Andrew Forest Muir, "Tories in Texas, 1836," *Texas Military History* 4, no. 2 (Summer 1964): 86.

68. Muir, 89.

69. Hervey Whiting to Colonel James Morgan, May 3, 1836, in Jenkins, *Papers of the Texas Revolution,* vol. 6, 157.

70. Whiting to Colonel James Morgan, 157.

71. Whiting to Colonel James Morgan, 157.

72. Sam Houston to the People East of the Brazos, March 31, 1836, in Jenkins, *Papers of the Texas Revolution,* vol. 5, 253.

73. David G. Burnet to Henry Raguet, Committee of Safety, April 7, 1836, in Jenkins, 356.

74. Harris, "Reminiscences, II," 164.

Chapter 4

1. Letter from Thomas J. Green to Adolphus T. McCall, March 30, 1836, *The Papers of the Texas Revolution,* ed. John H. Jenkins, vol. 5, *1835–1836,* (Austin: Presidial Press, 1973), 241–42.

2. Thomas J. Green to "The Friends of Liberty Throughout the World," April 5, 1836, *The Papers of the Texas Revolution, 1835–1836,* in Jenkins, 328.

3. Richard Ellis to the People of the United States, March 16, 1836, in Jenkins, 89. Also see Burnet address, March 17, 1836, in Jenkins, 101.

4. Mark E. Kann, *A Republic of Men: The American Founders, Gendered Language, and Patriarchal Politics* (New York: New York University Press, 1998), 30.

5. Thomas J. Chambers to unknown, March 1836, in Jenkins, *Papers of the Texas Revolution,* 263. The demand referred to in the quote was an absolute, unconditional submission to the will of a military despot.

6. David G. Burnet to the Citizens of Texas, March 29, 1836, in Jenkins, 226.

7. Burnet to Henry Raguet, April 7, 1836, in Jenkins, 356.

8. Harry S. Laver, "Refuge of Manhood: Masculinity and the Militia Experience in Kentucky," in *Southern Manhood: Perspectives on Masculinity in the Old South,* ed. Craig Thompson Friend and Lorri Glover (Athens: University of Georgia Press, 2004), 6.

9. E. Thomas to his father, March 10, 1836, in Jenkins, *Papers of the Texas Revolution,* 45.

10. Sam Houston to James Collingsworth, chairman of the Military Committee, March 17, 1836, in Jenkins, 123.

11. Sam Houston to the People East of the Brazos, March 31, 1836, in Jenkins, 253.

12. Peter Guardino, "Gender, Soldiering, and Citizenship in the Mexican-American War of 1846–1848," *American Historical Review* 119, no. 1 (February 2014): 32.

13. Ordinance to Organize the Militia of the Republic of Texas, March 12, 1836, at Washington, in Jenkins, *Papers of the Texas Revolution,* 58.

14. Brazoria Meeting held on March 17, 1836, in Jenkins, 98–99.

15. Benjamin Briggs Goodrich to Edmund Goodrich, March 15, 1836, in Jenkins, 81.

16. Thomas J. Chambers to unknown, March 1836, in Jenkins, 266.

17. David G. Burnet, Inaugural Address, March 17, 1836, in Jenkins, 101.

18. Guardino, Peter, "Gender, Soldiering, and Citizenship in the Mexican-American War of 1846–1848," *American Historical Review* 119, no. 1 (February 2014): 23.

19. Guardino, 46. On citizen soldiers, also see Robert E. Nye, "Western Masculinities in War and Peace," *American Historical Review* 112, no. 2 (April 2007): 417–38.

20. Guardino, 30.

21. See Noah Smithwick, *The Evolution of a State or Recollections of Old Texas Days* (Austin: Steck Company, 1935), 123; letter of March 15, 1836, published in the *Houston Post,* March 15, 1959; Jenkins, *Papers of the Texas Revolution,* 58, 89, 101, 226, 227, 241, 418, 448.

22. David Weber addressed long-standing negative stereotypes of Mexican Americans, particularly men, in "'Scarce More than Apes': Historical Roots of Anglo-American Stereotypes of Mexicans in the Border Region," in *Myth and the History of the Hispanic Southwest* (Albuquerque: University of New Mexico, 1988). Of note, the quote in Weber's title comes from Noah Smithwick's assertion: "I looked on the Mexicans as scarce more than apes." He also cites a similar ape comparison from Stephen Austin during his travels to Mexico City in the 1820s (pp. 154, 157). Smithwick, *Evolution of a State,* 45.

23. See Jenkins, *Papers of the Texas Revolution,* 81, 89, 103, 127, 241.

24. Edward L. Ayers, *Vengeance & Justice: Crime and Punishment in the 19th Century American South* (New York: Oxford University Press, 1984), 13.

25. Stephanie McCurry, *Masters of Small Worlds: Yeoman Households, Gender Relations, & the Political Culture of the Antebellum South Carolina Low Country* (New York: Oxford University Press, 1995), 261.

26. Thomas J. Chambers to unknown, March 1836, in Jenkins, *Papers of the Texas Revolution,* 265.

27. David F. Marley, *Mexico at War: From the Struggle for Independence to the 21st-Century Drug Wars* (Santa Barbara: ABC-CLIO, 2014), 451.

28. T. J. Green to Adolphus T. McCall, dated March 30, 1836, in Jenkins, *Papers of the Texas Revolution,* 241–42.

29. Stoking fears of rape to garner support for war is by no means exclusive to the Texas Revolution. During World War I, for example, British war propagandists produced the Bryce Report, which was widely circulated in the United States. The report included accounts of Germans raping women in Belgium. Bryce Report into German Atrocities in Belgium, 12 May 1915, firstworldwar.com, August 22, 2009, https://www.firstworldwar.com/source/brycereport.htm.

30. Emily West was a free black who signed a one-year contract with James Morgan to work as a housekeeper at a hotel located in New Washington. She was taken captive by the Mexican army when they came through the area during their

1836 march. Margaret Swett Henson, "West, Emily D. (unknown–unknown," *Handbook of Texas Online,* updated April 1, 2021, https://www.tshaonline.org/handbook/entries/west-emily-d.

31. Will Fowler, "All the Presidents Women: The Wives of General Antonio López in 19th Century Mexico," *Feminist Review*, no. 79, Latin America: History, War, and Independence (2005): 57.

32. Fowler, 59.

33. Guardino, "Gender, Soldiering, and Citizenship," 30.

34. Amy S. Greenberg, *Manifest Manhood and the Antebellum American Empire* (New York: Cambridge University Press, 2005), 12.

35. Gail Bederman, *Manliness & Civilization: A Cultural History of Gender and Race in the United States, 1880–1917* (Chicago: University of Chicago Press, 1995), 11–12.

36. Holly Beachley Brear, *Inherit the Alamo: Myth and Ritual at an American Shrine* (Austin: University of Texas Press, 1995), 48. Also see James E. Crisp, *Sleuthing the Alamo: Davy Crockett's Last Stand and Other Mysteries of the Texas Revolution* (New York: Oxford University Press, 2005), 188–95. Brear identifies Morgan as a slave, although other sources dispute this claim, noting her contractual arrangement with James Morgan.

37. Arnoldo de León, *They Called Them Greasers: Anglo Attitudes toward Mexicans in Texas, 1821–1900* (Austin: University of Texas Press, 1983), 10–11.

38. James W. Fannin to J. W. Robinson, February 7, 1836, in *The Papers of the Texas Revolution,* ed. John H. Jenkins, vol. 4, *1835–1836,* (Austin, Presidial Press, 1973), 280.

39. De León, *The Called Them Greasers,* 11.

40. *Nashville Banner & Nashville Whig,* April 11, 1836, as cited in Gary S. Zaboly, *An Altar for Their Sons: The Alamo and the Texas Revolution in Contemporary Newspaper Accounts* (Buffalo Gap, TX: State House Press, 2011), 295–96.

41. Paul Lack, ed., *The Diary of William Fairfax Gray: From Virginia to Texas, 1835–1837* (Dallas: De Golyer Library & William P. Clements Center, 1997), 152.

42. Jane Hallowell Hill, "Recollections of Jane Hallowell Hill," Thompson Family Papers Texas, 1832–1998, folder 1, MS288, Fondren Library, Rice University, Houston, Texas, 50–52.

43. Milly R. Gray, "Diary of Mrs. Milly R. Gray," Gray Family Papers, Box MC033, 32–3, Albert and Ethel Herzstein Library, San Jacinto Museum of History, LaPorte, Texas, 88.

44. Laura Clark Shire, *The Threshold of Manifest Destiny: Gender and National Expansion in Florida* (Philadelphia: University of Pennsylvania Press, 2016), 84.

45. Shire, 86, 87, 88, 94.

46. Shire, 123.

47. Shire, 125–25.

48. Mrs. T. C. Allan and Mrs. Thomas O'Connor, "Reminiscences of Mrs. Annie Fagan Teal," *Southwestern Historical Quarterly* 34, no. 4 (April 1931): 325.

49. Samuel Tabor Allen, letter to his brother, May 18, 1836, Samuel Tabor Allen Family Papers, 1759–1931, Box 3P153 vertical files, Dolph Briscoe Center for American History, University of Texas at Austin.

50. Ann B. Cardwell, "Attended First Texas Presbytery in 1849," newspaper clipping on Mrs. Ann B. Cardwell (no date), Kenney (Martin McHenry) Papers, Box 2E290 vertical files, Dolph Briscoe Center for American History, University of Texas at Austin.

51. C. Richard King, ed., *Victorian Lady on the Texas Frontier: The Journal of Ann Raney Coleman* (Norman: University of Oklahoma Press, 1971), 85.

52. Cardwell, "Attended First Texas Presbytery."

53. For a comprehensive analysis of the captive-exchange system during the Spanish and Mexican eras in New Mexico, see James F. Brooks, *Captives and Cousins: Slavery, Kinship, and Community in the Southwest Borderlands* (Chapel Hill: University of North Carolina Press, 2002).

54. The Horn family settled near the village of Dolores, which was part of a colonization project located between the Rio Grande and the Nueces rivers, established by empresario John Charles Beales, in the early 1830s (near present-day Eagle Pass, Texas).

55. Sarah Ann Horn and E. House, *A Narrative of the Captivity of Mrs. Horn, and Her Two Children with Mrs. Harris, by the Camanche Indians* (St. Louis: C. Keemle, printer, 1839), 15.

56. Horn and House, 17.

57. Gregory Michno and Susan Michno, *A Fate Worse than Death: Indian Captivities in the West, 1830–1885* (Caldwell, ID: Caxton Press, 2007), 24.

58. Shire, *Threshold of Manifest Destiny*, 61.

59. Shire, 62

60. Barbara Welter, "The Cult of True Womanhood, 1820–1860," *American Quarterly* 18 (Summer 1966): 151–75.

61. June Namias, *White Captives: Gender and Ethnicity on the American Frontier* (Chapel Hill: University of North Carolina Press, 1993), 36, 37, 40.

62. Noah Smithwick, "Reminiscences of an Old Texas," *Santa Ana Standard*, January 22, 1898. Interestingly, when Smithwick's daughter, Mrs. Nanna Smithwick Donaldson, compiled his memoirs into *The Evolution of a State*, she (or the editor) changed Smithwick's reference to "hordes of ruthless savages" to "thousands of Indians." Smithwick, *Evolution of a State*, 104.

63. Smithwick, *Evolution of a State*, 118.

64. Smithwick, 118–23.

65. President Jackson's Message to Congress "On Indian Removal," December 6, 1830, https://www.nps.gov/museum/tmc/MANZ/handouts/Andrew_Jackson

_Annual_Message.pdf. For sources on Jackson and Indian Removal, see Sean Wilentz, *Andrew Jackson* (New York: Times Books, Henry Holt & Company, 2005); Jon Meacham, *American Lion: Andrew Jackson in the White House* (New York: Random House, 2008); Alfred Cave, *Sharp Knife: Andrew Jackson and the American Indians* (Santa Barbara: Praeger, 2017).

66. Jacqueline Jones, *A Dreadful Deceit: The Myth of Race from the Colonial Era to Obama's America* (New York: Basic Books, 2013), xi.

67. Shire, *Threshold of Manifest Destiny*, 85.

68. Lack, *Texas Revolutionary Experience*, 168.

69. Lack, 169.

70. Lack, 170. Part of the evidence is a document that connected Vicente Córdova with Manuel Flores, an emissary of Santa Anna who reportedly passed through east Texas in late 1835 or early 1836. Flores is the individual at the heart of most reports of collusion between the Mexican forces and tribes surrounding east Texas. Sworn testimony placed Flores in east Texas seeking an alliance with the Caddo Indians. See Jenkins, *Papers of the Texas Revolution, 1835–1836*, vol. 5, 375, 376, 446, 447, 506, 507, 508.

71. Lack, *Texas Revolutionary Experience*, 171.

72. Henry Raguet to emissary, March 19, 1836, in Jenkins, *Papers of the Texas Revolution*, vol. 5, 144. Also see pp. 288, 289, 429, 430

73. A. Hotchkiss Report, March 21, 1836, in Jenkins, vol. 5, 153–54.

74. Members of the Committee of Vigilance and Safety to John Mason, April 11, 1836, in Jenkins, vol. 5, 432, 433.

75. R. A. Irion to John Mason, April 12, 1836, in Jenkins, vol. 5, 448.

76. John Mason to General Gaines, April 13, 1836, in Jenkins, vol. 5, 459–60.

77. Thomas W. Cutrer, "Gaines, Edmund Pendleton (1777–1849)," *Handbook of Texas Online*, updated October 30, 2019, https://www.tshaonline.org/handbook/entries/gaines-edmund-pendleton.

78. John Mason to unknown, April 16, 1836, in Jenkins, *Papers of the Texas Revolution*, vol. 5, 489.

79. Edmund P. Gaines to Secretary of War, dated April 20, 1836, in Jenkins, vol. 5, 510.

80. Brazoria Meeting, Committee M, March 17, 1836, in Jenkins, vol. 5, 99.

81. Andrew J. Torget, *Seeds of Empire: Cotton, Slavery, and the Transformation of the Texas Borderlands, 1800–1850* (Chapel Hill: University of North Carolina Press, 2015), 171–72.

82. Torget, 173.

83. King, *Victorian Lady*, 85.

84. See Jenkins, *Papers of the Texas Revolution, 1835–1836*, vol. 5, 81, 89, 103, 127, 241.

Chapter 5

1. S. F. Sparks, as cited in William Ransom Hogan, "Pamelia Mann: Texas Frontierswoman," *Southwest Review* 20, no. 4 (July 1935): 362.

2. Noah Smithwick, *The Evolution of a State or Recollections of Old Texas Days* (Austin: Steck Company, 1935), 111.

3. John Milton Swisher, *Early Days in Texas: Reminiscences of Colonel Swisher*, photocopy of transcript, A976.4 SW, Austin History Center, Austin, Texas, 18.

4. James T. DeShields, ed., *Tall Men with Long Rifles: The Glamorous Story of the Texas Revolution, As Told by Captain Creed Taylor, Who Fought in That Heroic Struggle from Gonzales to San Jacinto* (San Antonio: Naylor Company, 1935), 119.

5. Mann is sometimes referred to as a widow, which is accurate; however, when she moved to Texas in January 1834, she had remarried Marshall Mann. She had two sons from her previous marriages, Flournoy Hunt (from first marriage) and Samuel Allen (second marriage).

6. S. F. Sparks, as cited in Hogan, "Pamelia Mann," 362; Robert Hancock Hunter Diary, Box 2R 56 vertical files, Dolph Briscoe Center for American History, University of Texas at Austin, 13.

7. Hogan, "Pamelia Mann," 360–70; Andrew Forest Muir, "In Defense of Mrs. Mann," in *Mexican Border Ballads and Other Lore*, ed. Mody Boatright (Austin: Texas Folklore Society, 1946; Denton: University of North Texas Press, 2000), 113–35.

8. Paul D. Lack, *The Texas Revolutionary Experience: A Political and Social History, 1835–1836* (College Station: Texas A&M University Press, 1992), 227; Fane Downs, "'Tryels and Trubbles': Women in Early Nineteenth-Century Texas," *Southwestern Historical Quarterly* 90, no. 1 (July 1986): 47–48; James L. Haley, *Sam Houston* (Norman: University of Oklahoma Press, 2004), 140; Mary L. Scheer, ed., "'Joys and Sorrows of Those Dear Old Times': Anglo-American Women during the Era of the Texas Revolution," in *Women and the Texas Revolution* (Denton: University of North Texas Press, 2012), 87. A popular history of Pamelia Mann is Gene Shelton, *Houston Madam: The Story of Pamelia Mann, Texas* (Pecos, TX: Pecos Press, 2016).

9. Hogan, "Pamelia Mann," 360.

10. DeShields, *Tall Men*, 109–10.

11. Hunter, "Diary of Robert Hancock Hunter," Box 2R 56 vertical files, Dolph Briscoe Center for American History, University of Texas at Austin, 13.

12. Hunter, 13–14.

13. Hunter, 14.

14. Beulah Gayle Green, ed., *Narrative of Robert Hancock Hunter, 1813–1902, from His Arrival in Texas, 1822, through the Battle of San Jacinto, 1836* (Austin: Cook Printing Company, 1936), 19.

15. Lack, *Texas Revolutionary Experience,* 227.

16. S. F. Sparks, as cited in Hogan, "Pamelia Mann," 362. Also see John Holmes Jenkins III, ed., *Recollections of Early Texas: The Memoirs of John Holland Jenkins* (Austin: University of Texas Press, 1958), 264. This encounter between Sam Houston and Pamelia Mann is familiar terrain for many historians of the revolutionary era. It was retold, for example, in the relatively recent popular biography of Sam Houston by Haley, *Sam Houston,* 140.

17. Hogan, "Pamelia Mann," 370.

18. Hogan, 365.

19. Muir, "In Defense of Mrs. Mann," 124.

20. The reminiscences of Reverend O. M. Addison in O. M. Addison Papers, unpublished memoir, as cited in Hogan, "Pamelia Mann," 363. Flournoy Hunt's nickname was apparently Nimrod. Muir, "In Defense of Mrs. Mann," 114.

21. Mrs. P. Mann to Sam Houston, February 3, 1836, in *The Papers of the Texas Revolution,* ed. John H. Jenkins, vol. 4, *1835–1836,* (Austin: Presidial Press, 1973), 248.

22. In his diary, Fairfax wrote: "Entered as a boarder at Mrs. Mann's at $1.25 per day." Note that Fairfax described the boardinghouse as Mrs. Mann's, not her husband's. Lack, *Diary of William Fairfax Gray,* 116.

23. Muir, "In Defense of Mrs. Mann," 114. Initially recorded in Robert M. Coleman's *Houston Displayed, or Who Won the Battle of San Jacinto?* (Velasco, TX: Velasco Herald Office, 1837; Austin: Brick Row Book Shop, 1964). According to Muir, Silas Dinsmore identified the woman in Houston's tent as Mrs. Mann, 130n20.

24. Muir, "In Defense of Mrs. Mann," 117.

25. *Texas Almanac,* "The Capitals of Texas," accessed June 22, 2020, https://texasalmanac.com/topics/history/capitals-texas.

26. Muir, "In Defense of Mrs. Mann," 118. The level of licentiousness at the Mansion House was a matter of debate between her biographers. In his earlier account, Hogan claimed, "Boarding Houses, often dignified with the name of hotels, were set up to care for this portion of the male population which had to exist without benefit of wifely solicitude. In this last respect, Mrs. Mann and her 'girls' achieved a satisfying success" ("Pamelia Mann," 364). Muir, commenting on her later relationship with Tandy Brown, wrote, "She lived with Brown without benefit of clergy, but she was neither prostitute nor brothel mistress" ("In Defense of Mrs. Mann," 129). With "notorious" almost ubiquitously applied to Mrs. Mann by her contemporaries, perhaps it is not surprising that future writers might question the nature of her business undertakings. The record is inconclusive.

27. Dilue Rose Harris, "Reminiscences of Mrs. Dilue Harris, II," *Quarterly of the Texas State Historical Association* 4, no. 3 (January 1901): 180.

28. Ellen Garwood, "Early Texas Inns: A Study in Social Relationships," *Southwest Historical Quarterly* 60, no. 2 (October 1956): 231.

29. William Ransom Hogan, "Rampant Individualism in the Republic of Texas," *Southwest Historical Quarterly* 44, no. 4 (April 1941): 458.

30. Garwood, "Early Texas Inns," 226.

31. Muir, "In Defense of Mrs. Mann," 119.

32. Muir, 119–20. In the summer of 1838, the marriage of Pamelia's son Flournoy Hunt to Miss Mary Henry took place at the Mansion House, and the event was the outstanding social event of the season.

33. Muir, 120.

34. Muir, 120–21; Hogan, "Pamelia Mann," 367.

35. Muir, "In Defense of Mrs. Mann," 122.

36. The 150 men described in Travis's correspondence on February 23 (denoting the arrival of Santa Anna's forces) were joined by 32 men from Gonzales who arrived in the early morning, before the sun arose, on March 1, 1836 (with one courier arriving later in the day). William Barret Travis to Andrew Ponton, Judge and Citizens of Gonzales, dated February 23, 1836, in Jenkins, *Papers of the Texas Revolution*, 420; William Barret Travis to the President of the Convention, March 3, 1836, in Jenkins, 502.

37. Hogan, "Pamelia Mann," 366.

38. Muir, "In Defense of Mrs. Mann," 122.

39. Muir, 122–23.

40. Muir, 123.

41. Hogan, "Pamelia Mann," 366.

42. Hogan, 366; Muir, "In Defense of Mrs. Mann," 123.

43. Muir, 126–27. This assault charge against Tandy Brown was not a lone occurrence. On April 7, 1840, he was charged with assaulting Ann Tucker, a free black, quite likely over a property dispute with Mann. There were no white witnesses, so he was initially discharged, only to be rearrested later that day.

44. Garwood, "Early Texas Inns," 233.

45. Muir, "In Defense of Mrs. Mann," 126.

46. Mary L. Scheer, "Unequal Citizens," in *Texas Identities: Moving Beyond Myth, Memory, and Fallacy in Texas History*, ed. Light Townsend Cummins and Mary L. Scheer (Denton: University of North Texas Press, 2016), 79.

47. Lack notes that this was also a failure of the Revolution itself. Lack, *Texas Revolutionary Experience*, 259.

48. Muir, "In Defense of Mrs. Mann," 128–29.

49. Mary Crownover Rabb, *Travels and Adventures in Texas in the 1820s: Being the Reminiscences of Mary Crownover Rabb* (Waco, TX: W. M. Morrison, 1962), 14.

50. This is an often-repeated quote with challenging origins. Citing as his source the *Texas Almanac 1860* where the letter appears (dated April 1836), see Eugene C. Barker, "Communication: The San Jacinto Campaign," *Quarterly of the Texas State Historical Association* 4, no. 4 (April 1901): 249. Galveston News,

The Texas Almanac, for 1860, with Statistics, Historical and Biographical Sketches, &c., Relating to Texas (Galveston: W & D Richardson, 1860~), University of North Texas Libraries, Texas State Historical Association, https://texashistory.unt.edu/ark:/67531/metapth123766/m1/62/?q=burnet.

James L. Haley discusses the missing letter and the earliest reference to the letter (June 1841) in a footnote. Haley, *Sam Houston,* 444n14.

51. Cited in Stephen L. Hardin, "The San Jacinto Campaign: The Generalship of Sam Houston," accessed July 5, 2020, http://www.sonsofdewittcolony.org//adp/archives/feature/hardin.html.

52. Mark E. Kann, *A Republic of Men: The American Founders, Gendered Language, and Patriarchal Politics* (New York: New York University Press, 1998), 30.

53. David T. Moore, "Southern Baptists and Southern Men: Evangelical Perceptions of Manhood in Nineteenth-Century Georgia," *Journal of Southern History* 81, no. 3 (August 2015): 569, 602.

54. Randolph B. Campbell, *Sam Houston and the American Southwest* (New York: Pearson Longman, 2007), 75.

55. Bryan, Letter from Guy M. Bryan to Kate S. Terrell, August 15, 1895, Guy Morrison Bryan Papers, file #2N247, folder #8, Dolph Briscoe Center for American History, University of Texas at Austin.

56. DeShields, *Tall Men,* 125–26.

57. DeShields, 126.

58. W. P. Zuber, "The Runaway Scrape," *The Home and State,* January 1907, VF-General File, Texas Revolution, 1835–1836, Runaway Scrape, Daughters of the Republic of Texas Library at the Alamo, San Antonio, Texas. Taylor expressed a similar sentiment, stating "Many of the boys believed that Houston would never halt as long as the road was open to the Sabine." DeShields, *Tall Men,* 125.

59. Swisher, *Early Days in Texas,* 17–18.

60. Swisher, 18.

61. Campbell, *Sam Houston and the American Southwest,* 80.

62. Campbell, 81; Randolph B. Campbell, *Gone to Texas: A History of the Lone Star State* (New York: Oxford University Press, 2003), 153.

63. "The Battle of the Alamo: By One Who Fought in It," *The Living Age* 2 (August–October 1844): 262–63. https://babel.hathitrust.org/cgi/pt?id=chi.55225984&view=1up&seq=273&q1=san%20jacinto.

64. Amy S. Greenberg, *Manifest Manhood and the Antebellum American Empire* (New York: Cambridge University Press, 2005), 12.

65. David G. Burnet to the People of Texas, proclamation, September 1836, in *The Papers of the Texas Revolution,* ed. John H. Jenkins, vol. 8, *1835–1836* (Austin: Presidial Press, 1973), 401.

66. The Treaty of Velasco (Private), May 14, 1836, Texas State Library and Archives Commission, https://www.tsl.texas.gov/treasures/republic/velasco-private-2.html.

67. David G. Burnet to the People of Texas, September 1836, in Jenkins, *Papers of the Texas Revolution,* vol. 8, 399; Burnet to Peter W. Grayson and James Collinsworth, June 20, 1836, in *The Papers of the Texas Revolution,* ed. John H. Jenkins, vol. 7, *1835–1836* (Austin: Presidial Press, 1973), 207.

68. Sam T. Allen to Caleb Allen, May 18, 1836, Samuel Tabor Allen Family Papers, 1759–1931, Box 3P153 vertical file, Dolph Briscoe Center for American History, University of Texas at Austin.

69. Memucan Hunt to David G. Burnet, June 3, 1836, Executive Record Books, Texas Secretary of State, Archives and Information Services Division, Texas State Library and Archives Commission, Updated July 27, 2011, https://www.tsl.texas.gov/exhibits/presidents/burnet/mem_hunt_jun3_1836_1.html.

70. Citizens of Municipalities of Austin & Harrisburg to Cabinet of Texas, June 7, 1836, in Jenkins, *Papers of the Texas Revolution,* vol. 7, 50.

71. Adèle B. Looscan, "Sketch of the Life of Oliver Jones, and of his Wife, Rebecca Jones," *Quarterly of the Texas State Historical Association* 10, no. 2 (Oct. 1906): 177–78.

72. George R. Nielson, "Lydia Ann McHenry and Revolutionary Texas," *Southwestern Historical Quarterly* 74, no. 3 (January 1971): 402.

73. Nielson, 403.

74. Marguerite Starr Crain, *Two Glass Buttons: A Story of the Runaway Scrape* (Midland, TX: Nita Stewart Haley Memorial Library, 1988), 128, 136.

75. Hardin, "The San Jacinto Campaign."

76. Cited in Hardin, "The San Jacinto Campaign."

77. Hardin, "The San Jacinto Campaign."

78. Gordon S. Wood, "The Greatness of George Washington," *Virginia Quarterly Review* 68, no. 2 (Spring 1992): 196–97.

79. Anthony Rotundo, *American Manhood: Transformations in Masculinity from the Revolution to the Modern Era* (New York: Basic Books, 1994), 170.

80. Admittedly, his popularity took a significant hit with his opposition to secession in the prelude to the Civil War and his removal from the governorship in March 1861.

81. Hogan, "Pamelia Mann," 360.

82. Muir, "In Defense of Mrs. Mann," 128.

83. Beulah Gayle Green, *Narrative of Robert Hancock Hunter,* 19.

84. Greenberg, *Manifest Manhood,* 216.

Conclusion

1. Mary Crownover Rabb, *Travels and Adventures in Texas in the 1820s: Being the Reminiscences of Mary Crownover Rabb* (Waco, TX: W. M. Morrison, 1962), 14.

2. Rosa Kleberg, "Some of My Early Experiences in Texas," *Quarterly of the Texas State Historical Association* 1, no. 4 (April 1898), 300; Dilue Rose Harris,

"Reminiscences of Mrs. Dilue Harris, II," *Quarterly of the Texas State Historical Association* 4, no. 3 (January 1901): 160.

3. James W. Fannin to J. W. Robinson, February 7, 1836, in *The Papers of the Texas Revolution*, ed. John H. Jenkins, vol. 4, *1835–1836* (Austin: Presidial Press, 1973), 280.

4. Paula Fass, "The Memoir Problem," *Reviews in American History* 34, no. 1 (March 2006): 107–8.

5. Elizabeth Y. Enstam, "Using Memoirs to Write Local History," *History News* 37, no. 11 (November 1982): 20.

6. Kelly McMichael, *Sacred Memories: The Civil War Monument Movement in Texas* (Denton: Texas State Historical Association, 2009).

7. Walter L. Buenger, *The Path to A Modern South: Northeast Texas Between Reconstruction and the Great Depression* (Austin: University of Texas Press, 2001), 258.

8. C. Richard King, ed., *Victorian Lady on the Texas Frontier: The Journal of Ann Raney Coleman* (Norman: University of Oklahoma Press, 1971), 92–93.

9. Rosa Kleberg, "Some of My Early Experiences in Texas," *Quarterly of the Texas State Historical Association* 1, no. 4 (April 1898): 301.

10. Rabb, *Travels and Adventures*, 14.

11. Rabb, 14.

12. James T. DeShields, ed., *Tall Men with Long Rifles: The Glamorous Story of the Texas Revolution, As Told by Captain Creed Taylor, Who Fought in That Heroic Struggle from Gonzales to San Jacinto* (San Antonio: Naylor Company, 1935), 122.

13. DeShields, 122.

14. John Milton Swisher, *Early Days in Texas: Reminiscences of Colonel Swisher*, photocopy of transcript, A976.4 SW, Austin History Center, Austin, Texas, 18.

15. Swisher, 18.

16. Amy S. Greenberg, *Manifest Manhood and the Antebellum American Empire* (New York: Cambridge University Press, 2005), 12.

17. Michael S. Kimmel, *Manhood in America: A Cultural History*, 2nd ed. (New York: Oxford University Press, 2006), 23–24.

18. Noah Smithwick, *The Evolution of a State or Recollections of Old Texas Days* (Austin: Steck Company, 1935), 123–24.

19. Smithwick, 123.

20. Smithwick, 118.

21. S. F. Sparks, as cited in William Ransom Hogan, "Pamelia Mann: Texas Frontierswoman," *Southwest Review* 20, no. 4 (July 1935): 362.

22. S. F. Sparks, "Recollections of S. F. Sparks," *Quarterly of the State Historical Association* 12, no. 2 (July 1908): 63.

23. Sparks, 63.

24. Hogan, "Pamelia Mann," 370.

Bibliography

Allan, Mrs. T. C., and Mrs. Thomas O'Connor, comps., eds. "Reminiscences of Mrs. Annie Fagan Teal." *Southwestern Historical Quarterly* 34, no. 4 (1931): 317–28.

Allen, Samuel Tabor. Letter to Caleb Allen, May 18, 1836. Samuel Tabor Allen Family Papers, 1759–1931. Box 3P153 vertical file. Dolph Briscoe Center for American History, University of Texas at Austin.

Allen, Winnie. "While Houston Battled at San Jacinto: Pioneer Women Left Record of Panic That Spread over Texas When Mexican Invasion Was On." *Dallas Morning News,* April 24, 1927.

Ames, Harriet A. "The History of Harriet A. Ames during the Early Days of Texas." Box 2Q403 vertical file. Dolph Briscoe Center for American History, University of Texas at Austin.

Atkinson, M. Jourdan. "Maria Bachman Atkinson, 1801–1863; Harriet Bachman Jourdan, 1815–1881." In *Women in Early Texas,* edited by Evelyn M. Carrington, 23–36. Austin: Texas State Historical Association, 1994.

Ayers, Edward L. *Vengeance & Justice: Crime and Punishment in the 19th Century American South*. New York: Oxford University Press, 1984.

Baptist, Edward E. *Creating an Old South: Middle Florida's Plantation Frontier before the Civil War*. Chapel Hill: University of North Carolina Press, 2002.

———. "'Cuffy,' 'Fancy Maids,' and 'One-Eyed Men': Rape, Commodification, and the Domestic Slave Trade in the United States." *American Historical Review* 106, no. 5 (December 2001): 1619–50.

Barker, Eugene C. "The San Jacinto Campaign." *Quarterly of the Texas State Historical Association* 4, no. 4 (April 1901): 238–345.

Baylor, Mary A. "Reminiscences of Mrs. Mary A. Baylor." Box 2Q430 vertical file. Dolph Briscoe Center for American History, University of Texas at Austin.

Bederman, Gail. *Manliness & Civilization: A Cultural History of Gender and Race in the United States, 1880–1917*. Chicago: University of Chicago Press, 1995.

Boswell, Angela. *Her Act and Deed: Women's Lives in a Rural Southern County, 1837–1873*. College Station: Texas A&M University Press, 2001.

———. "Traveling the Wrong Way down Freedom's Trail: Black Women and the Texas Revolution." In *Women and the Texas Revolution*, edited by Mary L. Scheer, 97–121. Denton: University of North Texas Press, 2012.

———. *Women in Texas History*. College Station: Texas A&M University Press, 2018.

Boydston, Jeanne. "Gender as a Question of Historical Analysis." *Gender & History* 20, no. 3 (November 2008): 558–83.

Brear, Holly Beachley. *Inherit the Alamo: Myth and Ritual at an American Shrine*. Austin: University of Texas Press, 1995.

Brooks, James F. *Captives and Cousins: Slavery, Kinship, and Community in the Southwest Borderlands*. Chapel Hill: University of North Carolina Press, 2002.

Bryan, Guy M. Letter to Kate S. Terrell. Guy Morrison Bryan Papers, file #2N247, folder #8. Dolph Briscoe Center for American History, University of Texas at Austin.

Bryan, Moses A. "Reminiscences of M. A. Bryan." Moses Austin Bryan Papers, MC 060, folder 91–31. Albert and Ethel Herzstein Library, San Jacinto Museum of History, La Porte, Texas.

Bryce Report into German Atrocities in Belgium, 12 May 1915. firstworldwar.com. August 22, 2009. https://www.firstworldwar.com/source/brycereport.htm.

Buenger, Walter L. *The Path to a Modern South: Northeast Texas between Reconstruction and the Great Depression*. Austin: University of Texas Press, 2001.

Callaway, Carolyn. "The Runaway Scrape: An Episode of the Texas Revolution." Master's thesis, University of Texas at Austin, 1942.

Campbell, Randolph B. *An Empire for Slavery: The Peculiar Institution in Texas, 1821–1865*. Baton Rouge: Louisiana State Press, 1991.

———. *Gone to Texas: A History of the Lone Star State*. New York: Oxford University Press, 2003.

———. *Sam Houston and the American Southwest*. 3rd ed. New York: Pearson Longman, 2007.

Cardwell, Ann B. "Attended First Texas Presbytery in 1849." Newspaper clipping on Mrs. Ann B. Cardwell (no date), Kenney (Martin McHenry) Papers, vertical files, box 2E290. Dolph Briscoe Center for American History, University of Texas at Austin.

Carroll, Mark M. *Homesteads Ungovernable Families, Sex, Race, and the Law in Frontier Texas, 1823–1860*. Austin: University of Texas Press, 2001.

Caughfield, Adrienne. *True Women Westward Expansion*. College Station: Texas A&M University Press, 2005.

Cave, Alfred. *Sharp Knife: Andrew Jackson and the American Indians*. Santa Barbara: Praeger, 2017.

Coleman, Robert M. *Houston Displayed, or Who won the battle of San Jacinto? By a farmer in the army.* Austin: Brick Row Book Shop, 1964. First published 1837 by Velasco Herald Office (Velasco, TX).

Crain, Marguerite Starr. "Hodge, Alexander Hodge (1760–1836)." In *Handbook of Texas Online.* Updated October 30, 2019, https://www.tshaonline.org/handbook/entries/hodge-alexander. Published by the Texas State Historical Association.

———. *Two Glass Buttons: A Story of the Runaway Scrape.* Midland, TX: Nita Stewart Haley Memorial Library, 1988, 130.

Crisp, James E. *Sleuthing the Alamo: Davy Crockett's Last Stand and Other Mysteries of the Texas Revolution.* New York: Oxford University Press, 2005.

Cummins, Light Townsend. "'Up Buck! Up Ball! Do Your Duty!': Women and the Runaway Scrape." In *Women and the Texas Revolution*, edited by Mary L. Scheer, 153–78. Denton: University of North Texas Press, 2012.

Cummins, Light Townsend, and Mary L. Scheer, eds. Introduction to *Texas Identities: Moving Beyond Myth, Memory, and Fallacy in Texas History.* Edited by Light Townsend Cummins and Mary L. Scheer, 1–27. Denton: University of North Texas Press, 2016.

Cutrer, Thomas W. "Gaines, Edmund Pendleton (1777–1849)." *Handbook of Texas Online.* Updated October 30, 2019. https://www.tshaonline.org/handbook/entries/gaines-edmund-pendleton. Published by the Texas State Historical Association.

de León, Arnoldo. *They Called Them Greasers: Anglo Attitudes toward Mexicans in Texas, 1821–1900.* Austin: University of Texas Press, 1983.

DeShields, James T., ed. *Tall Men with Long Rifles: The Glamorous Story of the Texas Revolution, As Told by Captain Creed Taylor, Who Fought in That Heroic Struggle from Gonzales to San Jacinto.* San Antonio: Naylor Company, 1935.

Donaldson, Colgate D'Eve. Letter to Lawson Moore. William Moore Papers, 2F58, Dolph Briscoe Center for American History, University of Texas at Austin.

Donovan, Jim. *The Blood of Heroes: The 13-Day Struggle for the Alamo—and the Sacrifice that Forged a Nation.* New York: Little, Brown, 2012.

Downs, Fane. "Texas Women: History at the Edges." In *Texas Through Time: Evolving Interpretations*, eds. Walter L. Buenger and Robert A. Calvert, 81–101. College Station: Texas A&M University Press, 1991.

———. "'Tryels and Trubbles': Women in Early Nineteenth-Century Texas," *Southwestern Historical Quarterly* 90, no. 1 (1986): 35–56.

Dunn, Jeffrey D. "To the *Devil* with Your Glorious History." In *Women and the Texas Revolution*, ed. Mary L. Scheer, 179–208. Denton: University of North Texas Press, 2012.

English, Linda. *By All Accounts: General Stores and Community Life in Texas and Indian Territory.* Norman: University of Oklahoma Press, 2013.

———. "'That Very Trying Time': Guy Morrison Bryan Recalls the Runaway Scrape." *Central Texas Studies: Journal of the Central Texas Historical Association,* vol. 3 (December 2018): 67–79.

Enstam, Elizabeth York. *Women and the Creation of Urban Life: Dallas, Texas, 1843–1920.* College Station: Texas A&M University Press, 1998.

———. "Using Memoirs to Write Local History." *History News* 37, no. 11 (November 1982): 19–26.

Exley, Jo Ella Powell. "Mary Sherwood Wightman Helm." In *Texas Tears and Texas Sunshine: Voices of Frontier Women.* College Station: Texas A&M University Press, 1985.

———. "Rachel Parker Plummer." In *Texas Tears and Texas Sunshine: Voices of Frontier Women.* College Station: Texas A&M University Press, 1985.

Fass, Paula. "The Memoir Problem." *Reviews in American History* 34, no. 1 (March 2006): 107–23.

Faust, Drew Gilpin. *Mothers of Invention: Women of the Slaveholding South in the American Civil War.* Chapel Hill: University of North Carolina Press, 1996.

Feimster, Crystal N. *Southern Horrors: Women and the Politics of Rape and Lynching.* Cambridge: Harvard University Press, 2011.

Friend, Craig Thompson, and Lorri Glover. *Southern Manhood: Perspectives on Manhood in the Old South.* Athens: University of Georgia Press, 2004.

Fowler, Will. "All the Presidents Women: The Wives of General Antonio López in 19th Century Mexico." *Feminist Review* 79, no. 1 (2005): 52–68.

Galveston News. *The Texas Almanac, for 1860, with Statistics, Historical and Biographical Sketches, &c., Relating to Texas.* Galveston: W & D Richardson, 1860~. University of North Texas Libraries, Texas State Historical Association. Accessed July 5, 2020, https://texashistory.unt.edu/ark:/67531/metapth123766/m1/62/?q=burnet.

Garrison, George P. "Guy Morrison Bryan." *Quarterly of the Texas State Historical Association* 5, no. 2 (October 1901): 121–36.

Garwood, Ellen Garwood. "Early Texas Inns: A Study in Social Relationships." *Southwest Historical Quarterly* 60, no. 2 (October 1956): 219–44.

Glenn, Myra C. "Troubled Men in the Early Republic: The Life and Autobiography of Sailor Horace Lane." *Journal of the Early Republic* 26, no. 1 (Spring 2006): 59–93.

Glover, Lorri. "An Education in Southern Masculinity: The Ball Family of South Carolina in the New Republic." *Journal of Southern History* 69, no. 1 (February 2003): 39–70.

———. *Southern Sons: Becoming Men in the Nation.* Baltimore: Johns Hopkins University Press, 2007.

Gray, Milly R. Gray. "Diary of Mrs. Milly R. Gray." Gray Family Papers, box MC033, 32–3. Albert and Ethel Herzstein Library, San Jacinto Museum of History, LaPorte, Texas.

Green, Beulah Gayle, ed. *Narrative of Robert Hancock Hunter, 1813–1902, from his arrival in Texas, 1822, through the battle of San Jacinto, 1836.* Austin: Cook Printing Company, 1936.

Greenberg, Amy S. *Manifest Manhood and the Antebellum American Empire.* New York: Cambridge University Press, 2005.

Guardino, Peter. "Gender, Soldiering, and Citizenship in the Mexican-American War of 1846–1848." *American Historical Review* 119, no. 1 (February 2014): 23–46.

Haley, James L. *Sam Houston.* Norman: University of Oklahoma Press, 2004.

Hardin, Stephen L. "'A Hard Lot:' Texas Women in the Runaway Scrape." *East Texas Historical Journal* 29, no. 1 (1991): 35–45.

———. "The San Jacinto Campaign: The Generalship of Sam Houston." Accessed July 5, 2020, http://www.sonsofdewittcolony.org//adp/archives/feature/hardin.html.

Harris, Dilue. "Reminiscences of Mrs. Dilue Harris, I." *Quarterly of the Texas State Historical Association* 4, no. 2 (October 1900), 85–127.

———. "Reminiscences of Mrs. Dilue Harris, II." *Quarterly of the Texas State Historical Association* 4, no. 3 (January 1901), 155–89.

———. "Reminiscences of Mrs. Dilue Harris, III." *Quarterly of the Texas State Historical Association* 7, no. 3 (January 1904), 214–22.

Helm, Mary S. *Scraps of Early Texas History: By Mary S. Helm, who, with her first husband, Elias R. Wightman, founded the city of Matagorda, in 1828–29.* Austin: B. R. Warner & Co., 1884.

Henson, Margaret Swett. "McCormick, Margaret (ca. 1788–1859)." *Handbook of Texas Online.* Updated June 25, 2015, https://www.tshaonline.org/handbook/entries/mccormick-margaret. Published by the Texas State Historical Association.

———. "West, Emily D. (unknown–unknown)." *Handbook of Texas Online.* Updated April 1, 2021, https://www.tshaonline.org/handbook/entries/west-emily-d. Published by the Texas State Historical Association.

Hill, James Monroe. "Recollections of James Monroe Hill." Thomson Family Papers, 1832–1905, MS 288, folder 1. Fondren Library, Woodson Research Center, Rice University, Houston, Texas.

Hill, Jane Hallowell. "Recollections of Jane Hallowell Hill." Thompson Family Papers Texas, 1832–1998, MS 288, folder 1. Fondren Library, Woodson Research Center, Rice University, Houston, Texas.

Horn, Sarah Ann, and E. House. *A Narrative of the Captivity of Mrs. Horn, and her two children with Mrs. Harris, by the Camanche Indians.* St. Louis: C. Keemle, printer, 1839.

Hogan, William Ransom. "Pamelia Mann: Texas Frontierswoman." *Southwest Review* 20, no. 4 (July 1935): 360–70.

———. "Rampant Individualism in the Republic of Texas." *Southwest Historical Quarterly* 44, no. 4 (April 1941): 454–80.

Hunt, Memucan. Letter to David G. Burnet, June 3, 1836. Executive Record Books, Texas Secretary of State, Archives and Information Services Division, Texas State Library and Archives Commission. Updated July 27, 2011, https://www.tsl.texas.gov/exhibits/presidents/burnet/mem_hunt_jun3_1836_1.html.

Hunter, Robert Hancock. "Diary of Robert Hancock Hunter." Box 2R 56 vertical files. Dolph Briscoe Center for American History, University of Texas at Austin.

Huson, Hobart. "James, John (1788–1836)." *Handbook of Texas Online.* Updated December 3, 2020, https://www.tshaonline.org/handbook/entries/james-john. Published by the Texas State Historical Association.

Jackson, President Andrew. Message to Congress "On Indian Removal," December 6, 1830. Records of the United States Senate, 1789–1990, record group 46. National Archives and Records. Accessed July 2, 2020. https://www.nps.gov/museum/tmc/MANZ/handouts/Andrew_Jackson_Annual_Message.pdf.

Jacobs, Margaret. "Western History: What's Gender Got to Do with It?" *Western Historical Quarterly* 42, no. 3 (Autumn 2011): 297–304.

Jameson, Elizabeth. "Women as Workers, Women as Civilizers; True Womanhood in the American West." In *The Women's West*, edited by Susan Armitage and Elizabeth Jameson, 145–64. Norman: University of Oklahoma Press, 1987.

Jeffrey, Julie Roy. "Permeable Boundaries: Abolitionist Women and Separate Spheres." *Journal of the Early Republic* 21, no. 1 (2001): 79–93.

Jenkins, John Holland. *Recollections of Early Texas: The Memoirs of John Holland.* Austin: University of Texas Press, 1958.

Jenkins, John Holmes. *The Papers of the Texas Revolution, 1835–1836.* 10 vol. Austin: Presidial Press, 1973.

Johnson, Susan Lee. "Nail This to Your Door: A Disputation on the Power, Efficacy, and Indulgent Delusion of Western Scholarship That Neglects the Challenge of Gender and Women's History." *Pacific Historical Review* 79, no. 4 (November 2010): 605–17.

Johnson, Walter. *Soul by Soul: Live Inside the Antebellum Slave Market.* Cambridge: Harvard University Press, 1999.

Jones, Allan C. *Texas Roots: Agriculture and Rural Life before the Civil War.* College Station: Texas A&M University Press, 2005.

Jones, Jacqueline Jones. *A Dreadful Deceit: The Myth of Race from the Colonial Era to Obama's America.* New York: Basic Books, 2013.

Kann, Mark E. *A Republic of Men: The American Founders, Gendered Language, and Patriarchal Politics.* New York: New York University Press, 1998.

Kelley, Sean. "'Mexico in His Head': Slavery and the Texas-Mexico Border, 1810–1860." *Journal of Social History* 37, no. 3 (Spring 2004): 709–23.

Kilman, Ed. "Texas Heartbeat: The March Day When Texas Reached Its Lowest Ebb and 'Died A-Borning,' As a Soldier Eye Witness Feared." *Houston Post,* March 15, 1959.

Kimmel, Michael S. *Manhood in America: A Cultural History.* 2nd ed. New York: Oxford University Press, 2006.

King, Richard C., ed. *Victorian Lady on the Texas Frontier: The Journal of Ann Raney Coleman.* Norman: University of Oklahoma Press, 1971.

Kleberg, Rosa. "Early Experiences in Texas II." *Quarterly of the Texas State Historical Association* 2 (July 1898-April 1899): 170–73.

———. "Some of My Early Experiences in Texas." *Quarterly of the Texas State Historical Association* 1, no. 4 (April 1898): 297–302.

Lack, Paul, ed. *The Diary of William Fairfax Gray: From Virginia to Texas, 1835–1837.* Dallas: De Golyer Library & William P. Clements Center, 1997.

Lack, Paul D. *The Texas Revolutionary Experience: A Political and Social History, 1835–1836.* College Station, TX: Texas A&M University Press, 1992.

Laver, Harry S. "Refuge of Manhood: Masculinity and the Militia Experience in Kentucky." In *Southern Manhood: Perspectives on Masculinity in the Old South,* eds. Craig Thompson Friend & Lorri Glover. Athens: University of Georgia Press, 2004: 1–21.

Linn, John J. *Reminiscences of Fifty Years in Texas.* Facsimile reproduction. Austin: Steck Company, 1935.

Lofaro, Michael A. *Davy Crockett: The Man, The Legend, the Legacy, 1786–1986.* Knoxville: University of Tennessee Press, 1985.

Looscan, Adèle B. "Elizabeth Bullock Huling: A Texas Pioneer," *Quarterly of the Texas State Historical Association* 11, no. 1 (July 1907): 66–69.

———. "Sketch of the Life of Oliver Jones, and of His Wife, Rebecca Jones." *Quarterly of the Texas State Historical Association* 10, no. 2 (1906): 172–80.

Marley, David F. *Mexico at War: From the Struggle for Independence to the 21st-Century Drug Wars.* Santa Barbara: ABC-CLIO, 2014.

Martin, Charles L. "Women and Old Men's Retreat before Mexican Invaders Big Page in the History of Texas." Unidentified newspaper clipping, VF-General

File, Texas Revolution, 1835–1836, Runaway Scrape. Alamo Research Center, Daughters of the Republic of Texas Library, San Antonio, Texas.

McArthur, Judith N. "Harriet A. Moore Page Potter Ames (1810–1902)." *Handbook of Texas Online.* Updated August 2, 2017, https://www.tshaonline.org/handbook/entries/ames-harriet-a-moore-page-potter. Published by the Texas State Historical Association.

McCurry, Stephanie. *Masters of Small Worlds: Yeoman Households, Gender Relations, & the Political Culture of the Antebellum South Carolina Low Country.* New York: Oxford University Press, 1995.

McGill, Sarah Ann. *Davy Crockett.* Toledo, OH: Great Neck Publishing, 2005.

McMichael, Kelly. *Sacred Memories: The Civil War Monument Movement in Texas.* Denton: Texas State Historical Association, 2009.

Meacham, Jon. *American Lion: Andrew Jackson in the White House.* New York: Random House, 2008.

Michno, Gregory, and Susan Michno. *A Fate Worse than Death: Indian Captivities in the West, 1830–1885.* Caldwell, ID: Caxton Press, 2007.

Mohl, Aurelia Hadley. "Mrs. Anson Jones." Women of the Texas Republic and Revolution Papers, Box 2R119 vertical files. Dolph Briscoe Center for American History, University of Texas at Austin.

———. "Mrs. Thomas J. Rusk." Women of the Texas Republic and Revolution Papers, Box 2R119 vertical files. Dolph Briscoe Center for American History, University of Texas at Austin.

Moore, David T. "Southern Baptists and Southern Men: Evangelical Perceptions of Manhood in Nineteenth-Century Georgia." *Journal of Southern History* 81, no. 3 (August 2015): 563–606.

Moore, Stephen. *Eighteen Minutes: The Battle of San Jacinto and the Texas Independence Campaign.* Austin: Republic of Texas Press, 2004.

Moore-Morse Family Papers, Creator Sketch, MC091. Albert and Ethel Herzstein Library, San Jacinto Museum, La Porte, TX.

Muir, Andrew Forest. "In Defense of Mrs. Mann." In *Mexican Border Ballads and Other Lore,* edited by Mody Boatright, 113–35. Denton: University of North Texas Press, 2000; first published by Texas Folklore Society, 1946.

———. "The Lady Was for Burning." *Southwest Review* 44, no. 2 (Spring 1959): 166–69.

———. "Tories in Texas, 1836." *Texas Military History* 4, no. 2 (Summer 1964): 81–94.

Namias, June. *White Captives: Gender and Ethnicity on the American Frontier.* Chapel Hill: University of North Carolina Press, 1993.

Nielson, George R. "Lydia Ann McHenry and Revolutionary Texas." *Southwestern Historical Quarterly* 74, no. 3 (January 1971): 393–408.

Nye, Robert E. "Western Masculinities in War and Peace." *American Historical Review* 112, no. 2 (April 2007): 417–38.

Oakes, James. *The Ruling Race: A History of American Slaveholders*. New York: Knopf, 1982.

Parsons, Uncle Jeff. Interview with *Galveston News*. Sons of DeWitt Colony Texas. Accessed July 24, 2020, http://www.sonsofdewittcolony.org/mustergon2.htm.

Peterson, Dorothy Burns, ed. *Daughters of the Republic of Texas, Patriot Ancestor Album,* vol. 1. Nashville, TN: Turner Publishing, 1995.

Priour, Rosalie B. Hart. "The Adventures of a Family of Emigrants Who Emigrated to Texas in 1834: An Autobiography by Rosalie B. Hart Priour." Box 2R154 vertical files. Dolph Briscoe Center for American History, University of Texas, Austin.

Rabb, Mary Crownover. *Travels and Adventures in Texas in the 1820s: Being the Reminiscences of Mary Crownover Rabb*. Introduction by Ramsey Yelvington. Waco, TX: W. M. Morrison, 1962.

Seth Thomas History. ClockHistory.com. Accessed December 23, 2020. https://clockhistory.com/sethThomas/company.

Sparks, S. F. "Recollections of S. F. Sparks," *Quarterly of the Texas State Historical Association* 12, no. 1 (1908): 61–79.

Rable, George C. *Civil Wars: Women and the Crisis of Southern Nationalism*. Urbana: University of Illinois Press, 1991.

Ragsdale, Crystal Sasse, ed. *The Golden Free Land: The Reminiscences and Letters of Women on an American Frontier*. Austin, TX: Landmark Press, 1976.

Rindfleisch, Brian C. "'What It Means to Be A Man': Contested Masculinity in the Early Republic and Antebellum America," *History Compass* 10, no. 11 (2012): 852–65.

Robinson, Victoria, and Diane Richardson. *Introducing Gender & Women's Studies*. 4th ed. London: Palgrave, 2015.

Rotundo, Anthony. *American Manhood: Transformations in Masculinity from the Revolution to the Modern Era*. New York: Basic Books, 1994.

Scott, Anne Firor. *The Southern Lady: From Pedestal to Politics, 1830 to 1930*. 25th anniversary edition. Charlottesville: University of Virginia Press, 1995.

Scott, Joan W. "Gender: A Useful Category of Historical Analysis. *American Historical Review* 91, no. 5 (December, 1986): 1053–75.

Scheer, Mary L. "'Joys and Sorrows of Those Dear Old Times': Anglo-American Women during the Era of the Texas Revolution." In *Women and the Texas Revolution*, edited by Mary L. Scheer, 65–96. Denton: University of North Texas Press, 2012.

———. "Unequal Citizens." In *Texas Identities: Moving Beyond Myth, Memory, and Fallacy in Texas History*, edited by Light Townsend Cummins and Mary L. Scheer, 61–86. Denton: University of North Texas Press, 2016.

Shelton, Gene. *Houston Madam: The Story of Pamelia Mann, Texas*. Pecos, TX: Pecos Press, 2016.

Shire, Laura Clark. *The Threshold of Manifest Destiny: Gender and National Expansion in Florida*. Philadelphia: University of Pennsylvania Press, 2016.

Sigourney, Lydia Howard. *Letters to Young Ladies*. 2nd ed. Hartford: William Watson, 1835.

Smithwick, Noah. *The Evolution of a State or Recollections of Old Texas Days*. Austin, TX: Steck Company, 1935.

———. "Reminiscences of an Old Texas," *Santa Ana Standard,* January 22, 1898.

Sutherland, Anne H. *The Robertsons, the Sutherlands, and the Making of Texas*. College Station: Texas A&M University Press, 2006.

Sutherland, [Frances] George. Letter to sister. Sutherland (George) Papers. Box 2K328 vertical files. Dolph Briscoe Center for American History, University of Texas at Austin, Texas.

Swisher, John Milton. *Early Days in Texas: Reminiscences of Colonel Swisher*. Photocopy of Transcript, A976.4 SW. Austin History Center, Austin, Texas.

Terrell, Kate Scurry. "Reminiscences of Kate Scurry Terrell" In *A Comprehensive History of Texas, 1685–1897*, edited by Dudley Wooten, 669–71. Dallas: William G. Scarff, 1898.

Texas Almanac. "The Capitals of Texas." Accessed June 22, 2020. https://texasalmanac.com/topics/history/capitals-texas.

"The Battle of the Alamo: By One Who Fought in It." *The Living Age* 2 (August–October 1844), 262–63. https://babel.hathitrust.org/cgi/pt?id=chi.55225984&view=1up&seq=273&q1=san%20jacinto.

The Treaty of Velasco (Private), May 14, 1836. Texas State Library and Archives Commission. https://www.tsl.texas.gov/treasures/republic/velasco-private-2.html.

Torget, Andrew J. *Seeds of Empire: Cotton, Slavery, and the Transformation of the Texas Borderlands, 1800–1850*. Chapel Hill: University of North Carolina Press, 2015.

Weber, David J. "'Scarce More than Apes': Historical Roots of Anglo-American Stereotypes of Mexicans in the Border Region." In *Myth and the History of the Hispanic Southwest,* 153–67. Albuquerque: University of New Mexico, 1988.

Welter, Barbara. "The Cult of True Womanhood, 1820–1860." *American Quarterly* 18 (1966): 151–75.

Wells, Ida B. Wells. *Southern Horrors and Other Writings: The Anti-Lynching Campaign of Ida B. Wells, 1892–1900*. Bedford Series in History and Culture, First Edition. Boston: Bedford/St. Martin's, 1997.

Whites, LeeAnn. *The Civil War as a Crisis in Gender, Augusta, Georgia, 1860–1890.* Athens: University of Georgia Press, 1995.

Whites, LeeAnn, and Alecia P. Long, editors. *Occupied Women: Gender, Military Occupation, and the American Civil War.* Baton Rouge: Louisiana State University Press, 2009.

Wilentz, Sean. *Andrew Jackson.* New York: Times Books, Henry Holt & Company, 2005.

Williams, John Hoyt. *Sam Houston: The Life and Times of the Liberator of Texas, an Authentic American Hero.* New York: Simon & Schuster, 1993.

Wood, Gordon S. "The Greatness of George Washington." *Virginia Quarterly Review* 68, no. 2 (Spring 1992): 189–207.

Van Winkle, Irene. "The Priour Family Has Long History." *West Kerr Current,* May 18, 2006. http://wkcurrent.com/priour-family-has-long-history-p838-71.htm.

Vinson, Michael. *Bluffing Texas Style: The Arsons, Forgeries, and High-Stakes Poker Capers of Rare Book Dealer Johnny Jenkins.* Norman: University of Oklahoma Press, 2020.

Von Hinueber, Caroline. "Life of German Pioneers in Early Pioneers." *Quarterly of the Texas State Historical Association* 2, no. 3 (January 1899): 227–32.

Zaboly, Gary S. *An Alter for Their Sons: The Alamo and the Texas Revolution in Contemporary Newspaper Accounts.* Buffalo Gap, TX: State House Press, 2011.

Zuber, W. P. "The Runaway Scrape." *The Home and State,* January 1907. VF-General File, Texas Revolution, 1835–1836, Runaway Scrape. Alamo Research Center, Daughters of the Republic of Texas Library at the Alamo. San Antonio, Texas.

Index

Adelsverein, 34
Alamo, 4–5, 17, 32, 38–39, 41, 45, 52, 61, 64, 69–70, 73, 87, 93, 95, 100–101, 106, 113, 125
Allen, Quintus, 38
Allen, Caleb, 121
Allen, Samuel, 95, 121
Almonte, Col. Juan, 80
American intervention, 85, 100–101, 103
American Revolution, 17, 77, 85–86, 88, 124
American South, 14, 17, 67, 88, 117, 130–131. *See* masculinity: southern notions of
Ames, Harriet A.: during the Runaway Scrape, 30–31; rustic living conditions, 30; unpublished reminiscences, 11
Atascosito Crossing, 71
Atkinson, M. Jourdan, 35
Atkinson, Maria Bachman: family members, 35; mantel clock, 35–36
Austin, Stephen F.: Austin colony, 25, 35, 42, 78; presidential candidate, 123; as a slaveholder, 15
Asbury, Dr. Samuel F., 11
Austin, Texas, 51, 122
Ayers, Edward, 89

babies: born during the Runaway Scrape, 2, 60; died during the escape, 40, 60
Baker, Mosely: on burning San Felipe, 37; on enlistment, 63, 73

Baltimore Gazette and Daily Advertiser, 37
Baptist, Edward, 25
Barrett, D. C., 101
Bastrop, Texas, 95, 97
Baylor, Mary A.: description of Runaway Scrape, 32; unpublished reminiscences, 11
Beaumont, Texas, 47
Beason's Ferry, 64–65
Bederman, Gail, 91
Bellville, Texas, 78
Bexar, 64
Billingsley, Jesse, 123
Birdsall, John, 114
Board of Examination, 37
Boswell, Angela, 10, 128
Bowie, James, 10, 105
Boyce, James, 79
Brazoria, Texas, 37, 87–88, 101–102
Brazos River, 15, 35, 37, 48, 58, 71, 93, 102, 116
Brear, Holly, 91–92
Brooks, Gilbert, 81
Brown, Tandy, 115
Bryan, Col. Guy Morrison: letter on Runaway Scrape, 13, 14, 32–33, 77, 117; published account of rebellion, 13
Buenger, Walter, 131
Buffalo Bayou, 119
Burnet, David G.: age of military service, 48; armistice terms, 121–122; deserters and noncombatants, 73–75; on the

enemy, 88; on Houston's courage and character, 116, 124; Houston's retreat, 52; impressment, 76, 78–79; on manly obligations, 1, 7, 64, 73–74, 82, 86; personal property, 79, 81–82
Burnham's Crossing, 64

Callaway, Caroline, 14
Campbell, Randolph, 67, 119
Caney Creek (Cany Creek), 25, 34, 42
Cardwell, Ann, 95–96
Carroll, Mark, 29
Caughfield, Adrienne, 23
Chambers, Thomas, 85, 88, 90
Clear Creek, 2, 32
Coahuila y Tejas (Texas), 3, 30, 98
Coleman, Ann Raney: disagreements with husband, 44, 49, 54–57, 131–132; enemy threat, 95–96, 103; enslaved laborers, 15; image of, 22; leaving possessions, 21, 23, 25; published memoir, 11, 128; rustic living, 27
Coleto Creek, 5
Colorado River: crossings, 60, 64, 71; Houston's decision to fall back, 4, 17, 32, 52, 64–66, 70–71, 82, 116–118; settlements along, 15
Columbus, Texas, 71
Columbus Herald, 37
Committee of Safety, 70, 75
Constitution of 1824, 3–4
Constitutional Convention: on enlistment, 87; General Convention for independence, 13, 51–52, 110, 113
convicts, 86–87
Córdova, Vicente, 99–100
Cos, General, 119
criminals, 17, 77–79, 80–82, 83
Crockett, Davy, 9, 61, 68, 105
Cummins, Light Townsend, 10, 14, 128

Dallas Morning News, 33–34, 72
De León, Arnoldo, 92
De Zavala, Gen. Lorenzo, 122
Department of the Brazos, 50
deserters, 17, 50, 64, 68–71, 73–74, 82–83, 132
DeShields, James T., 12, 45

Dickinson, Capt. Almaron, 106
Dickinson, Susanna: Alamo survivor, 106; fellow survivors, 106
Dimmit, Philip, 54
disease, 39–40, 58, 60
dishonorable, 17, 86–89, 92–93, 94, 97–98, 103, 134
Dolph Briscoe Center for American History, 11
domestic security, 16, 21–23, 39, 43, 93–95, 97, 99, 102–103, 132
Donaldson, Colgate D'Eve: description of Runaway Scrape, 28; lack of religion in Texas, 42; rustic living conditions, 27–29
Donaldson, William, 29
Downs, Fane, 14, 62, 107, 128

Ellis, Richard, 85, 87
empresario contracts: 14, 15
enslaved laborers: building fortifications, 88; conspiring with enemies, 101–103; constructing homes, 14, 29; patriarchal authority over, 66–67; rebellion, 102; during the Runaway Scrape, 15, 21, 36, 47–48, 55–56
Ernst, Friedrich, 30, 34

Fagan, Nicholas, 54
Fannin, Col. James W., 5, 37, 48, 54, 64, 66, 92
Fass, Paula, 130
Fort Jesup, Louisiana, 100
"frail flower" (archetype), 97
Frazier, Hugh McDonald, 54

Gaines, Maj. Gen. Edmund P., 100–101, 103
Galveston, Texas, 30–31
Galveston News, 13
Galveston-Dallas News, 13, 47
Garrison, George P., 11, 13
Garwood, Ellen, 112, 115
gender: definition and application of, 6–7; notions of, 130. *See* manliness; masculinity; womanhood
German migrants: Ernsts, 10, 30, 34; Klebergs, 2, 3, 42–43, 132; von Hinueber 10, 30, 34, 58; von Roeders, 2

Glenn, Myra, 77
Glover, Lorri, 67
Goliad, 4–5, 17, 37, 41, 48, 52, 54, 62, 64–66, 69–70, 90, 100, 106, 111, 117, 122, 125; town, 54
Goliad County, 5
Gonzales, Texas: battle of, 2, 4, 24, 64, 95, 99, 134; burning of, 38; reinforcements from, 5; town of, 95–96
Goodrich, Benjamin, 88
Grass Fight, 64
Gray, Milly R., 93
Gray, William Fairfax: on Convention, 52, 110; diary, 13; threat to families, 93
Green, Beulah Gayle, 13
Green, Brig. Gen. Thomas, 84–85, 90, 122
Greenberg, Amy, 67, 77, 117, 125
Greenwood, Capt. J. H., 60–61
Grimes County, 45
Groce's Crossing (Groce's Landing), 35–36
Groce, Jared, 35
Guadalupe River, 4
Guardino, Peter, 88–89, 91

Hall, John W., 92
Hardin, Stephen, 14, 123, 128
Hardy, Mrs. Mary, 113
Harris, Dilue Rose: description of early Houston, 111–112; description of Runaway Scrape, 58, 60; enslaved laborers, 15, 47; father's journal, 48; on men who left the front, 71, 82–83; photograph, 12; published account of the Runaway Scrape 10, 128; on Tories, 80
Harris, Ira, 48
Harris County, 2, 113–114
Harrisburg, Texas, 51, 108, 111, 117, 119, 122
Hart, Elizabeth, 53–54, 62
Hart, Tom, 53
Haley, James, 107
Helm, Mary Sherwood Wightman: description of Runaway Scrape, 26; domestic role, 23; enslaved laborers, 15, 47; on lack of churches, 41; published memoir, 11; rustic living conditions, 25
Hibbons family, 98
Hill, Asa, 71

Hill, James Monroe, 71
Hill, Jane Hallowell, 31–32, 93
Hill, William W., 71
Hodge, Alexander: faith, 41; plantation, 36; preference for Austin over Houston, 123; during the Runaway Scrape, 36–37, 48
Hogan, William Ransom, 107, 109, 113–114, 136
homes: burning homes, 16, 36, 37–39, 42, 94–95; centrality of, 8, 23; creating new homes, 8, 14–15, 23, 25. 27, 29–30. *See* domestic security
Horn, John, 96
Horn, Sarah Ann, 96–97
Houston, General Sam: administration, 113; contentious female encounters, 9, 61, 107–109, 118; on deserters, 69–71, 73–76, 82; early relationship with Pamelia Mann, 110–11; on government officials' removal to Harrisburg, 51–52; illustration of, 106; on the Mexican enemy, 86–87; on noncombatants, 71–73, 82; notoriety, 10, 105–6, 123–124, 126; order to burn towns, 37; political ambitions, 105, 123–125, 132; questions of courage, decision making 18, 61–62, 105, 116, 123, 125, 132–133; retreat from the enemy, 3–6, 17, 24, 32, 52, 64–65, 70, 82–83, 102, 105, 117–118, 125, 128; victory at San Jacinto, 6, 90, 105–6, 119–120
Houston, Texas, 48, 111–112
Houston and Birdsall, 114
Huling, Elizabeth Bullock, 60
Hunt, Flournoy, 110, 115
Hunt, Memucan, 122
Hunter, Robert Hancock: account of Pamelia Mann incident, 107–108; published diary, 13

impressment: animals, 18, 60–61, 75–76, 107–108, 135; property, 36, 75–79, 83, 118
Indian Removal Act, 98
Irion, R. A., 100

Jackson, Andrew, 68, 98
Jackson, Mrs., 52

Jacobs, Margaret, 10
James, John, 53
Jefferson, Thomas, 98
Jenkins, John Holmes, III, 13
"Joe" (enslaved person), 15
Jones, Allan C., 29
Jones, Jacqueline, 98–99
Jones, Mrs. Anson, 70
Jones, Rebecca Westover, 62, 122

Kann, Mark, 85
Karnes, Captain, 38
Kegans, Clarinda Pevehouse: account of the Runaway Scrape, 11, 128; enslaved persons, 48; prized possessions, 36; during the Runaway Scrape, 36–37, 41; on Sam Houston, 123
Kimmel, Michael, 68, 133–134
King, C. Richard, 22
Kleberg, Rosa [von Roeder], 2–4, 8, 10, 42–43, 128, 132
Kleberg, Rudolph Jr., 2, 10
Kokernot, Lt. David, 82

Labardee, Texas (La Bahia), 33, 54
Labardie, Dr. Nicholas, 60
Lack, Paul: the criminal element, 79; Convention members, 52; on deserters, 69; noncombatants and class, 50–51; religion in Texas, 41–42; on Tejanos' loyalty, 99–100; on Tories, 80; William Fairfax Gray's diary, 13
Laver, Harry, 86
Lamar, Mirabeau Buonaparte, 114–115, 122
Las Vegas, New Mexico, 97
Law of April 6, 1830, 3
Liberty, Texas, 60
Lion of the West, The, 68
Long, Alecia P., 58
Looscan, Adele, 11
Lost Cause, 130
Lynch's Ferry, 119
Lynchburg, Texas, 76, 80–81

manliness (manly, manhood): acting manly, 7, 18, 74, 77–78, 86, 91, 103, 117, 132, 136; martial manhood, 67, 68, 82, 124–125, 133. *See* masculinity
Mann, Marshall, 110, 112, 115
Mann, Pamelia: brazenness and notoriety, 18, 107–110, 112–113, 115–116, 125–126, 135–136; courier role, 110; encounter with Sam Houston, 9, 104, 106–109; legal entanglements, 109–115, 125; as a property owner, entrepreneur, 110–112
Mansion House, 111–113
maps: Texas and Mexican troop advances, 65; Texas rivers and creeks, 59; Texas settlements, 26
Mason, John, 100–101
masculinity: depictions of Mexican army, 86–88, 92–93; gendered rhetoric of the American Revolution, 17, 77, 85–86, 103, 117; hypermasculinity, 68, 133; Mexican ideals of, 88–89, 91; nineteenth century notions of, 7, 91; and political service, 124; restrained vs. martial manhood, 67–68, 76–77, 83, 117, 125; southern notions of, 14, 57, 66–68, 89–90, 103 117
Matagorda, Texas: county, 26; town, 25
Matamoros, Mexico, 96
McCall, Adolphus T., 90
McCormick, Margaret "Peggy," 61
McCormick, Michael, 81
McCurry, Stephanie, 67
McHenry, Lydia Ann: on criminal plundering, 78; Methodist camp meeting, 42; on Santa Anna's release, 122–123
McHenry, John Hardin, 78
McMichael, Kelly, 130–131
Mexico City, Mexico, 102
Mexican troops. *See* dishonorable; Santa Anna
Military Committee, 69–70, 86–87
Mobile, Alabama, 54
Morning Star, 114
Moore, Charcila "Chess," 27, 29
Moore, David T., 68
Moore, William, 27–29
Morgan, Col. James, 80–81, 90

INDEX   181

Morgan, Emily. *See* West, Emily D.
Moss, Mrs., 61, 107
Muir, Andrew Forest, 107, 111, 113, 116

Nacogdoches, Texas: lack of religious services, 41; protection of, 49–50, 99–101; road to, 108, 118
Namias, June, 97
Nashville Banner & Nashville Whig, 93
Native Americans: Black Hawk War, 94; captives, 96–97; conspiring with Tejanos/Mexicans, 99–101, 103; characterizations, 17, 86, 94–95, 97–99, 134; domestic threat,18, 94, 96, 134; Seminoles in Florida, 24, 39, 94, 97, 99; threat of raids, 6, 34, 49–50, 94–95, 100–102
Navidad River, 38
Neches River, 27, 60
New Orleans, Louisiana, 31, 54
New York City, 68
noncombatants, 17, 50, 71–72, 74, 80, 83, 133
Nueces River, 64

Oyster Creek, 41

Page, Solomon, 31
Paine, Mr. George, 49
Papers of the Texas Revolution, 13
Parsons, Uncle Ned, 47
Peace Party, 3
Perry, James, 117
Possessions: hiding from enemy, 2, 34–35, 72; leaving behind, 16, 21, 32–35; loss of, 42–43, 78, 93
Potter, Col. Robert, 30–31
Priour, Rosalie B. Hart: description of Runaway Scrape, 33, 53–54; religion and loss, 40; unpublished account of Runaway Scrape, 11

Quarterly of the Texas State Historical Association, The, 2, 10, 12, 13, 128

Rabb, Mary Crownover: dangers during the escape, 127; loss of her child, 40–41, 132; published account of Runaway Scrape, 11; on Sam Houston, 66, 116, 132
Rable, George, 57
Raguet, Henry, 100
religion, 39–42
Robinson, J. W., 116
Rohrer, Captain, 108
Roger, Samuel, 38
Rose, Dr. Pleasant W., 10, 47
Rotundo, Anthony (historian), 66, 124
Runaway Scrape: defined, 3; early months, peak period 5–6; historical marker, 129
Rusk, John Rusk Jr., 49–50
Rusk, Mary, 49–50
Rusk, Thomas: armistice, 120; on desertions, 7, 73–74; husband to Mary, 49

Sabine Lake, 27
Sabine River, 3, 8, 16, 24, 27, 36, 47, 61, 70, 75, 83, 96, 101, 103
Salinas, Francisco Garcia, 90
San Antonio, 5
San Antonio River, 54
San Augustine, 61, 100
San Bernard River (Bernard River), 47, 72
San Felipe, Texas, 37, 70–71, 110
San Jacinto: battle of, 3, 39–40, 61, 78, 90, 106, 119–120, 123; painting of battle, 120; river, 58
San Patricio, Texas, 96
San Phillippe. *See* San Felipe
Santa Anna, General Antonio López de: advancing army, 4–5, 15, 32, 46, 64, 66, 80, 93, 95, 99; characterizations of, 17, 62, 85, 89–94, 96, 103, 121–122, 134; communication with Whiting, 81; correspondence, 38; defeat and capture, 6, 93, 105, 119–120; fear of liberating enslaved laborers, 102; shift from federalist to centralist, 3–4, 64; terms of release, 121–123; Yellow Rose allegations, 90–92, 106
Sargent, Texas, 25
Scheer, Mary, 10, 14, 107, 116, 128
Scott, Anne Firor, 57
Scott, Joan Wallach, 6–7
Scounton, Antonio, 111

Seguin, Juan, 10
Sesma, General Joaquim Ramirez y, 38, 65, 118
Sharp, John, 38, 112
Shire, Laura Clark, 24, 39, 94, 97, 99
Siete Leyes (Seven Laws), 3–4
Sigourney, Lydia Howard, 23
slavery, 14–15. *See* enslaved laborers
Smith, Alice, 11
Smith, Deaf, 80
Smith, Governor Henry, 32, 123
Smithwick, Noah: on criminal element, 79; on the enemy, 95, 97–98, 134; published account of Texas Revolution, 11, 13; on Sam Houston, 105
Somervell, Colonel, 117
Sparks, S. F.: account of the Runaway Scrape, 53; dangers of impressment, 76–77; on Pamelia Mann encounter, 104, 107–109, 134–135; published account of Texas Revolution, 13
Sutherland, Mrs. Francis: enslaved laborers, 47; family loss and faith, 39; husband, 40; property loss, 42
Swisher, Col. John Milton: on deserters, 70; on Sam Houston, 66, 105, 118, 133; unpublished memoir, 13
Synot, Mrs., 33

Taylor, Creed: deserters, 69–70, 132–133; during the Runaway Scrape, 45, 60; on family home, 20, 24–25; men with families, 76, 133; noncombatants, 74–76; published account of Texas Revolution, 11–12; on Sam Houston, 66, 105, 117
Teal, Anna Fagan, 6, 79, 95
Tejanos: looting of property, 79; loyalty of, 99–101
Tennessee volunteers, 61, 107
Terrell, Kate Scurry, 13, 14, 46–47,
Texas Declaration of Independence, 51
Texas State Historical Association, 13
Thomas, John: disagreements with wife, Ann Raney Coleman, 21, 54–57, 131–132; missing military service, 49
Thompson, Craig, 67

Torget, Andrew, 102
Tories, 80–82
Travis, Lt. Col. William Barret, 5, 9, 15, 92, 105, 113
Treaty of Velasco, 120–121
Trinity River, 15, 71, 78
Tumlinson, Capt. John Jackson Jr., 95, 98

Uncle Ned, 47
Urrea, General José, 5

Velasco, Texas, 72, 122
Victoria, Texas, 5, 54
von Hinueber, Caroline Ernst, 10, 30; experience during the Runaway Scrape, 34–35, 58
von Roeders: Louis, 2; Ludwig, 2, 3; Pauline, 2; Rosa [von Roeder] Kleberg, 2, 3. *See* German migrants

Washington, George, 124
Washington (on-the Brazos), Texas, 37, 51–52, 69, 110, 135
West, Emily D. (Yellow Rose), 90–92, 106
West, Judge, 52
Westover, Ira, 54, 62, 122
Whites, LeeAnn, 58
Whiting, Hervey, 80–82
Wightman, Elias, 25–26
Williams, Sam, 122
womanhood: armed encounters, 16, 53, 56, 61, 106–109, 131–132, 135; brazen women, female pluck, 9, 10, 16, 18, 46, 61, 106–109, 112–113, 115, 125, 135–136; depictions of women of color, 92; domestic security, trauma, 16–17, 21 23–24, 39, 43, 93–94, 99, 100, 103, 128, 132; leadership, authority 19, 45–46, 57–58, 62, 106; Lost Cause memorials, 131; nineteenth century notions of, 8, 22, 115–116; prescriptive literature, 23, 25; sexual threats to white women, 92–93

Zacatecas, Mexico, 90
Zuber, Capt. W. P., 118